EPISODE ONE: DEAD STOCK

STORY
MICHAEL COAST
MATTHEW SUMMO
BILL JEMAS

SCRIPT
MATTHEW SUMMO
MIKE SOVIERO

LAYOUTS
YOUNG HELLER
JJ DZIALOWSKI

PENCILS
YOUNG HELLER
JJ DZIALOWSKI

COLORS
LEONARDO PACIAROTTI

INKS
LEONARDO PACIAROTTI
ALEJANDRO SICAT

COVER
RUIZ BURGOS

LETTERS
CAROLINE FLANAGAN

EDITOR
CAROLINE FLANAGAN

EPISODE TWO: MIDNIGHT SNACK

STORY
MICHAEL COAST
MATTHEW SUMMO
BILL JEMAS

SCRIPT
MATTHEW SUMMO
MIKE SOVIERO

LAYOUTS
YOUNG HELLER

PENCILS
YOUNG HELLER

COLORS
LEONARDO PACIAROTTI

INKS
ALEJANDRO SICAT
DENIS FREITAS

COVER
RUIZ BURGOS

LETTERS
CAROLINE FLANAGAN

EDITOR
CAROLINE FLANAGAN

EPISODE THREE: CHECKED OUT

STORY
MICHAEL COAST
MATTHEW SUMMO
BILL JEMAS

SCRIPT
MATTHEW SUMMO
MIKE SOVIERO

LAYOUTS
YOUNG HELLER

PENCILS
YOUNG HELLER

COLORS
LEONARDO PACIA

INKS
       SICAT

          S

          ANAGAN

EDITOR
CAROLINE FLANAGAN

EPISODE FOUR: CLEAN UP ON ISLE Z

STORY
MICHAEL COAST
BILL JEMAS
YOUNG HELLER

SCRIPT
MATTHEW SUMMO
MIKE SOVIERO
BILL JEMAS

LAYOUTS
YOUNG HELLER
DEAN KOTZ

PENCILS
DEAN KOTZ

COLORS
LEONARDO PACIAROTTI

INKS
ALEJANDRO SICAT
GLAUBER MATOS

COVER
RUIZ BURGOS

LETTERS
ELYSIA LIANG
CAROLINE FLANAGAN

EDITOR
CAROLINE FLANAGAN

EPISODE FIVE: Z-MART

STORY
BILL JEMAS

SCRIPT
MATTHEW SUMMO
BILL JEMAS
MICHAEL COAST

LAYOUTS
DEAN KOTZ
STAN CHOU

PENCILS
EZEQUIEL FERREIRA DE ASSIS
JUAN FRIGERI
ADRIANO VICENTE
ELTON THOMAS

COLORS
LEONARDO PACIAROTTI

COVER
RUIZ BURGOS

LETTERS
CAROLINE FLANAGAN
ELYSIA LIANG

EDITORS
CAROLINE FLANAGAN
LILLIAN TAN

D1451596

ULTIMATE
Cocktail Party

Sidecar
¾ ounce triple sec
¾ ounce lemon juice
1 ½ ounces cognac

Martini
2 ½ ounces dry gin
½ ounce dry vermouth
Green olive for garnish

Classic Onion Dip

Ingredients
1 ½ cups chopped onion
½ cup mayonnaise
3 tablespoons butter
1 teaspoon black pepper
¼ teaspoon salt
2 cups sour cream
1 tsp garlic powder

Directions:
• Heat butter in a saucepan. Add black pepper, salt, garlic powder, and onions. Sauté for 10 minutes.
• Mix mayonnaise, sour cream, and sautéed onions in large bowl. Serve at room temperature or chilled, if desired.

Manhattan
2 ounces bourbon whiskey
½ ounce sweet vermouth
½ ounce dry vermouth
2 dashes Angostura bitters
Maraschino cherry

Cosmo
2 ounces vodka
½ ounce triple sec
¾ ounce cranberry juice
¼ ounce fresh lime juic
1 2-inch orange peel/tw

Swiss Fondue

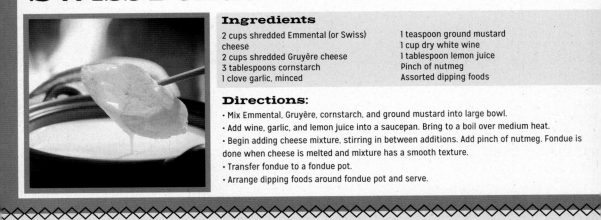

Ingredients
2 cups shredded Emmental (or Swiss) cheese
2 cups shredded Gruyère cheese
3 tablespoons cornstarch
1 clove garlic, minced

1 teaspoon ground mustard
1 cup dry white wine
1 tablespoon lemon juice
Pinch of nutmeg
Assorted dipping foods

Directions:
• Mix Emmental, Gruyère, cornstarch, and ground mustard into large bowl.
• Add wine, garlic, and lemon juice into a saucepan. Bring to a boil over medium heat.
• Begin adding cheese mixture, stirring in between additions. Add pinch of nutmeg. Fondue is done when cheese is melted and mixture has a smooth texture.
• Transfer fondue to a fondue pot.
• Arrange dipping foods around fondue pot and serve.

Deviled Eggs

Ingredients
6 eggs
2 tablespoons mayonnaise
1 teaspoon of yellow mustard

Salt and black pepper to taste
Paprika

Directions:
• Hard boil eggs and slice into halves.
• Separate yolks from egg whites and place yolks in a bowl.
• Mash yolks using a fork. Add mayonnaise, mustard, salt, and pepper and stir.
• Spoon mixture into egg whites using a teaspoon. Sprinkle paprika to garnish.
• Chill eggs for 1 hour and serve.

Fondue image by naito8/Shutterstock | Onion dip image by Adriana Nikolova/Shutterstock | Deviled eggs image by Igot Dutina/Shutterstock

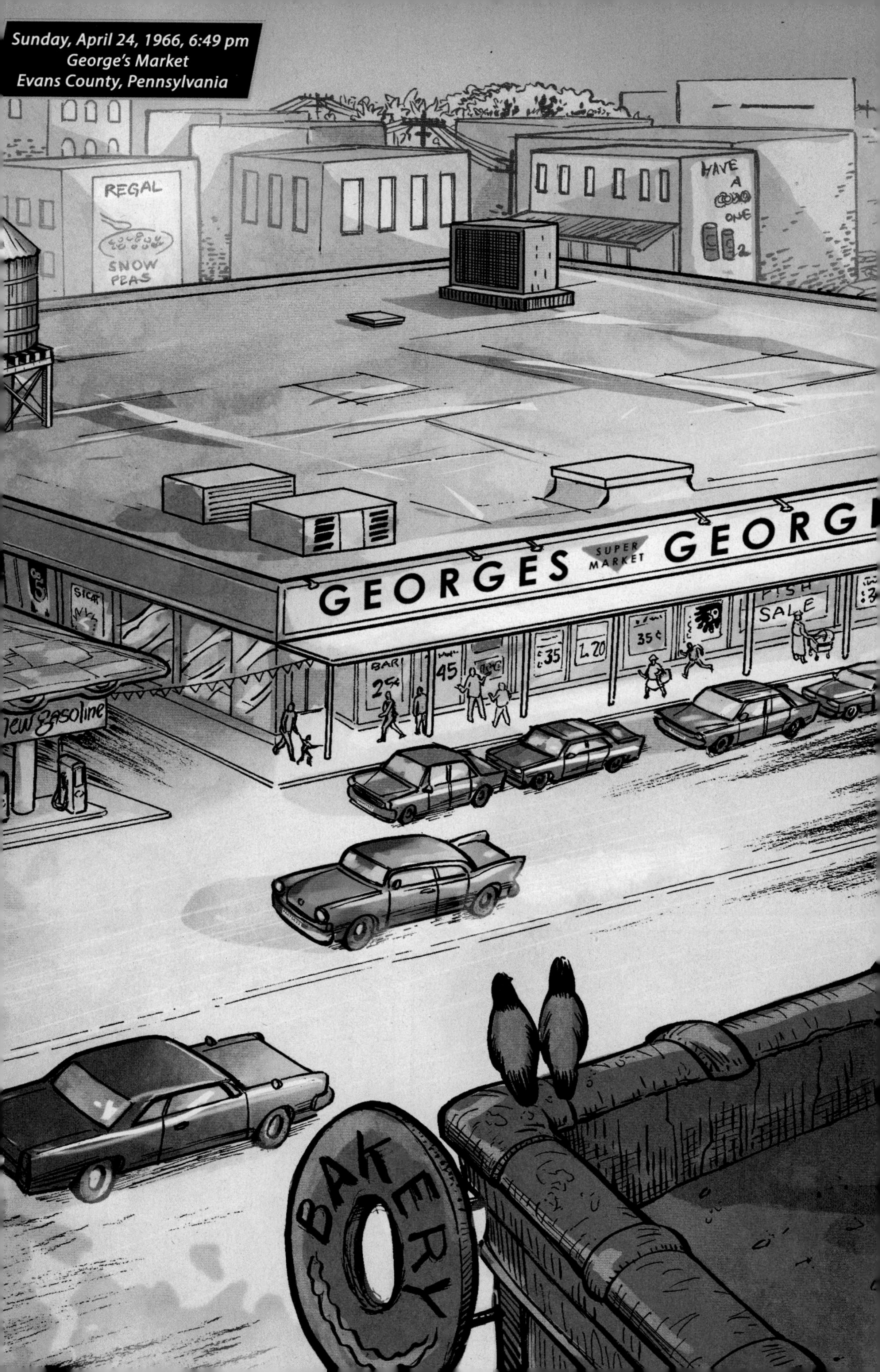
Sunday, April 24, 1966, 6:49 pm
George's Market
Evans County, Pennsylvania
REGAL
SNOW PEAS
HAVE A
ONE
GEORGES
SUPER MARKET
GEORGES
GEORG
FISH SALE
BAR 25¢
45
35
1.20
35¢
new Gasoline
BAKERY

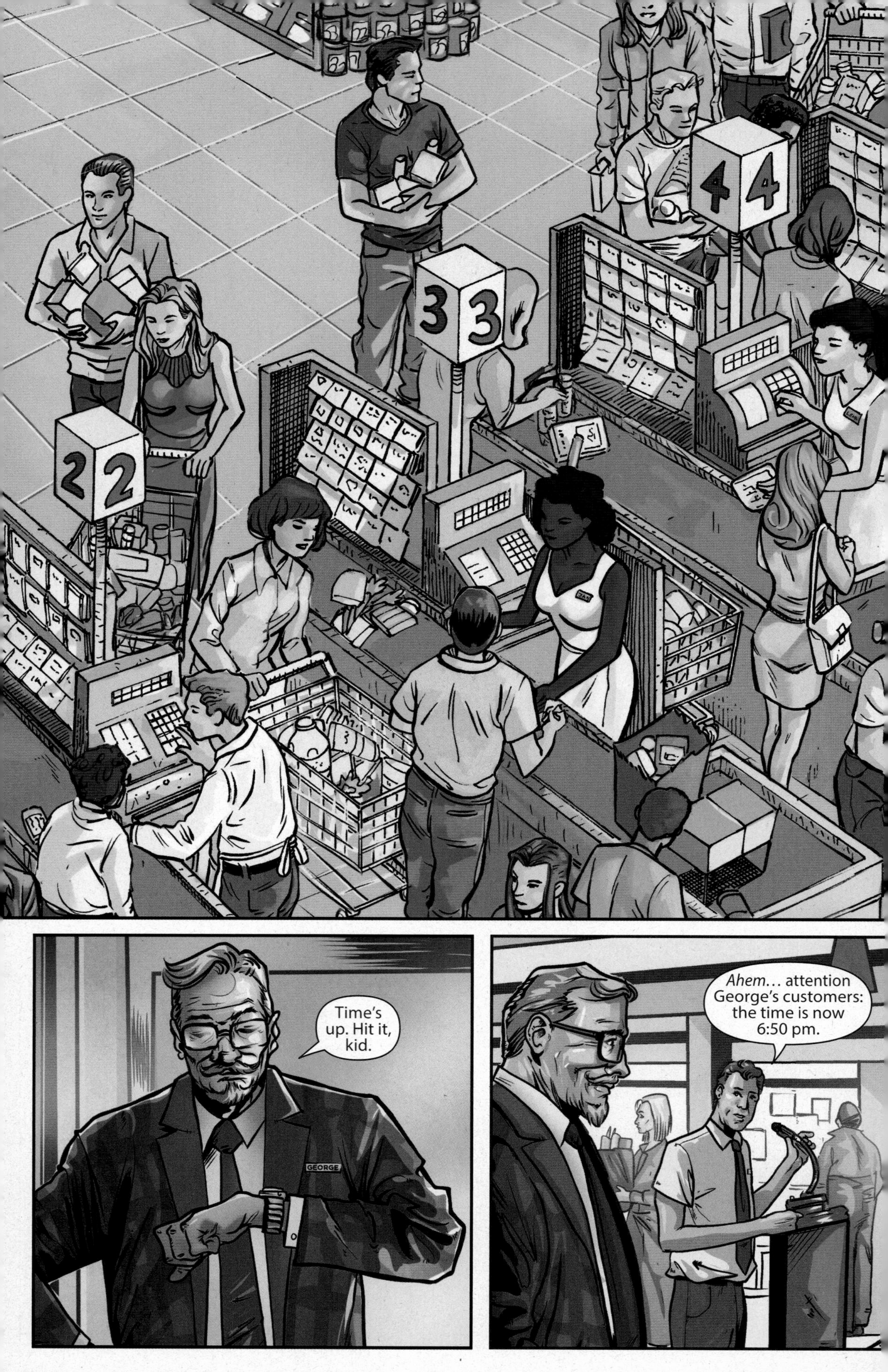
22
33
44
GEORGE
Time's up. Hit it, kid.
Ahem… attention George's customers: the time is now 6:50 pm.

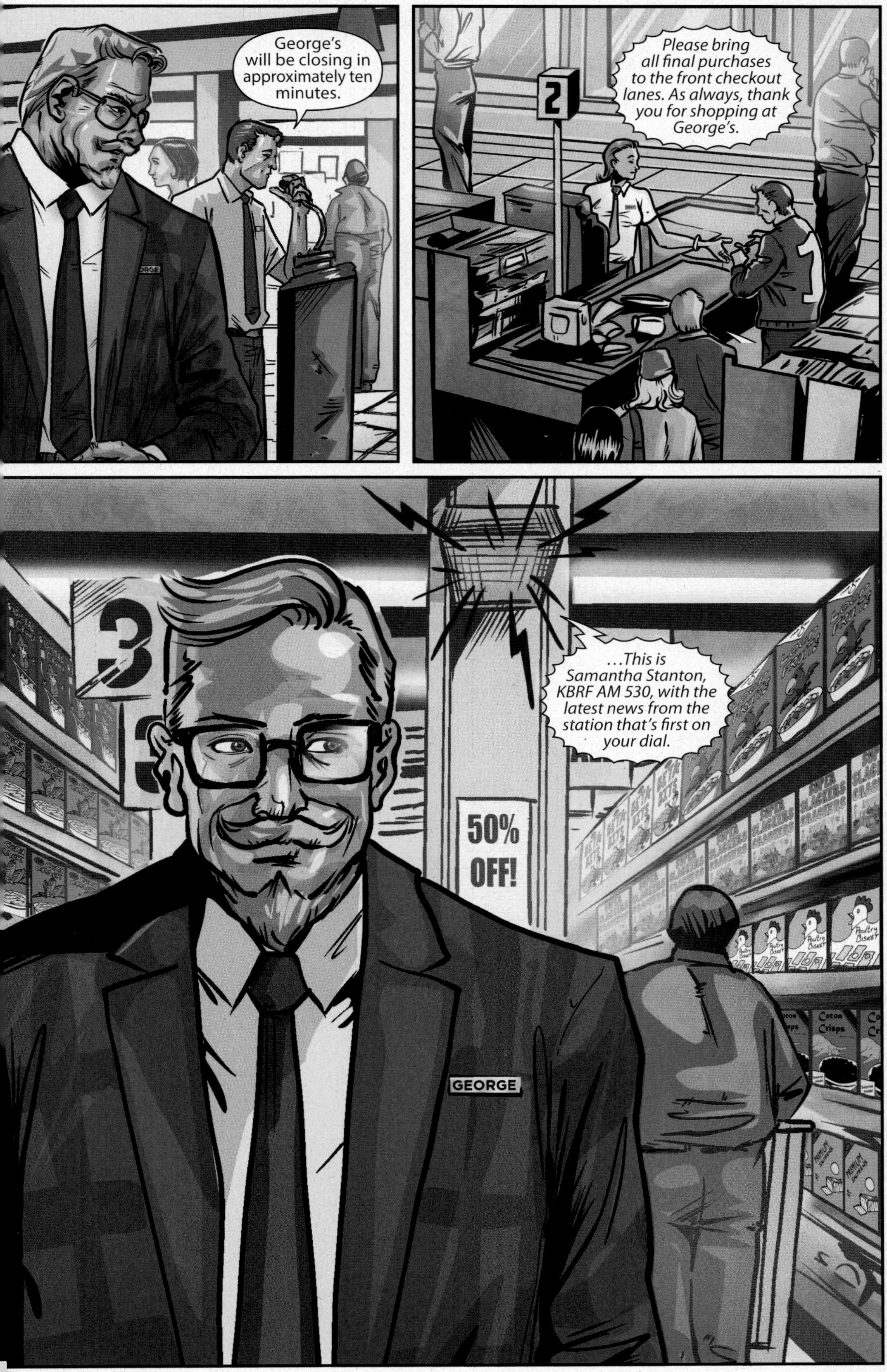
George's will be closing in approximately ten minutes.
GEORGE
2
Please bring all final purchases to the front checkout lanes. As always, thank you for shopping at George's.
3
3
...This is Samantha Stanton, KBRF AM 530, with the latest news from the station that's first on your dial.
50% OFF!
GEORGE
Poultry Bisket
Coco Crisps

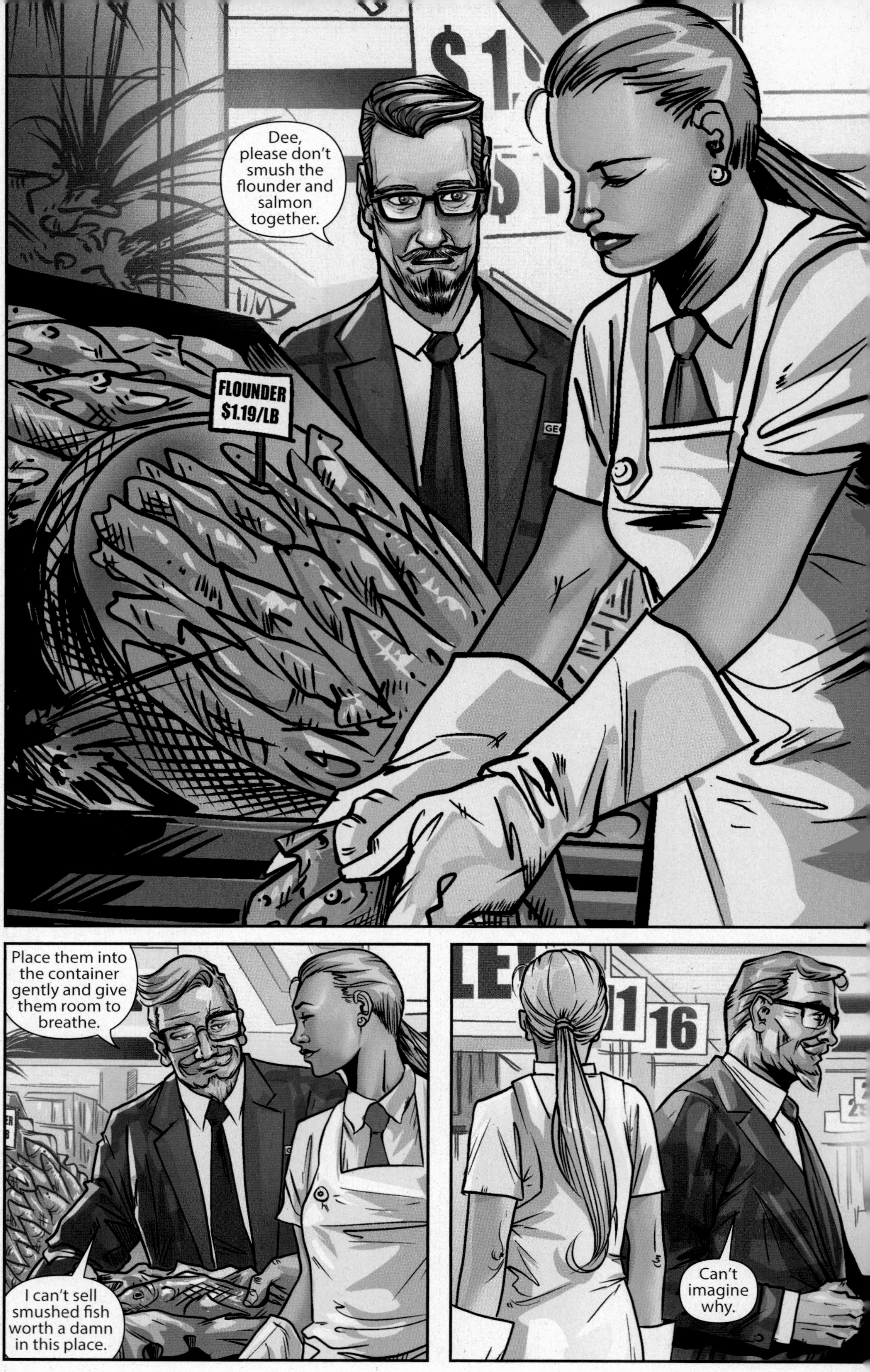
Dee, please don't smush the flounder and salmon together.
FLOUNDER $1.19/LB
Place them into the container gently and give them room to breathe.
I can't sell smushed fish worth a damn in this place.
16
Can't imagine why.

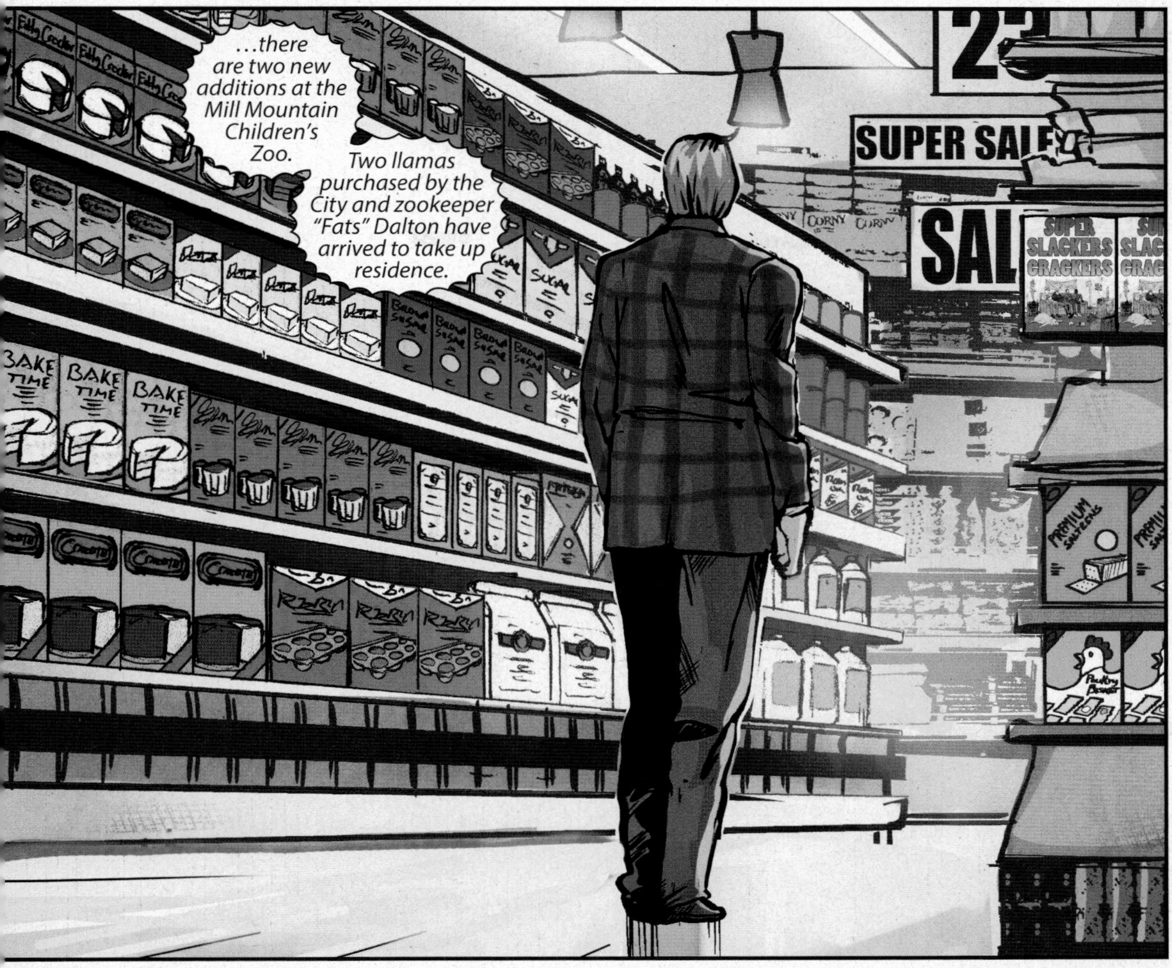
…there are two new additions at the Mill Mountain Children's Zoo.
Two llamas purchased by the City and zookeeper "Fats" Dalton have arrived to take up residence.
SUPER SLACKERS CRACKERS
BAKE TIME
CORNY

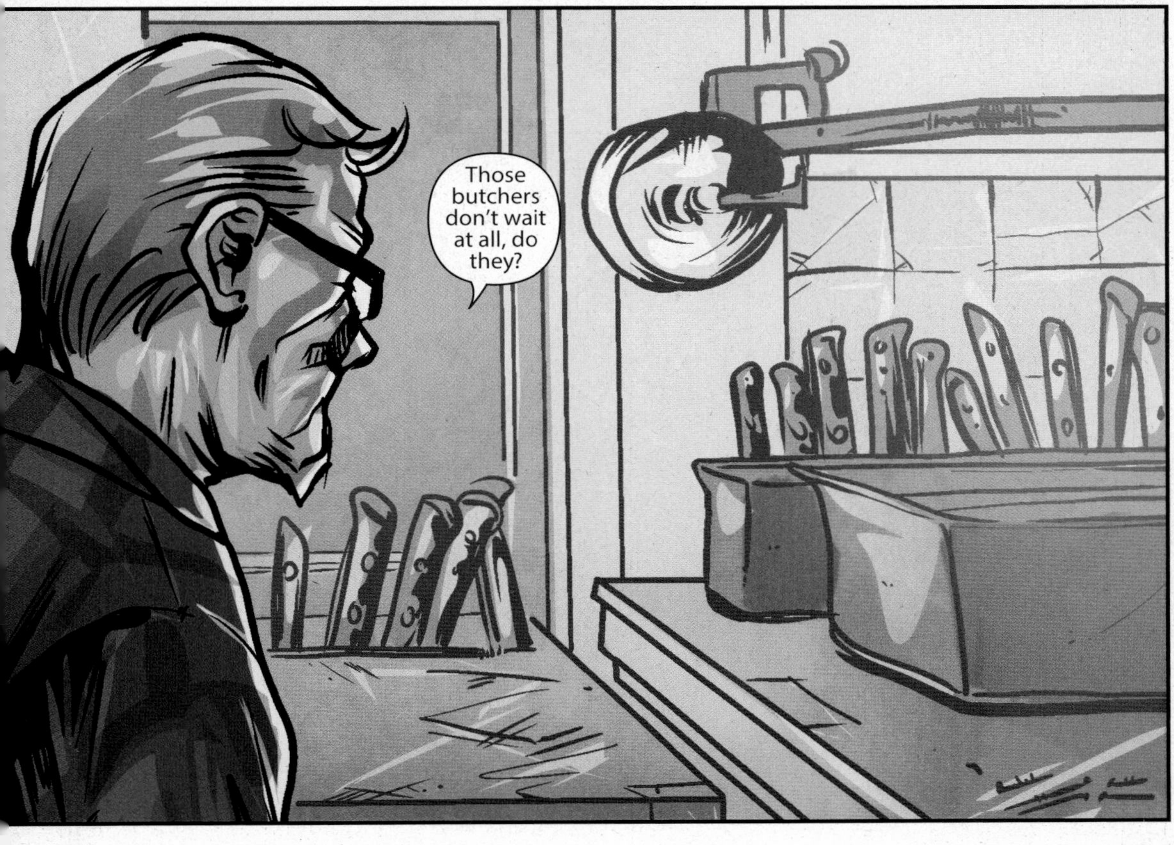
Those butchers don't wait at all, do they?

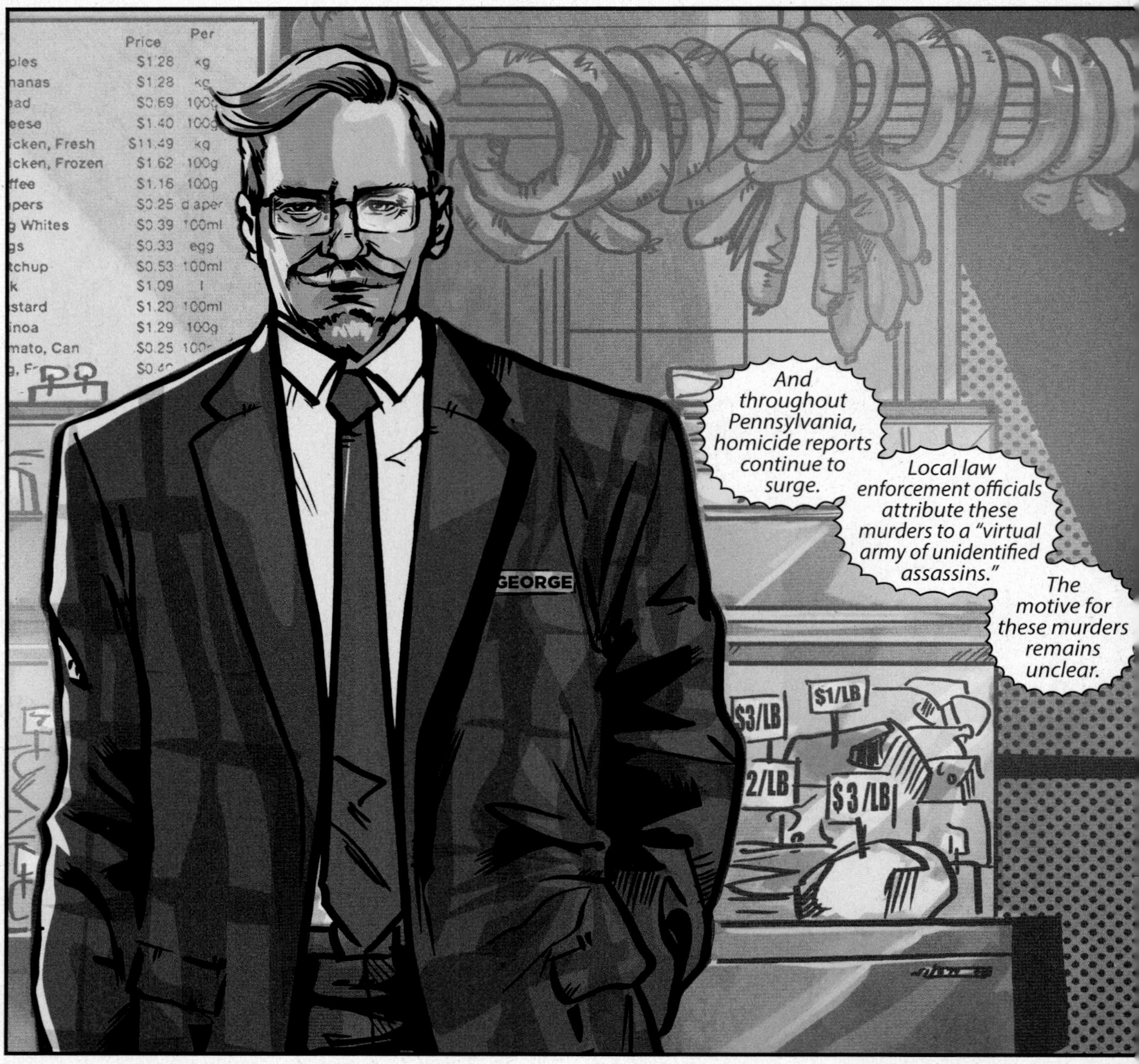
Price Per
And throughout Pennsylvania, homicide reports continue to surge.
Local law enforcement officials attribute these murders to a "virtual army of unidentified assassins."
The motive for these murders remains unclear.
GEORGE
$3/LB
$1/LB
2/LB
$3/LB

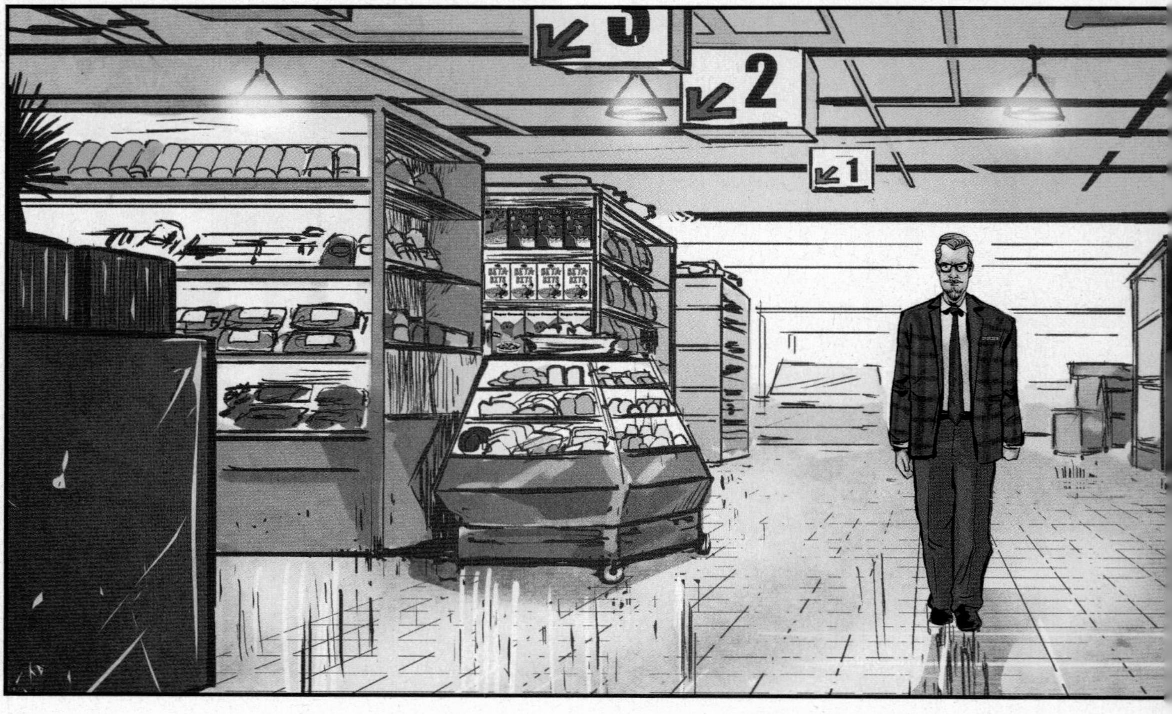
2
1

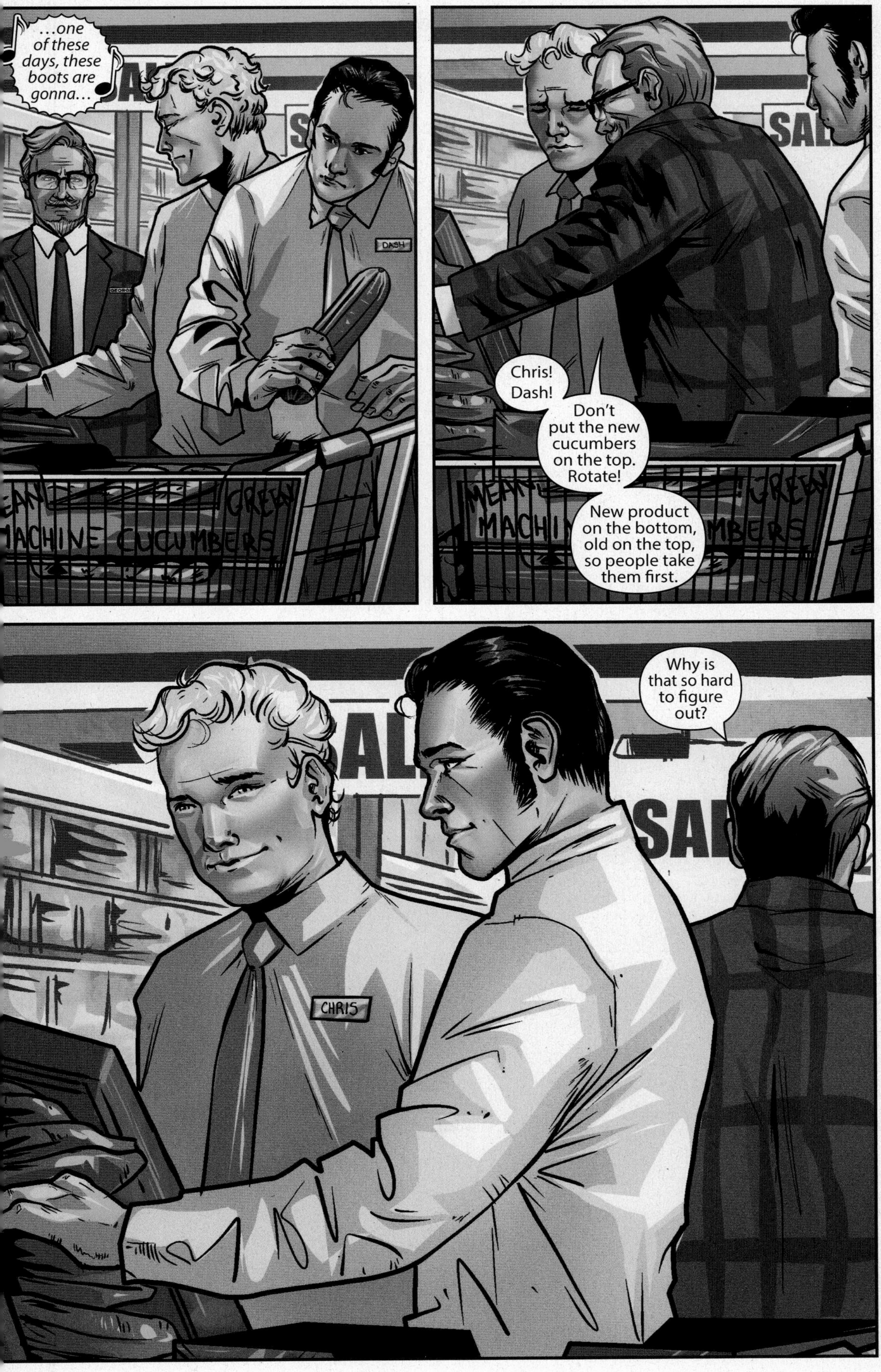
…one of these days, these boots are gonna…
DASH
MEAN GREEN MACHINE CUCUMBERS
Chris! Dash!
Don't put the new cucumbers on the top. Rotate!
New product on the bottom, old on the top, so people take them first.
Why is that so hard to figure out?
CHRIS

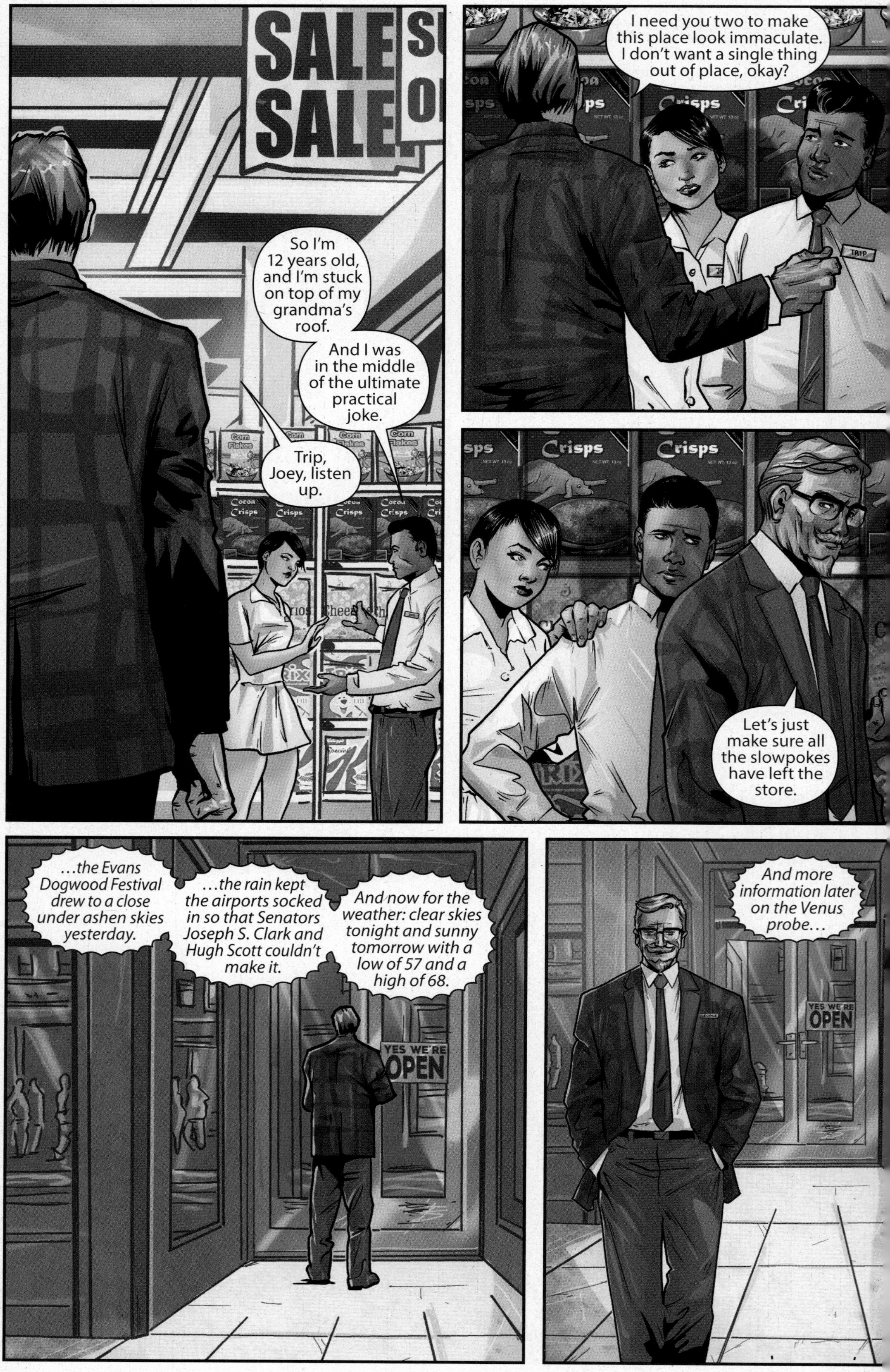
SALE
SALE
So I'm 12 years old, and I'm stuck on top of my grandma's roof.
And I was in the middle of the ultimate practical joke.
Trip, Joey, listen up.
I need you two to make this place look immaculate. I don't want a single thing out of place, okay?
Let's just make sure all the slowpokes have left the store.
…the Evans Dogwood Festival drew to a close under ashen skies yesterday.
…the rain kept the airports socked in so that Senators Joseph S. Clark and Hugh Scott couldn't make it.
And now for the weather: clear skies tonight and sunny tomorrow with a low of 57 and a high of 68.
YES WE'RE OPEN
And more information later on the Venus probe…
YES WE'RE OPEN

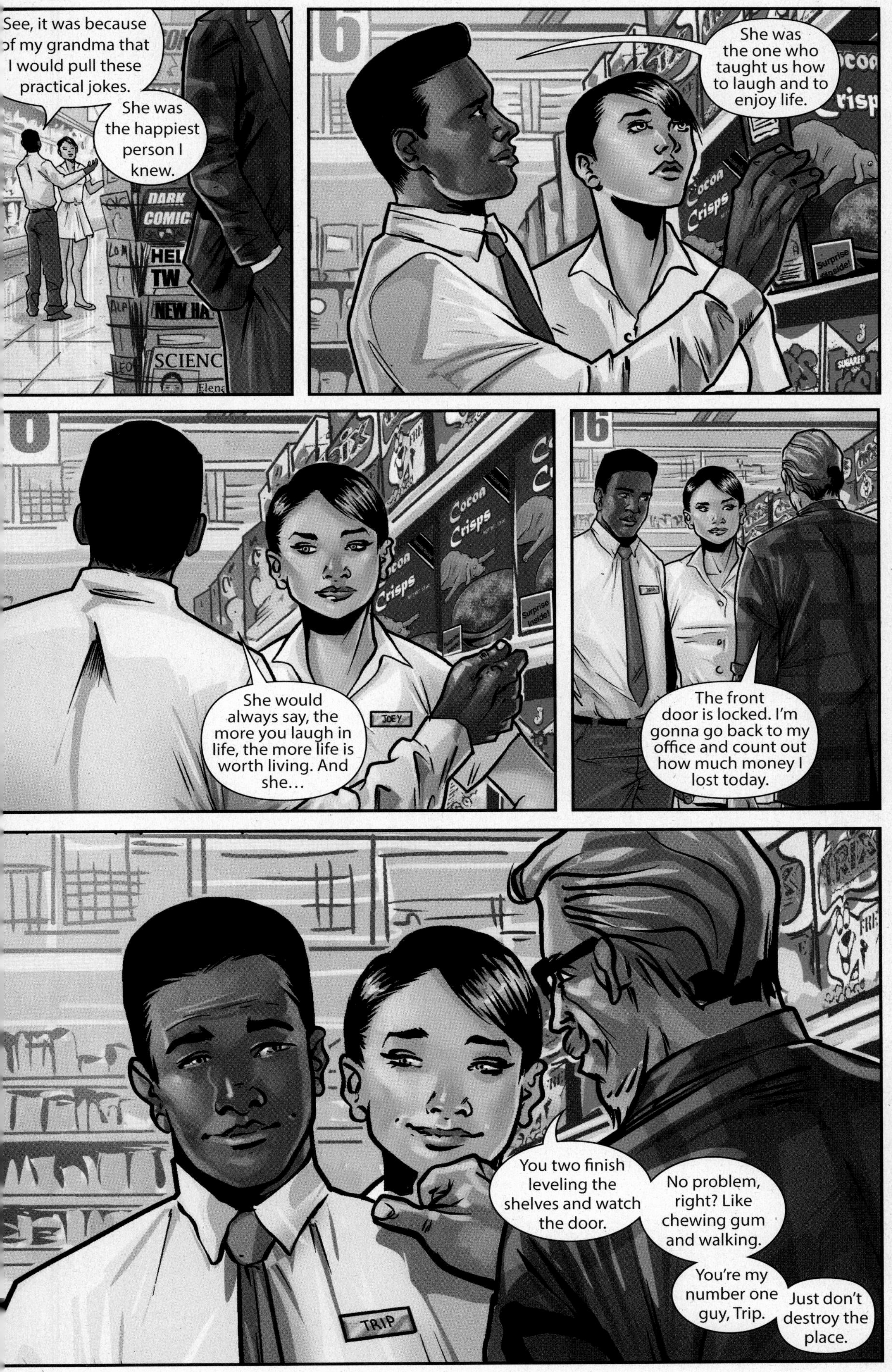
See, it was because of my grandma that I would pull these practical jokes.
She was the happiest person I knew.
DARK COMICS
HEL TW
NEW HA
SCIENC
She was the one who taught us how to laugh and to enjoy life.
Cocon Crisps
Surprise Inside!
She would always say, the more you laugh in life, the more life is worth living. And she…
JOEY
The front door is locked. I'm gonna go back to my office and count out how much money I lost today.
You two finish leveling the shelves and watch the door.
No problem, right? Like chewing gum and walking.
You're my number one guy, Trip.
Just don't destroy the place.
TRIP

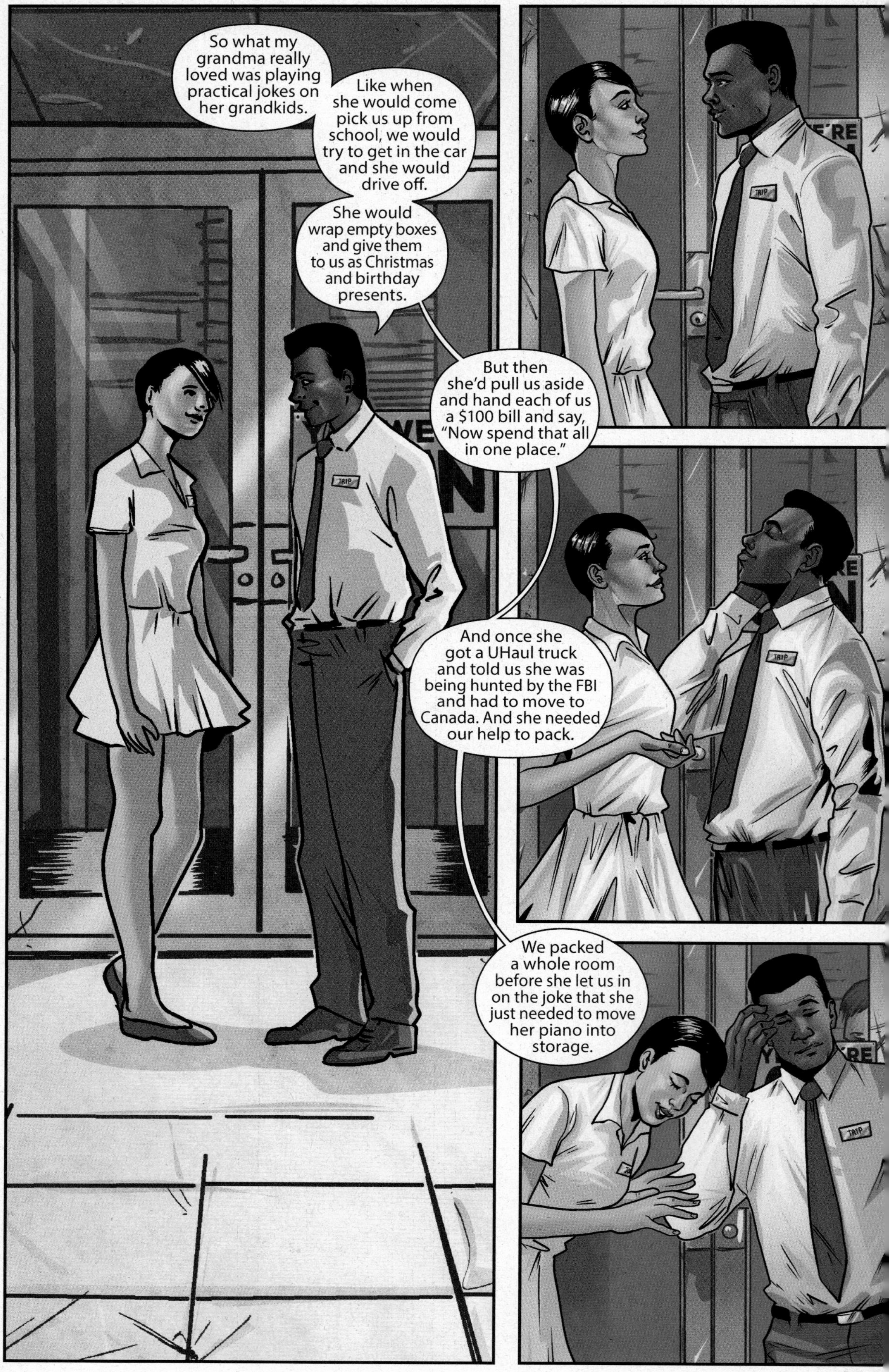
So what my grandma really loved was playing practical jokes on her grandkids.
Like when she would come pick us up from school, we would try to get in the car and she would drive off.
She would wrap empty boxes and give them to us as Christmas and birthday presents.
But then she'd pull us aside and hand each of us a $100 bill and say, "Now spend that all in one place."
And once she got a UHaul truck and told us she was being hunted by the FBI and had to move to Canada. And she needed our help to pack.
We packed a whole room before she let us in on the joke that she just needed to move her piano into storage.
TRIP
TRIP
TRIP
TRIP

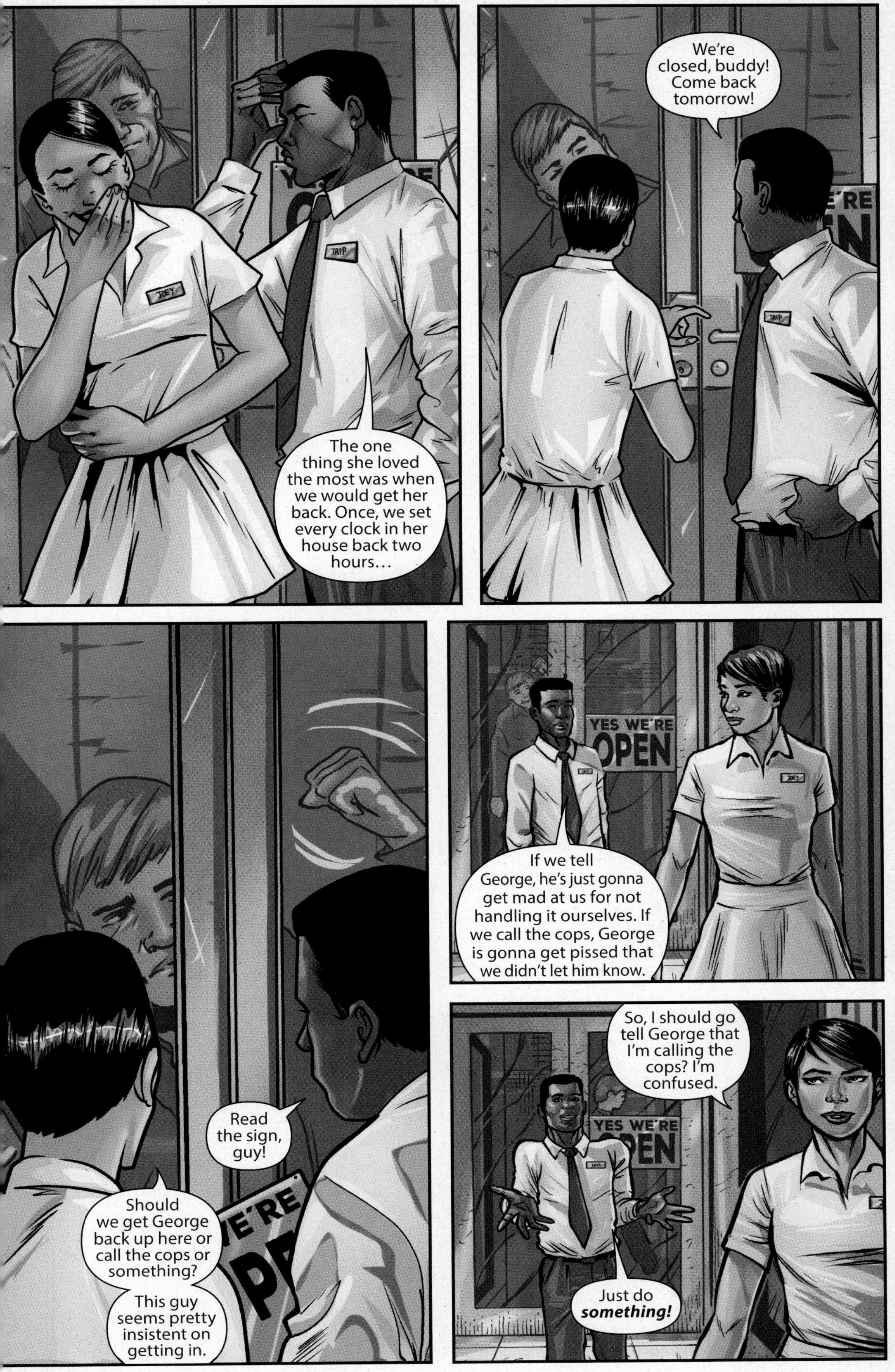
TAIP
JOEY
The one thing she loved the most was when we would get her back. Once, we set every clock in her house back two hours…
We're closed, buddy! Come back tomorrow!
Read the sign, guy!
Should we get George back up here or call the cops or something?
This guy seems pretty insistent on getting in.
YES WE'RE OPEN
If we tell George, he's just gonna get mad at us for not handling it ourselves. If we call the cops, George is gonna get pissed that we didn't let him know.
So, I should go tell George that I'm calling the cops? I'm confused.
Just do *something!*

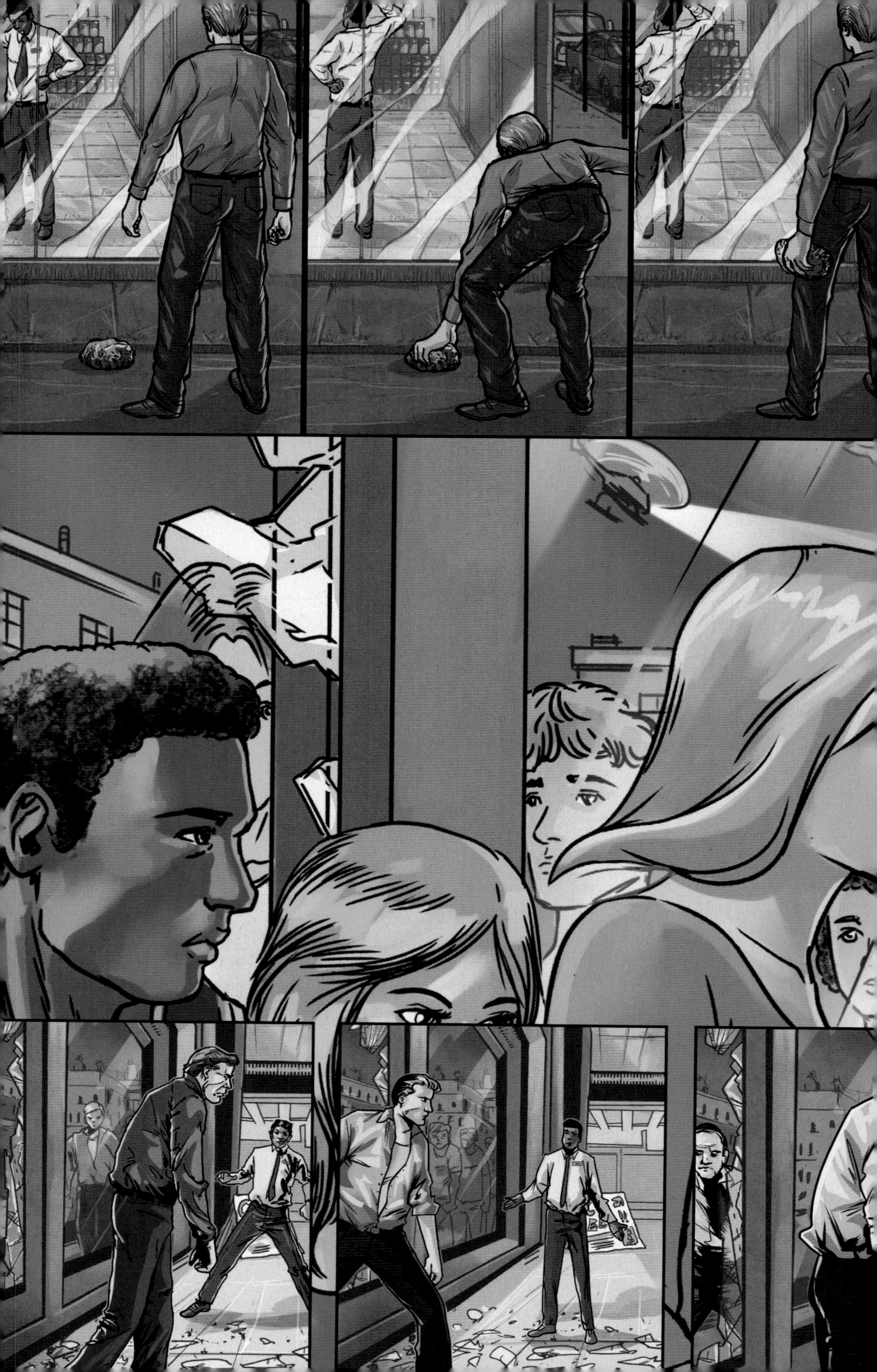

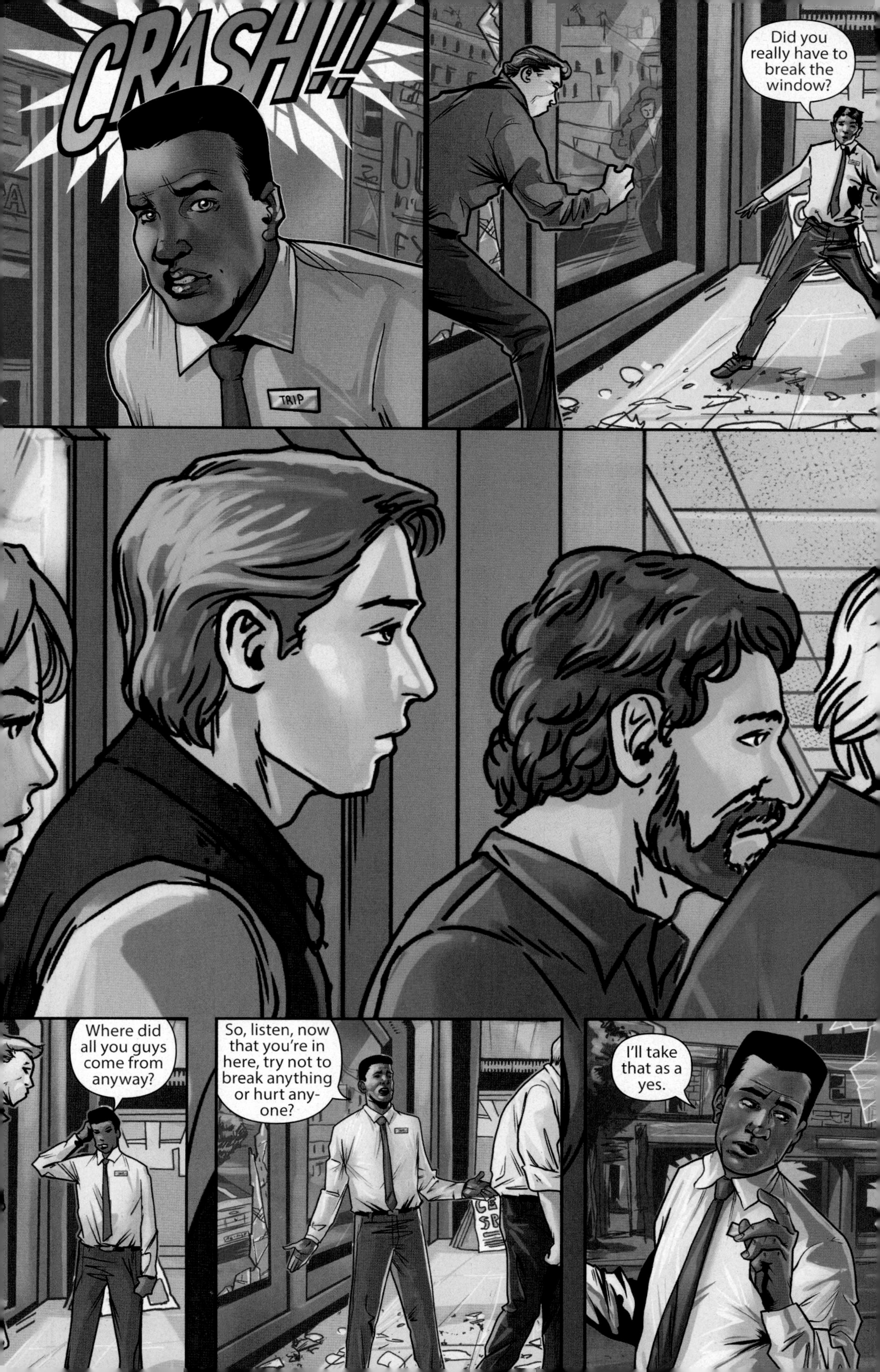
CRASH!!!
TRIP
Did you really have to break the window?
Where did all you guys come from anyway?
So, listen, now that you're in here, try not to break anything or hurt any-one?
I'll take that as a yes.

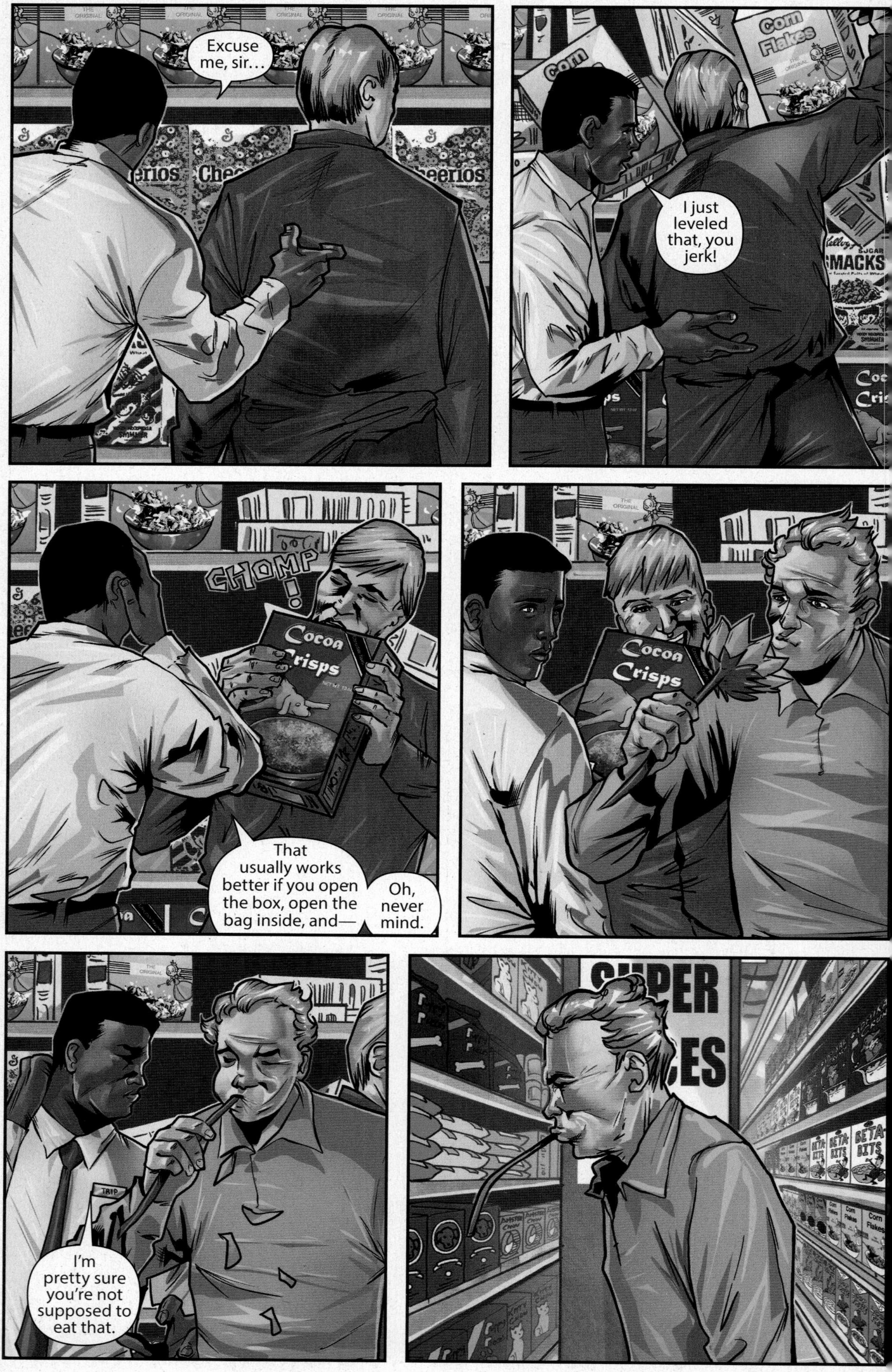
Excuse me, sir…
I just leveled that, you jerk!
CHOMP!
That usually works better if you open the box, open the bag inside, and—
Oh, never mind.
I'm pretty sure you're not supposed to eat that.

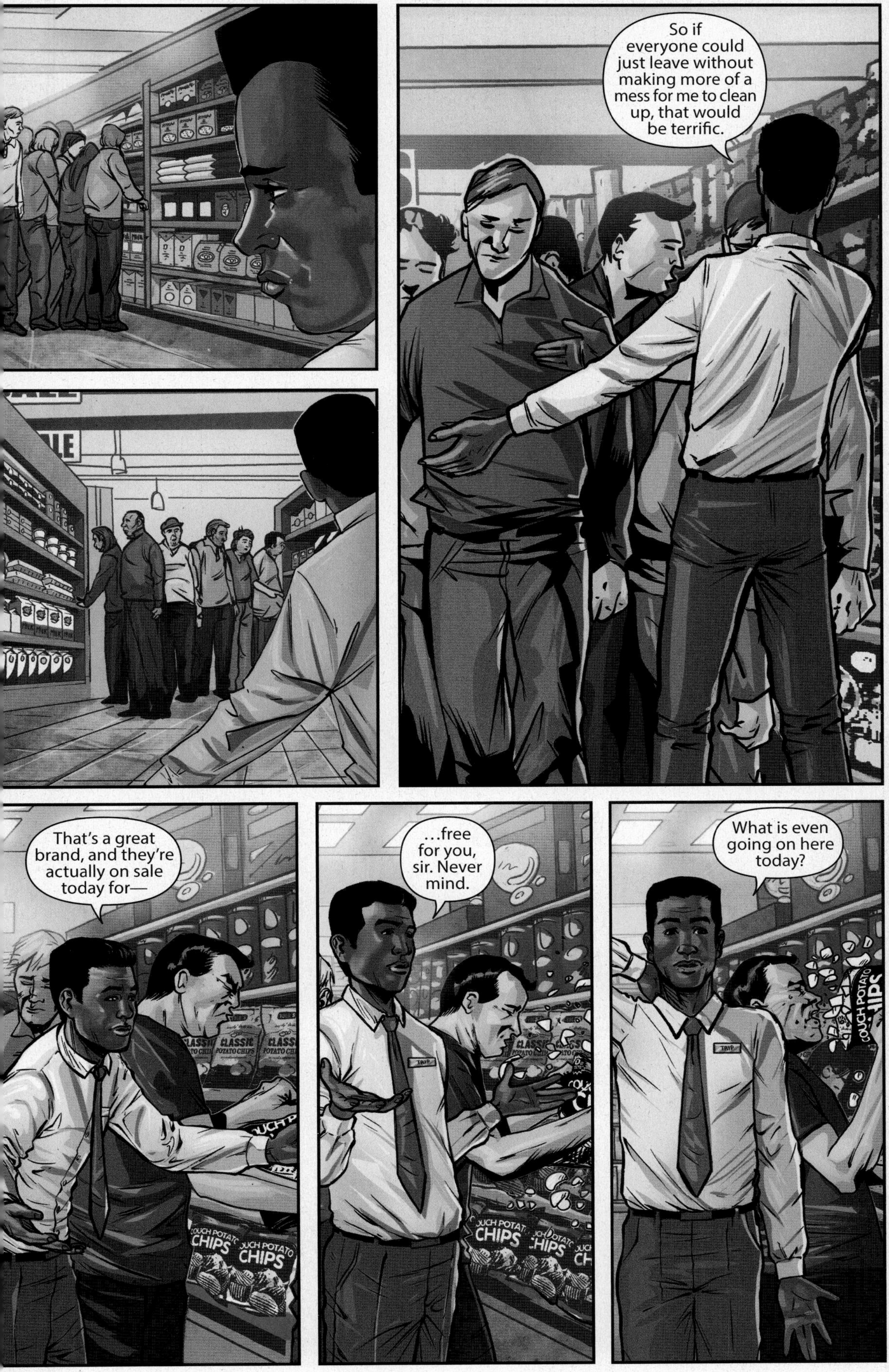
So if everyone could just leave without making more of a mess for me to clean up, that would be terrific.
That's a great brand, and they're actually on sale today for—
…free for you, sir. Never mind.
What is even going on here today?
CLASSIC POTATO CHIPS
COUCH POTATO CHIPS

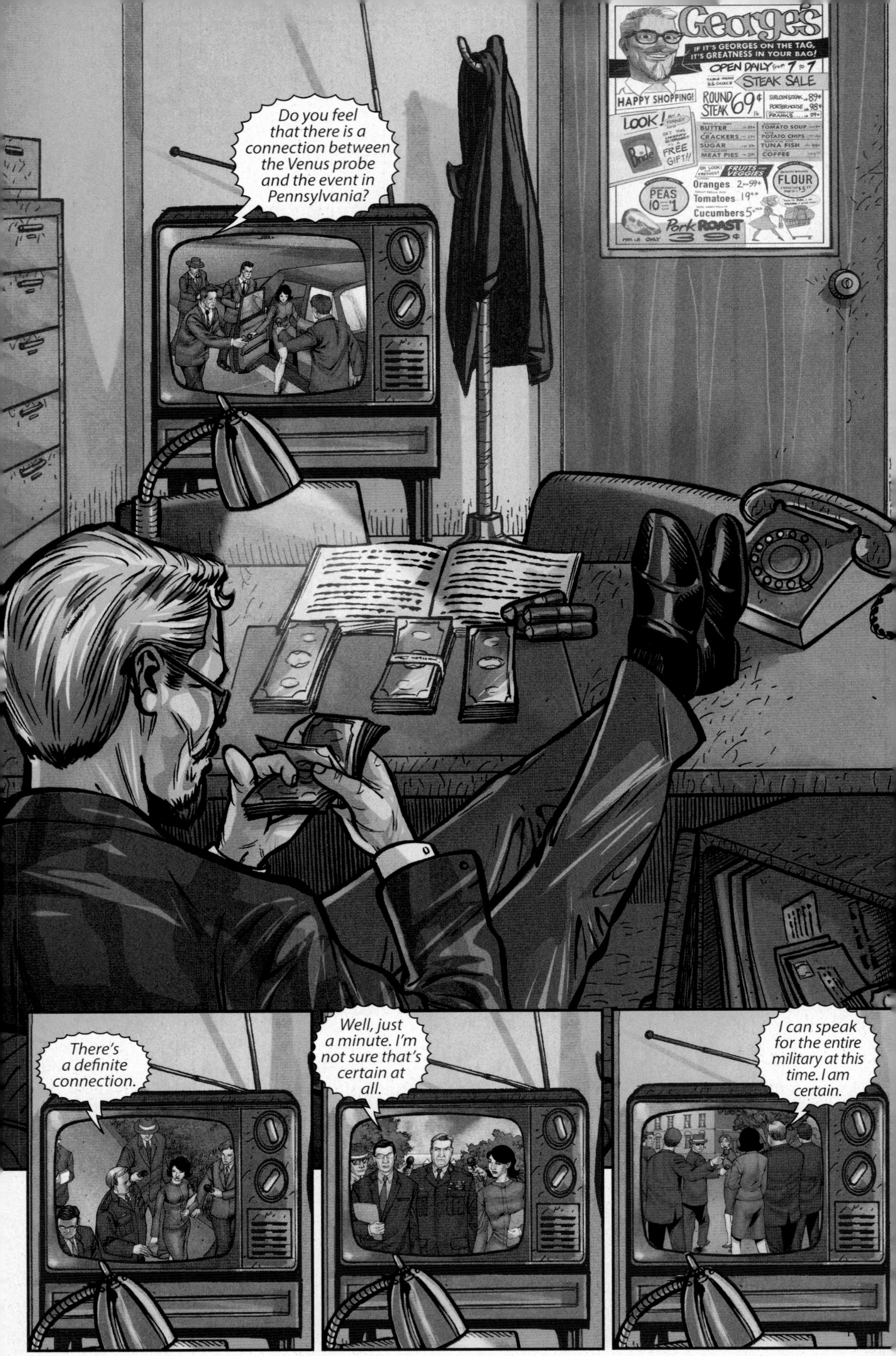
George's
IF IT'S GEORGES ON THE TAG, IT'S GREATNESS IN YOUR BAG!
OPEN DAILY from 7 to 7
STEAK SALE
HAPPY SHOPPING!
ROUND STEAK 69¢ lb
LOOK!
FREE GIFT!!
BUTTER
CRACKERS
SUGAR
MEAT PIES
TOMATO SOUP
POTATO CHIPS
TUNA FISH
COFFEE
FRUITS AND VEGGIES
PEAS 10 for $1
Oranges
Tomatoes
Cucumbers
FLOUR
Pork ROAST 39¢
Do you feel that there is a connection between the Venus probe and the event in Pennsylvania?
There's a definite connection.
Well, just a minute. I'm not sure that's certain at all.
I can speak for the entire military at this time. I am certain.

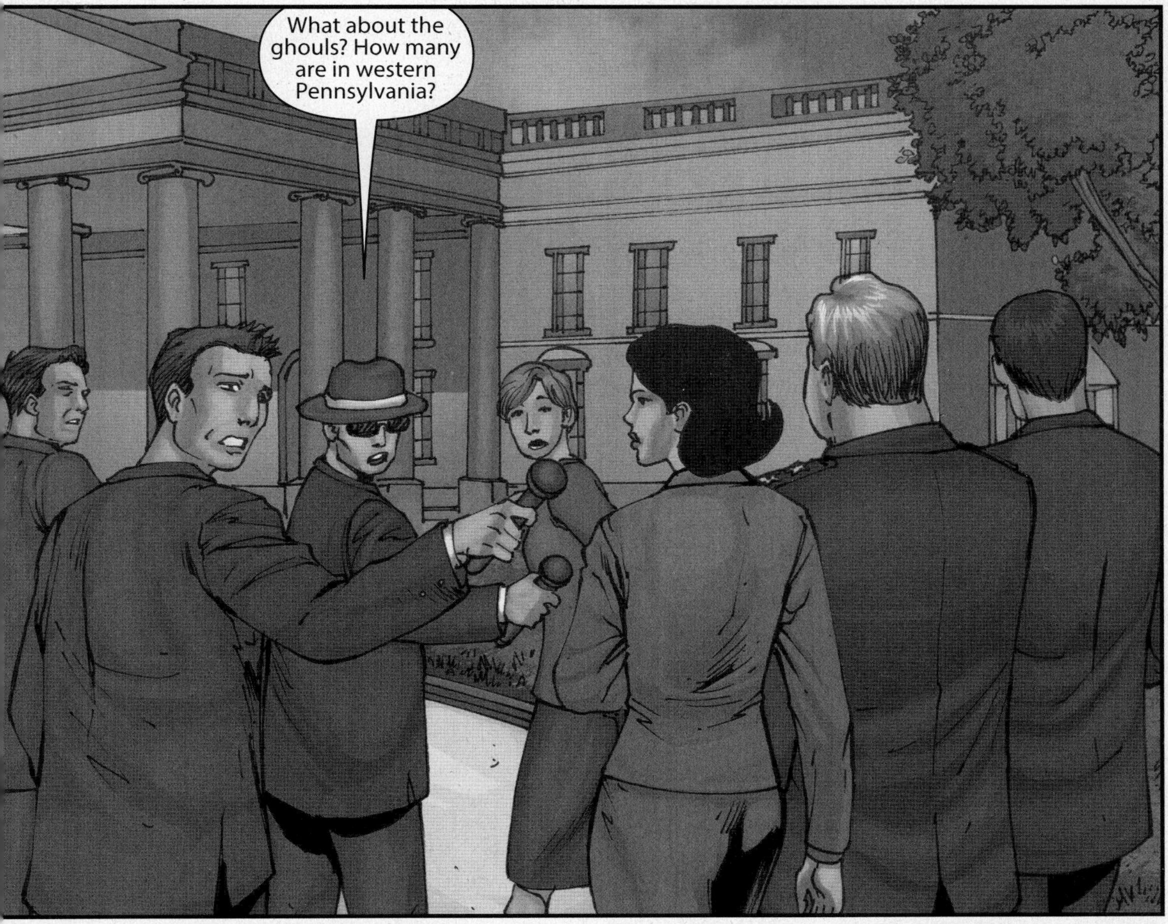
What about the ghouls? How many are in western Pennsylvania?

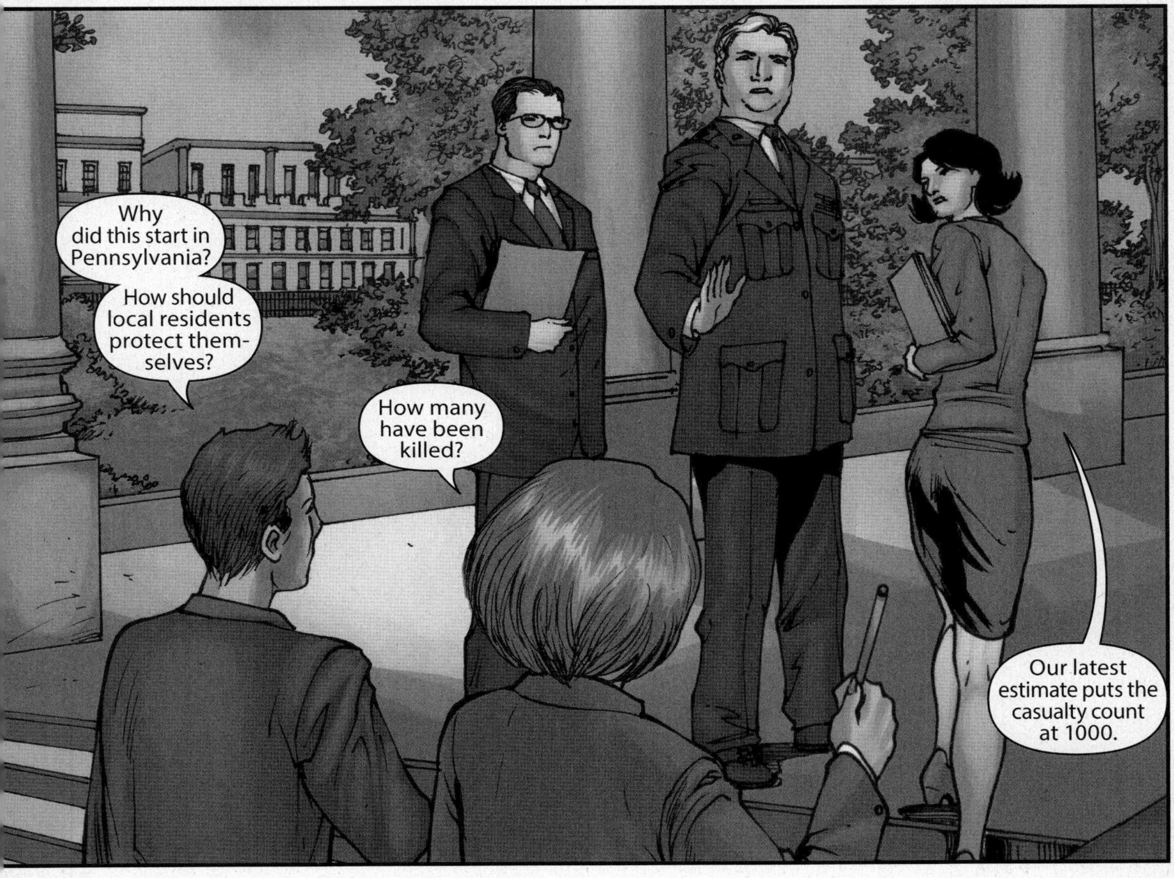
Why did this start in Pennsylvania?
How should local residents protect them-selves?
How many have been killed?
Our latest estimate puts the casualty count at 1000.

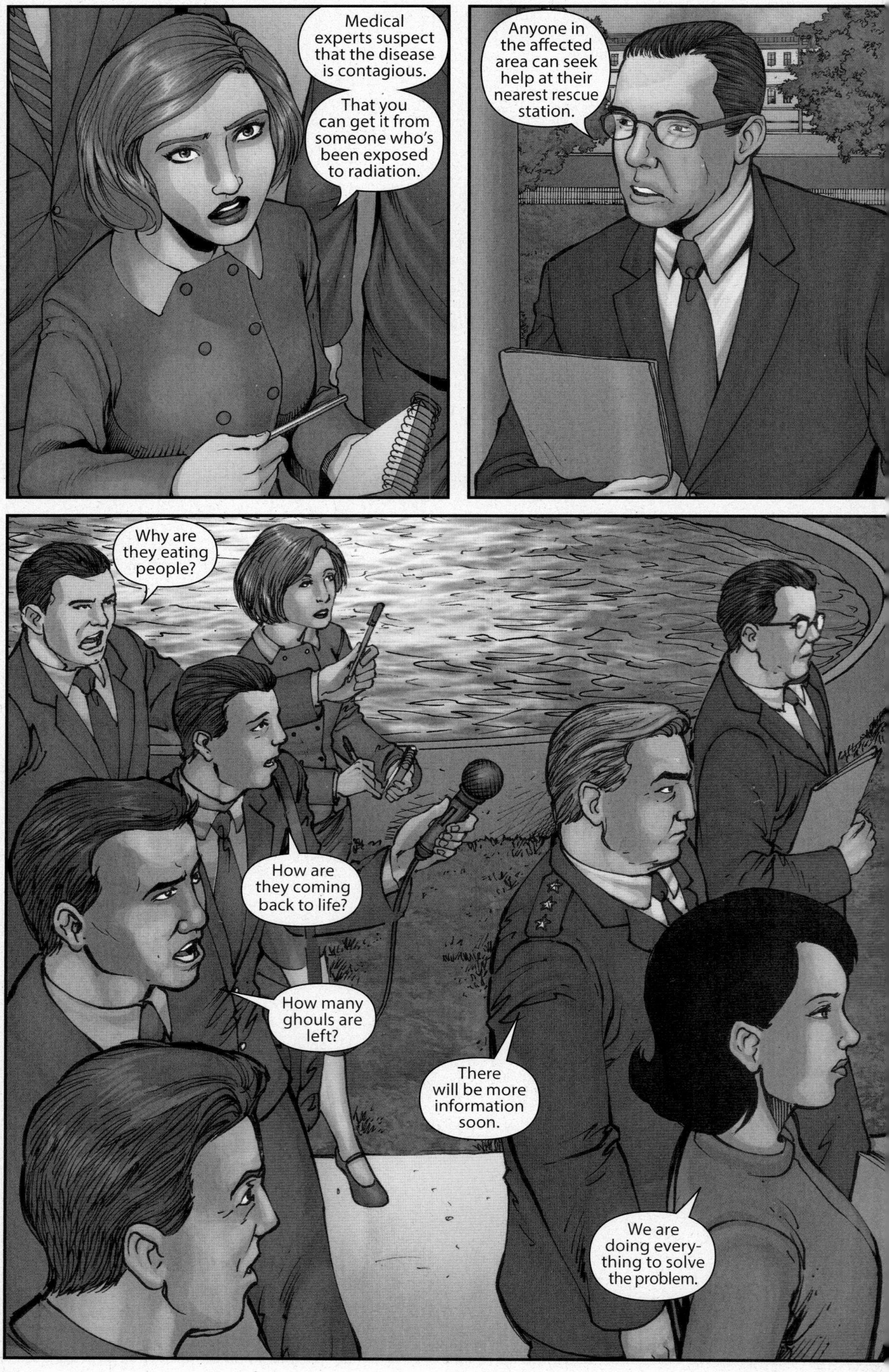
Medical experts suspect that the disease is contagious.
That you can get it from someone who's been exposed to radiation.
Anyone in the affected area can seek help at their nearest rescue station.
Why are they eating people?
How are they coming back to life?
How many ghouls are left?
There will be more information soon.
We are doing every-thing to solve the problem.

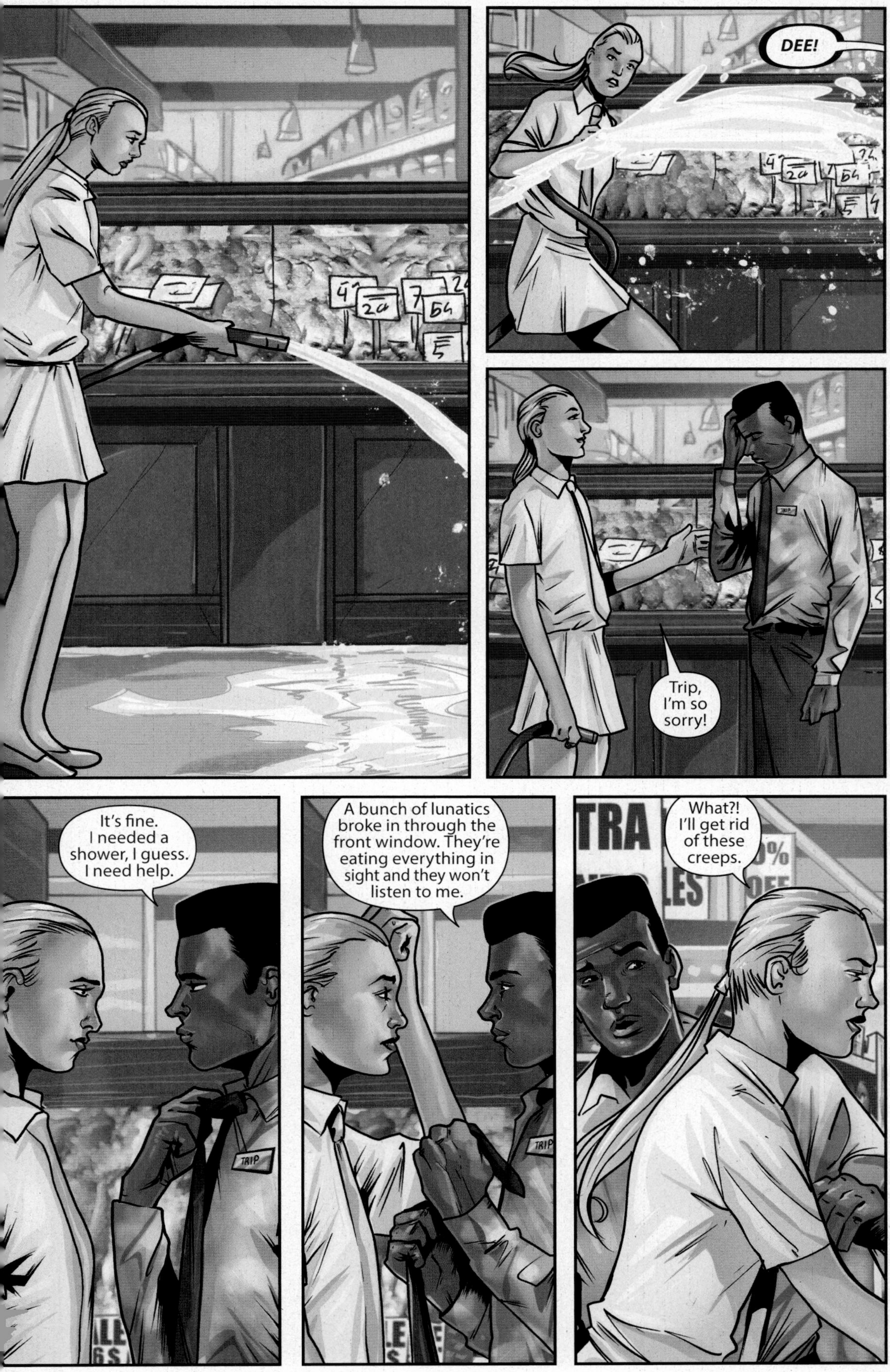
DEE!
Trip, I'm so sorry!
It's fine. I needed a shower, I guess. I need help.
A bunch of lunatics broke in through the front window. They're eating everything in sight and they won't listen to me.
What?! I'll get rid of these creeps.

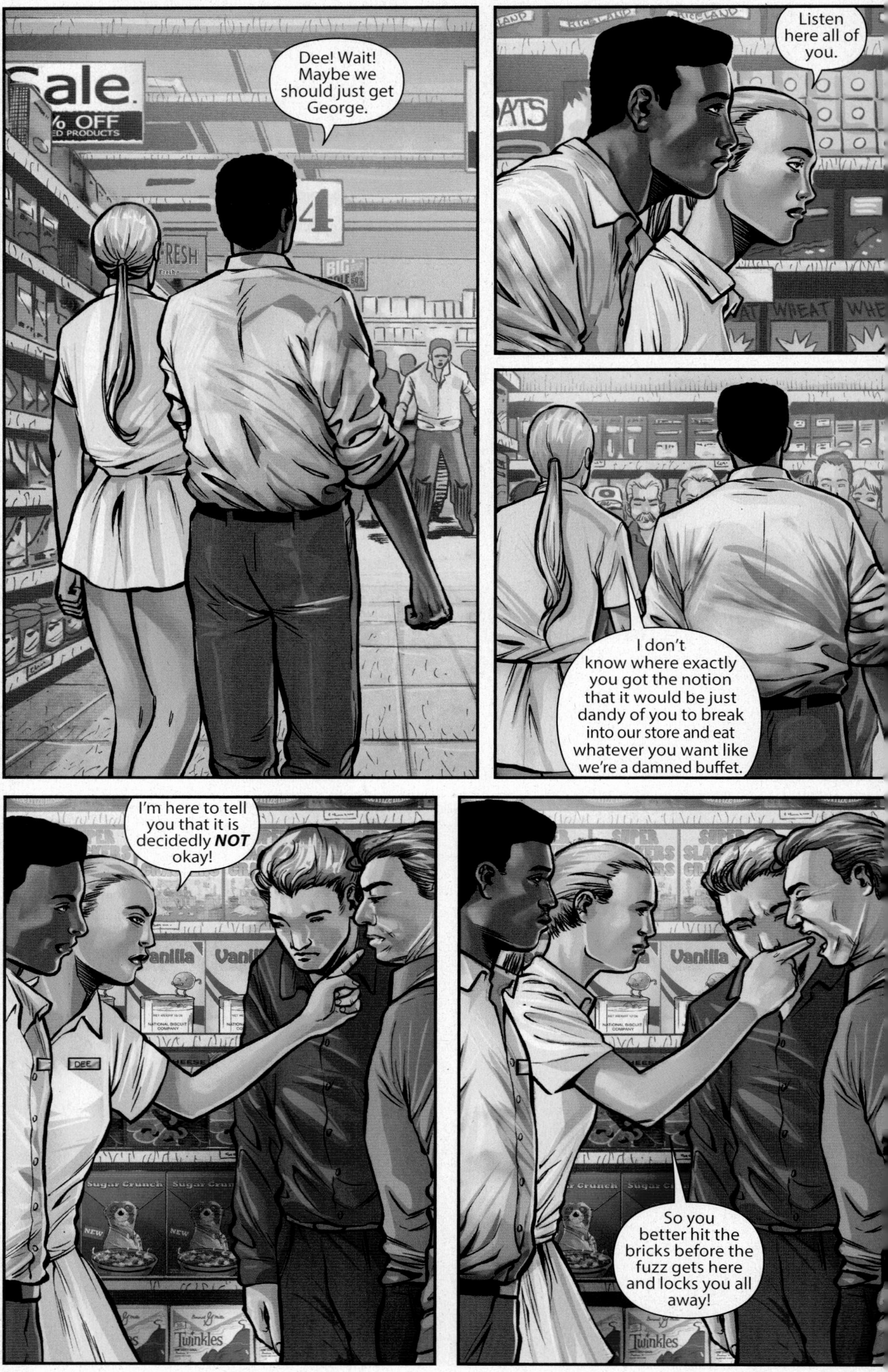
Sale.
% OFF
ED PRODUCTS
Dee! Wait! Maybe we should just get George.
FRESH
Listen here all of you.
I don't know where exactly you got the notion that it would be just dandy of you to break into our store and eat whatever you want like we're a damned buffet.
I'm here to tell you that it is decidedly ***NOT*** okay!
DEE
Vanilla
NATIONAL BISCUIT COMPANY
Sugar Crunch
Twinkles
So you better hit the bricks before the fuzz gets here and locks you all away!

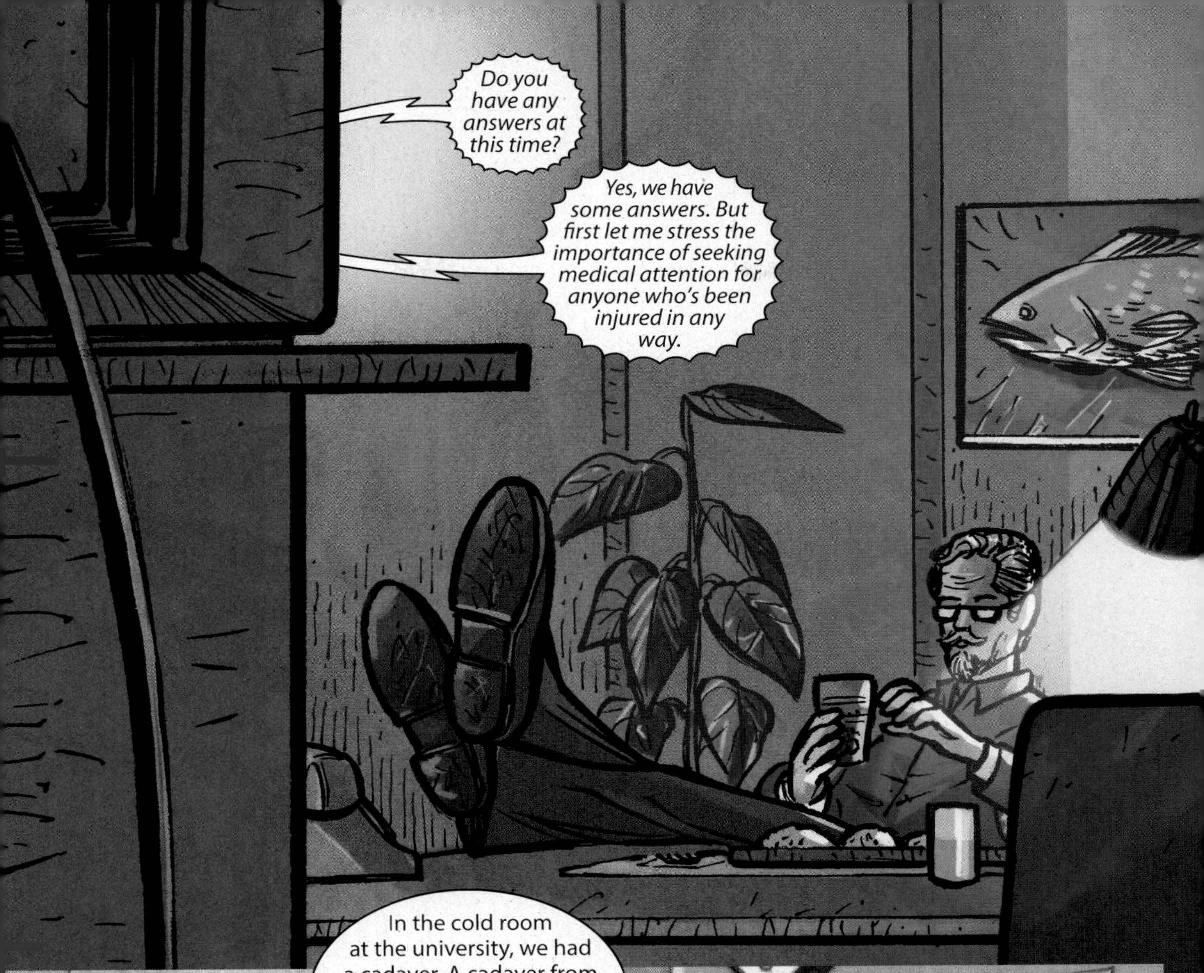
Do you have any answers at this time?
Yes, we have some answers. But first let me stress the importance of seeking medical attention for anyone who's been injured in any way.
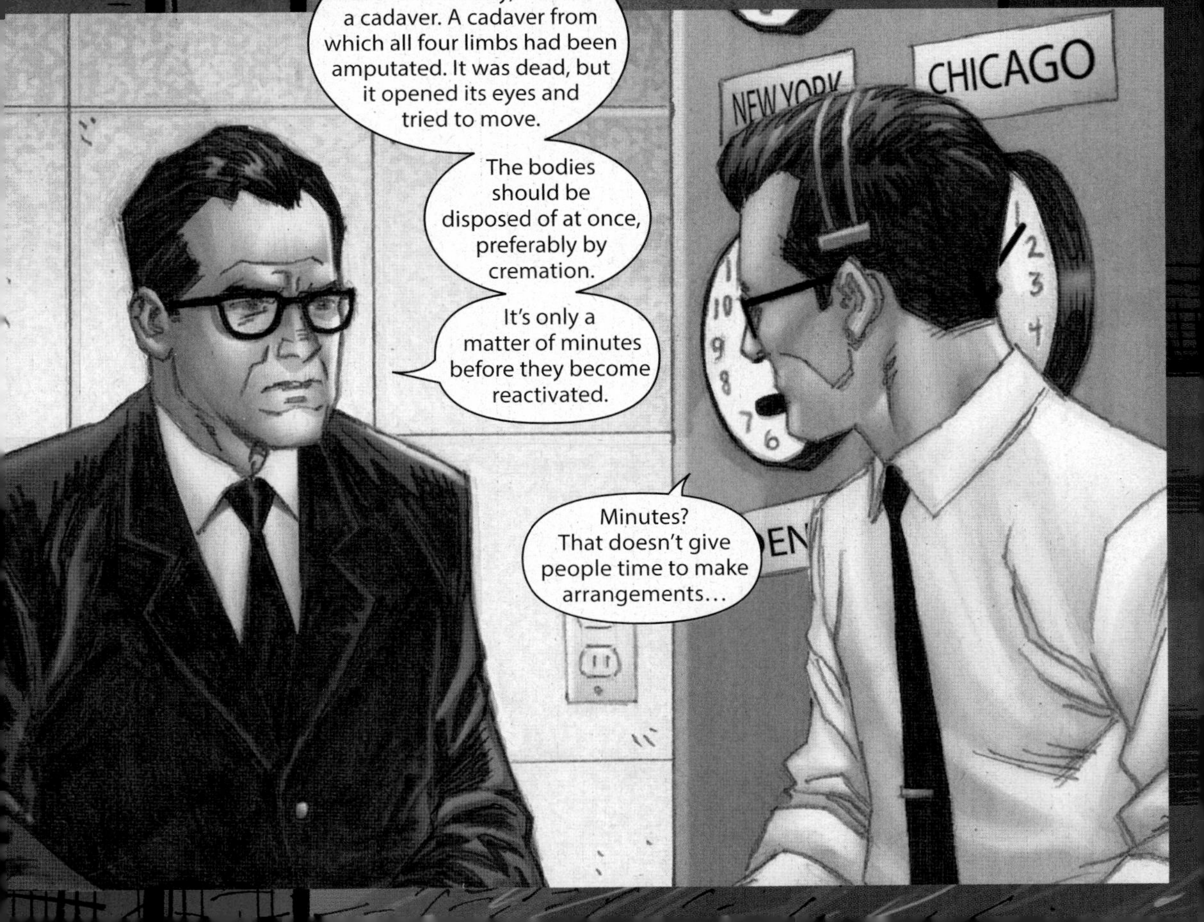
In the cold room at the university, we had a cadaver. A cadaver from which all four limbs had been amputated. It was dead, but it opened its eyes and tried to move.
The bodies should be disposed of at once, preferably by cremation.
It's only a matter of minutes before they become reactivated.
CHICAGO
Minutes? That doesn't give people time to make arrangements…

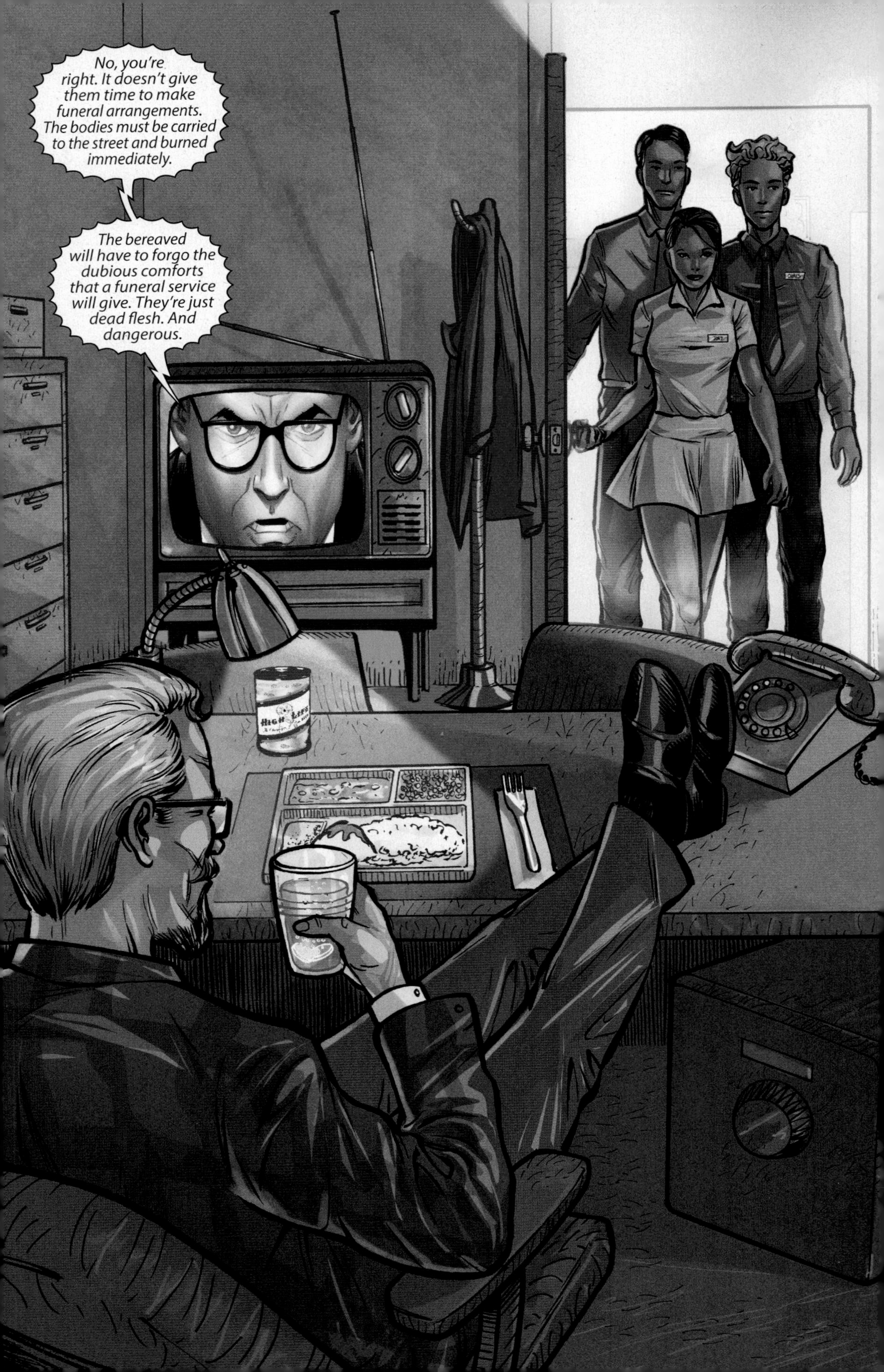
No, you're right. It doesn't give them time to make funeral arrangements. The bodies must be carried to the street and burned immediately.
The bereaved will have to forgo the dubious comforts that a funeral service will give. They're just dead flesh. And dangerous.

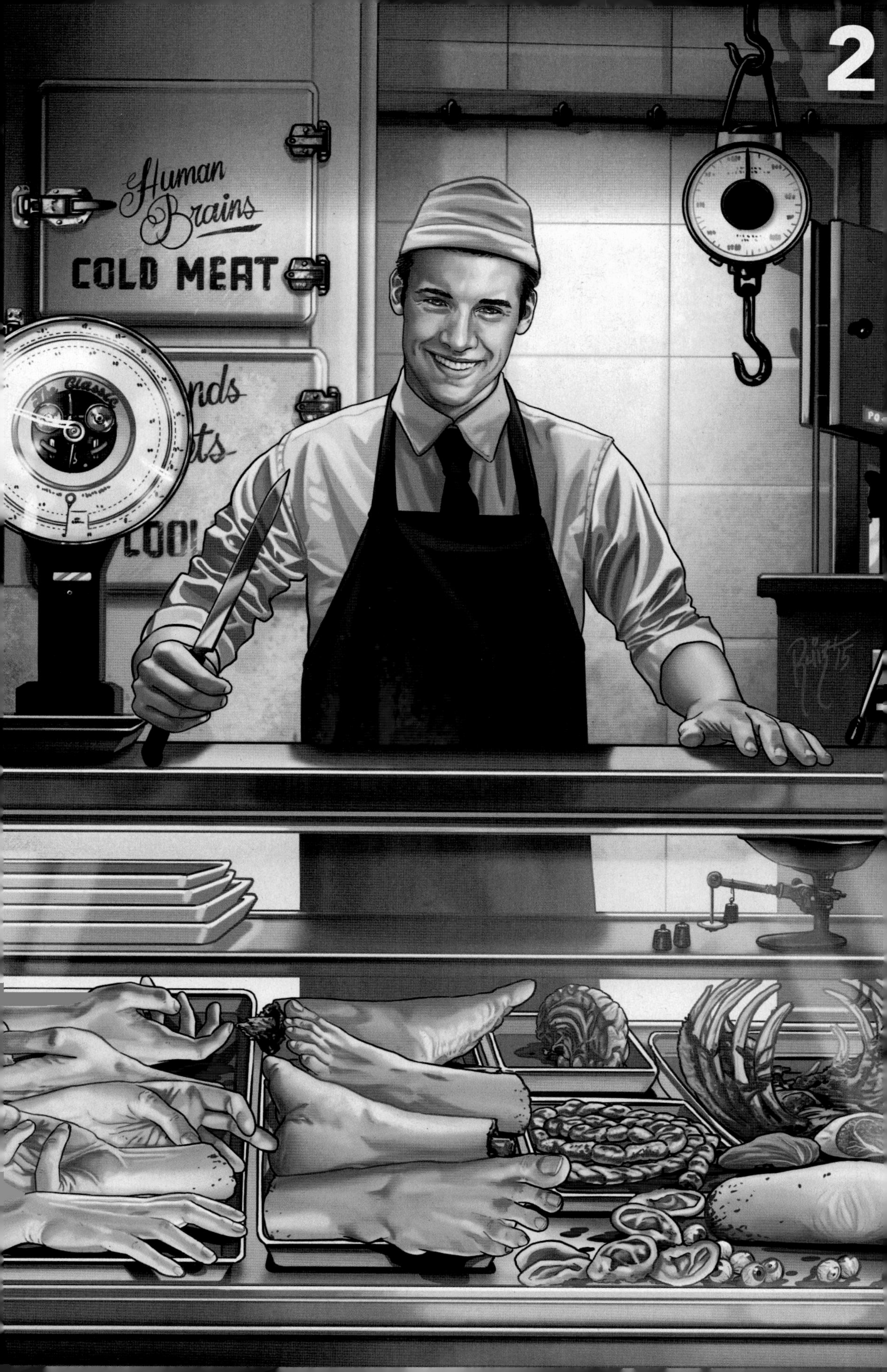
2
Human Brains
COLD MEAT

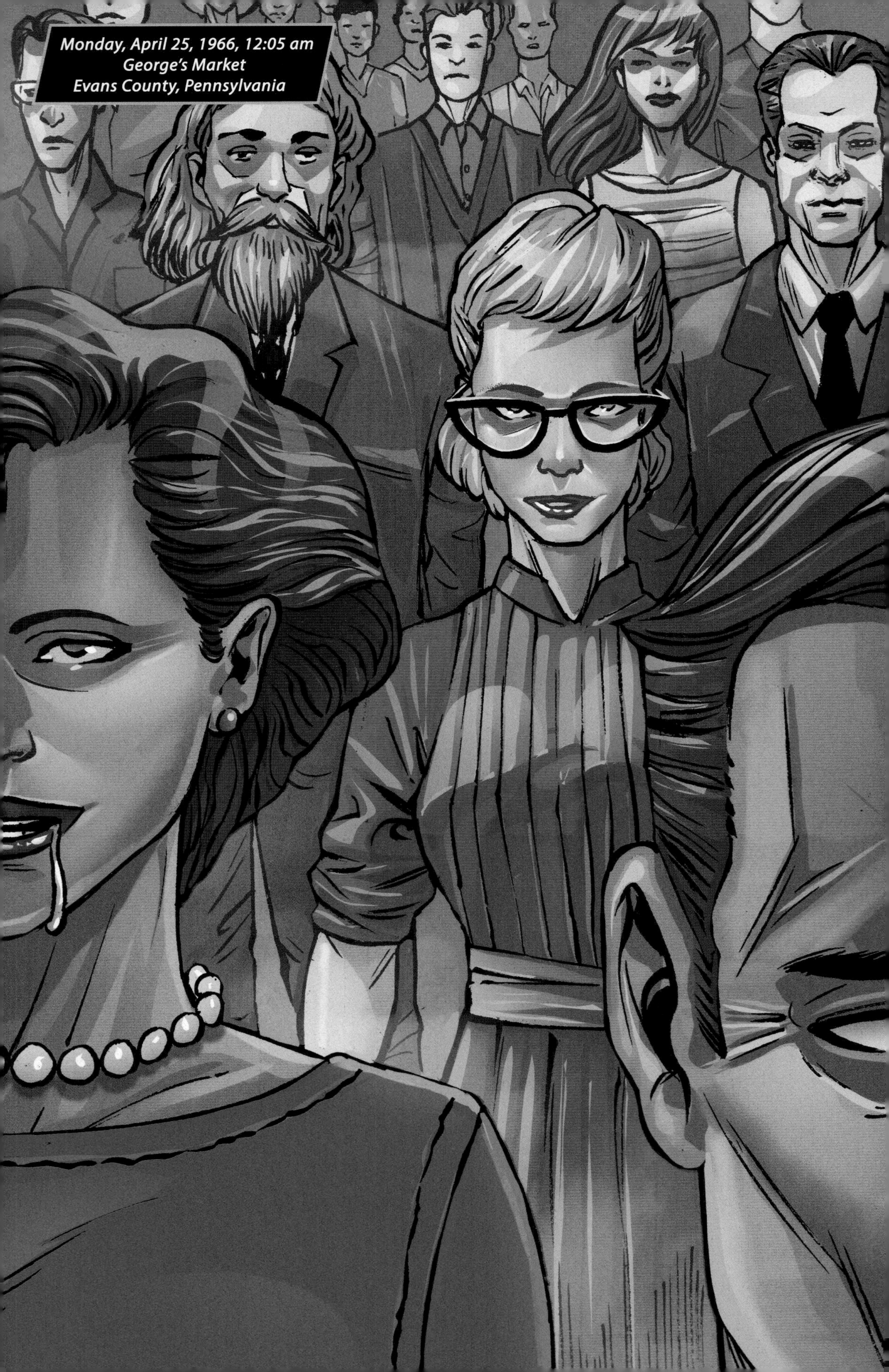
Monday, April 25, 1966, 12:05 am
George's Market
Evans County, Pennsylvania

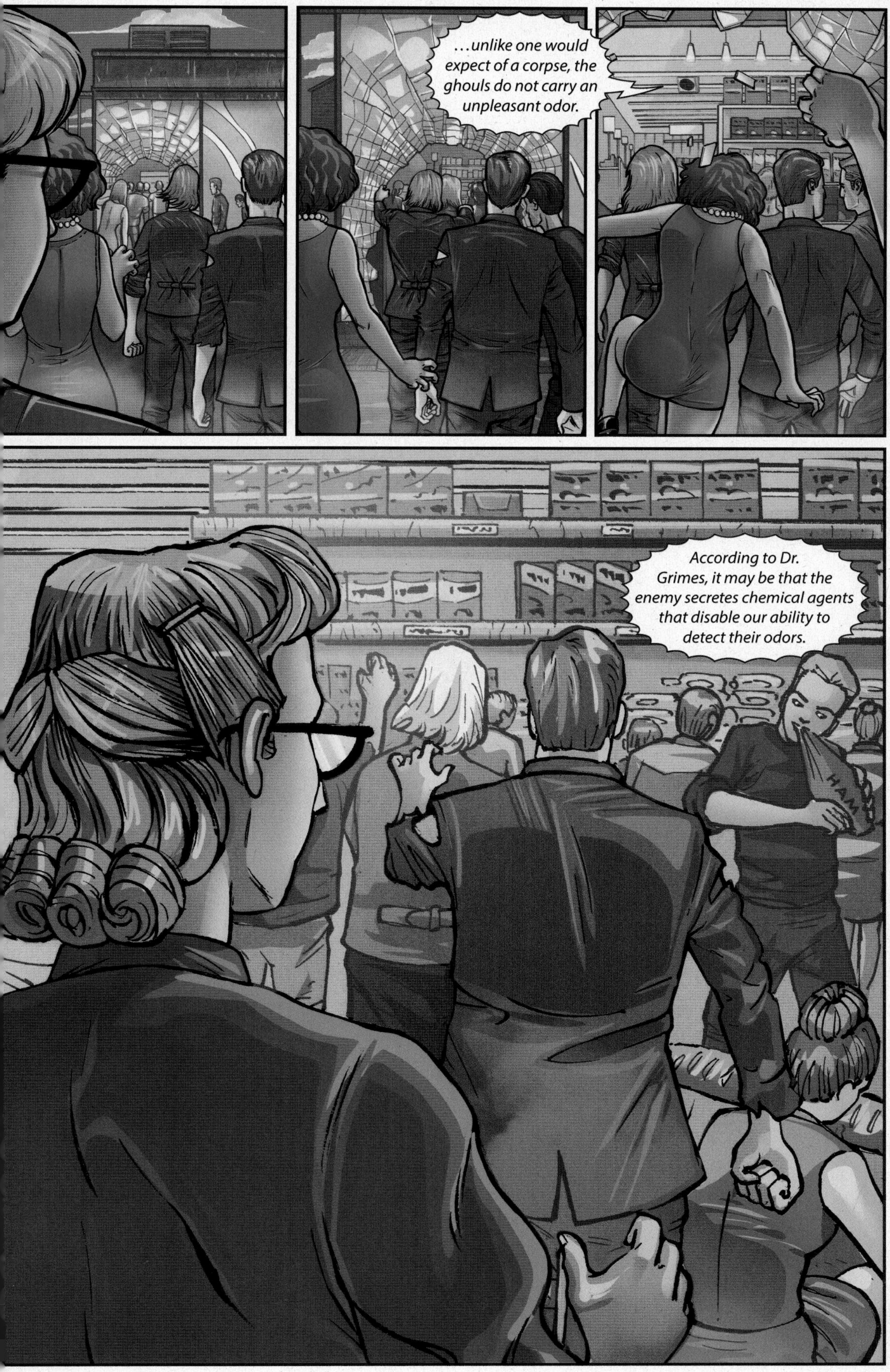
...unlike one would expect of a corpse, the ghouls do not carry an unpleasant odor.
According to Dr. Grimes, it may be that the enemy secretes chemical agents that disable our ability to detect their odors.
HAM

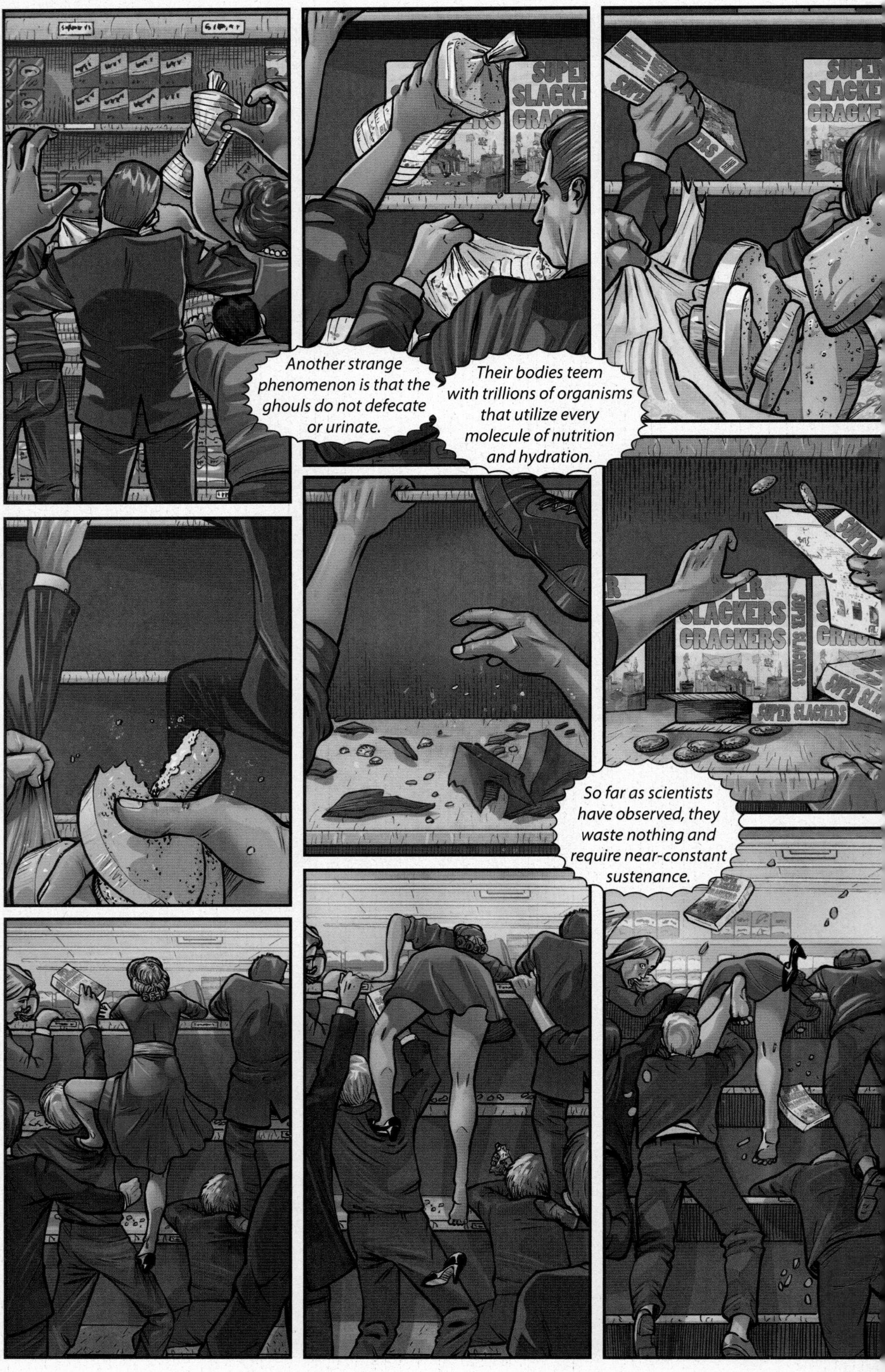
Another strange phenomenon is that the ghouls do not defecate or urinate.
Their bodies teem with trillions of organisms that utilize every molecule of nutrition and hydration.
So far as scientists have observed, they waste nothing and require near-constant sustenance.

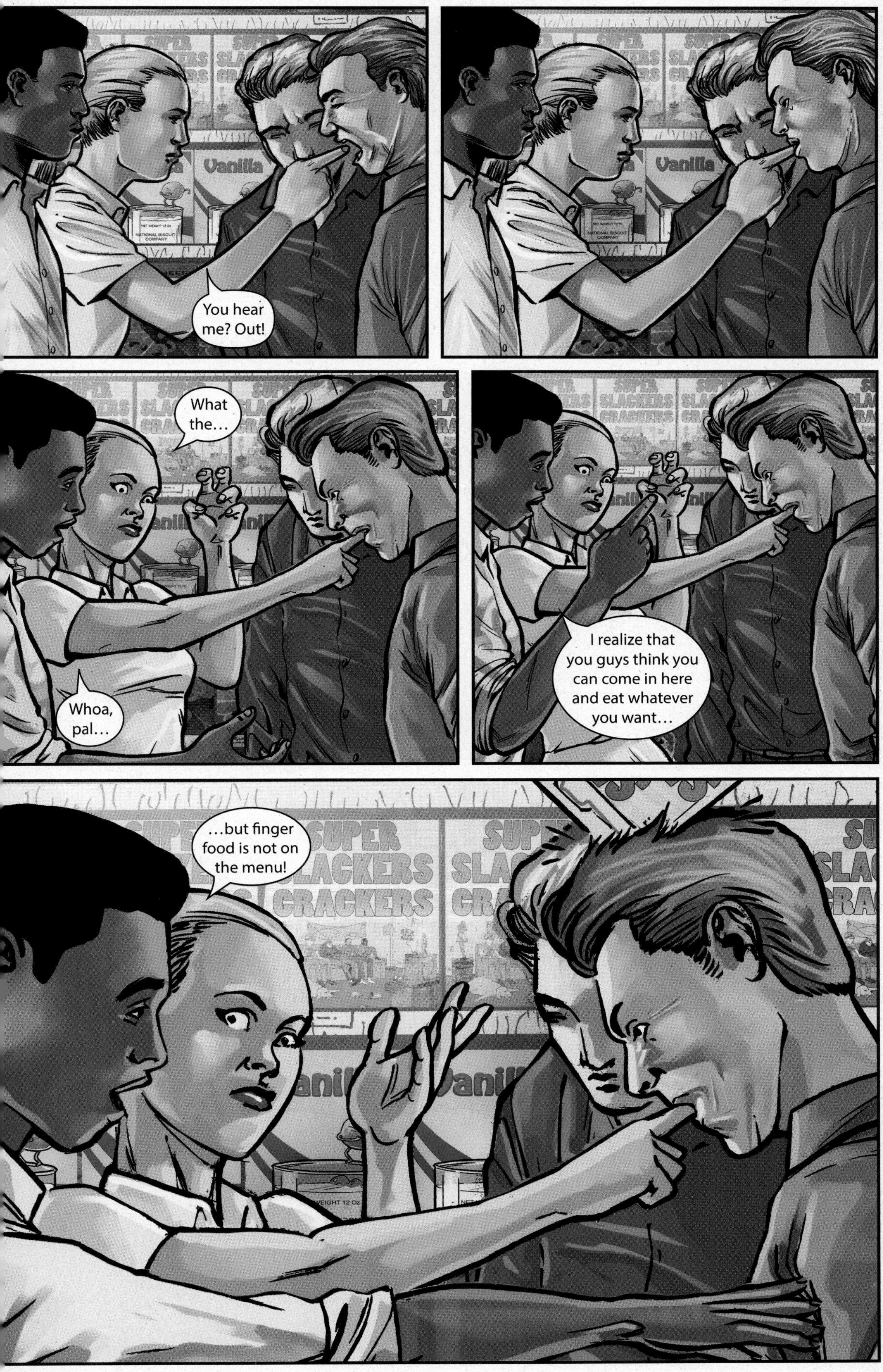
You hear me? Out!
What the…
Whoa, pal…
I realize that you guys think you can come in here and eat whatever you want…
…but finger food is not on the menu!
SUPER SLACKERS CRACKERS
Vanilla

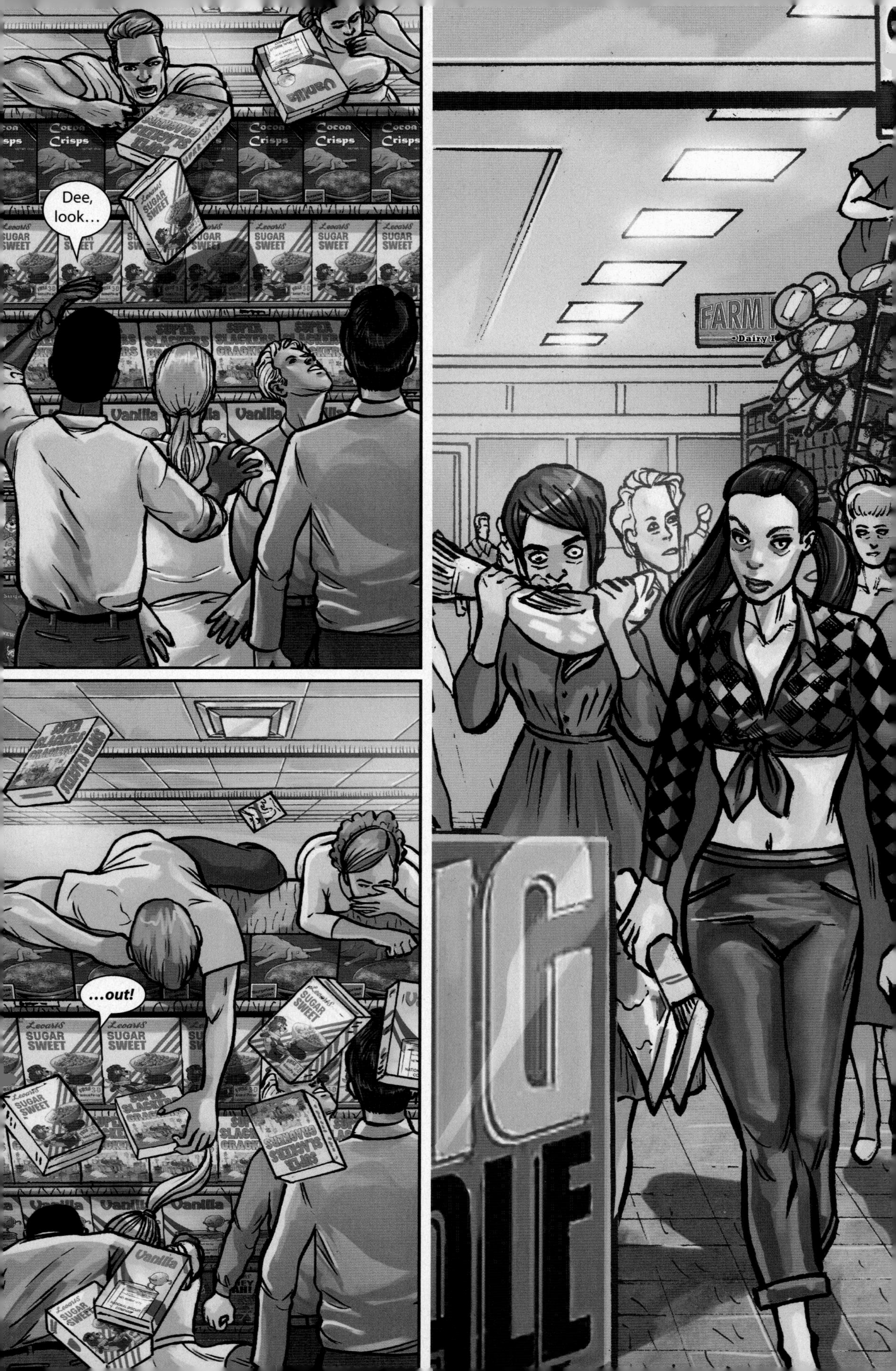
Dee, look…
…out!

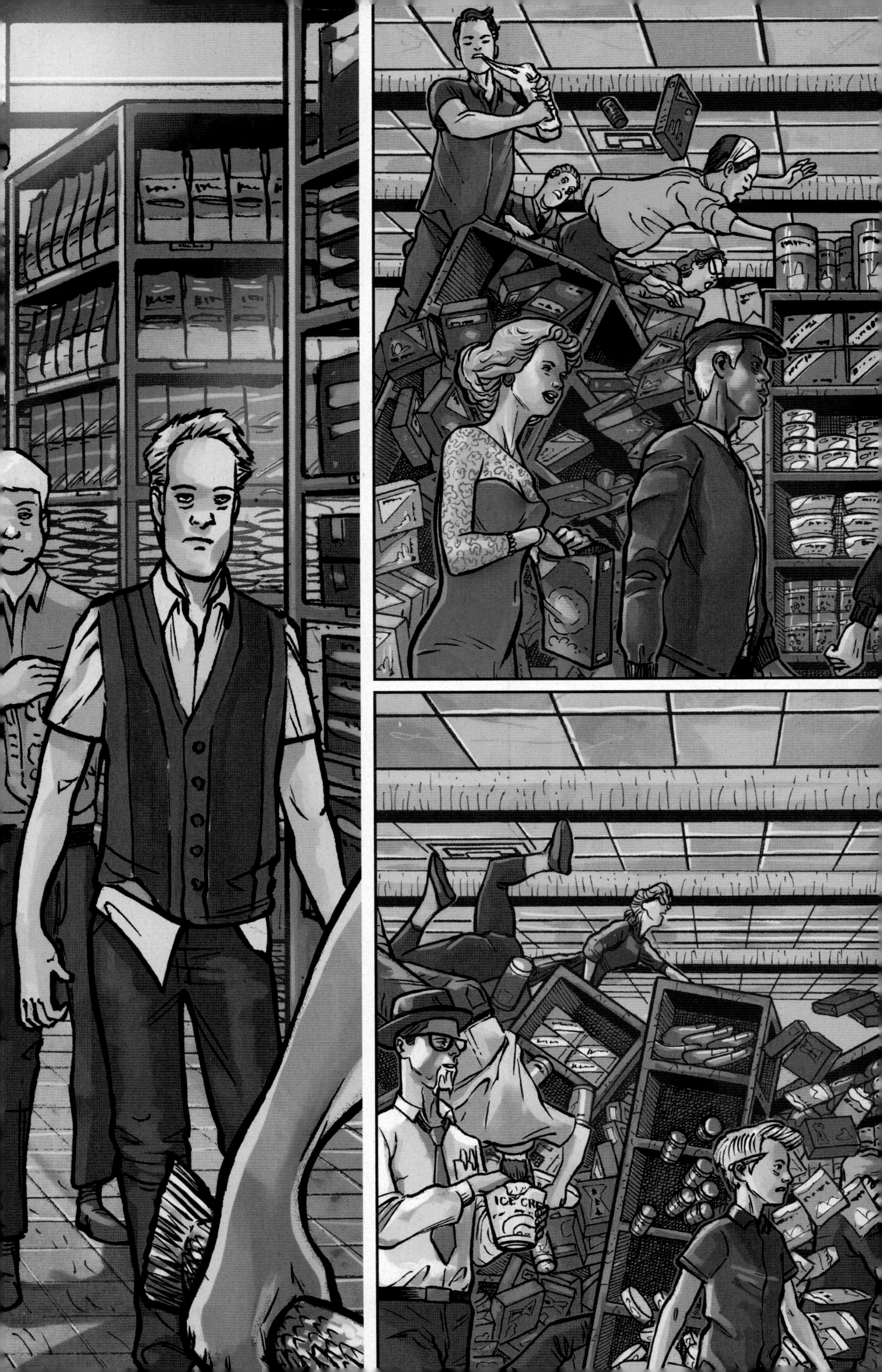
ICE

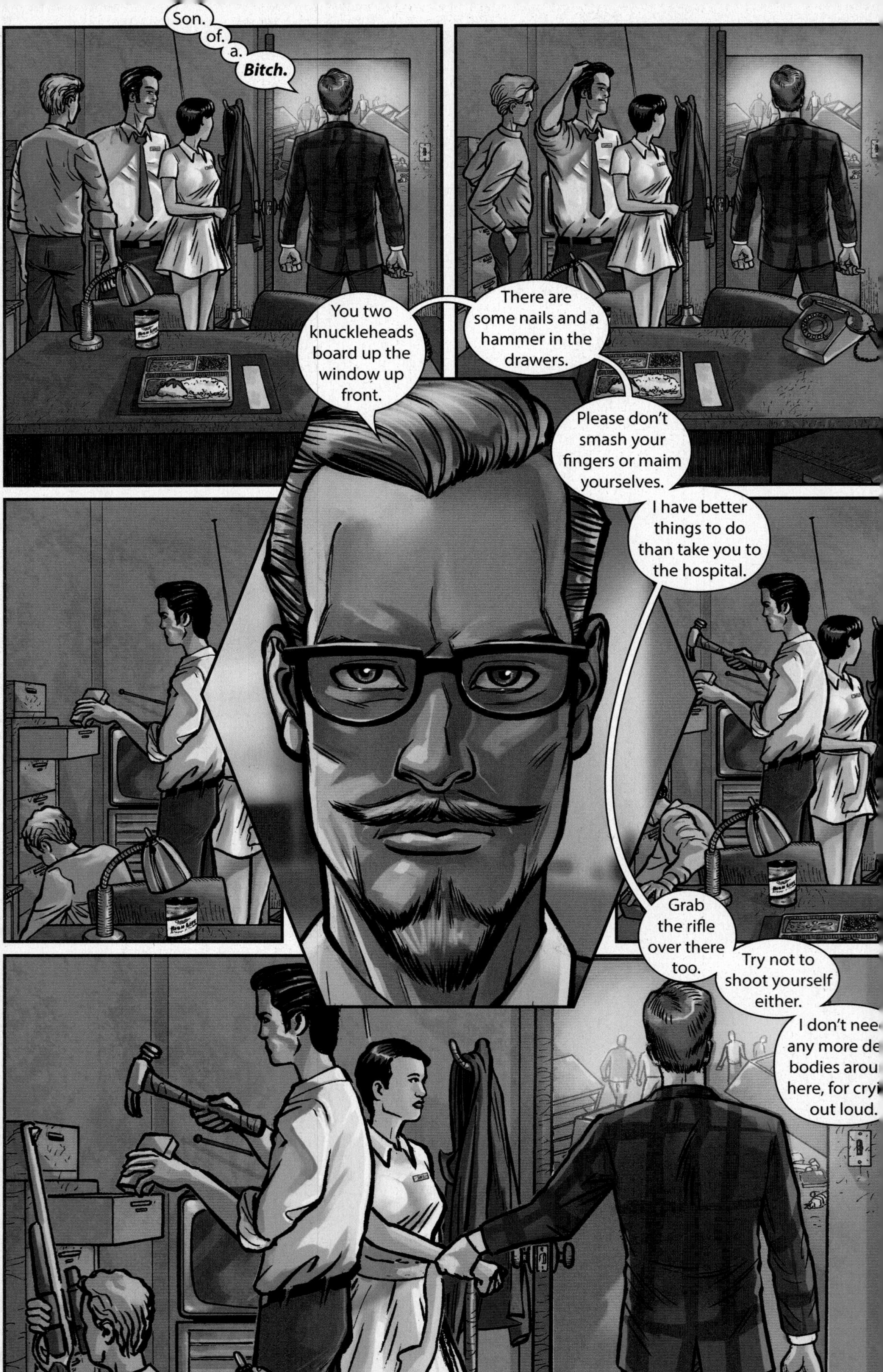

Son.
of.
a.
Bitch.
You two knuckleheads board up the window up front.
There are some nails and a hammer in the drawers.
Please don't smash your fingers or maim yourselves.
I have better things to do than take you to the hospital.
Grab the rifle over there too.
Try not to shoot yourself either.

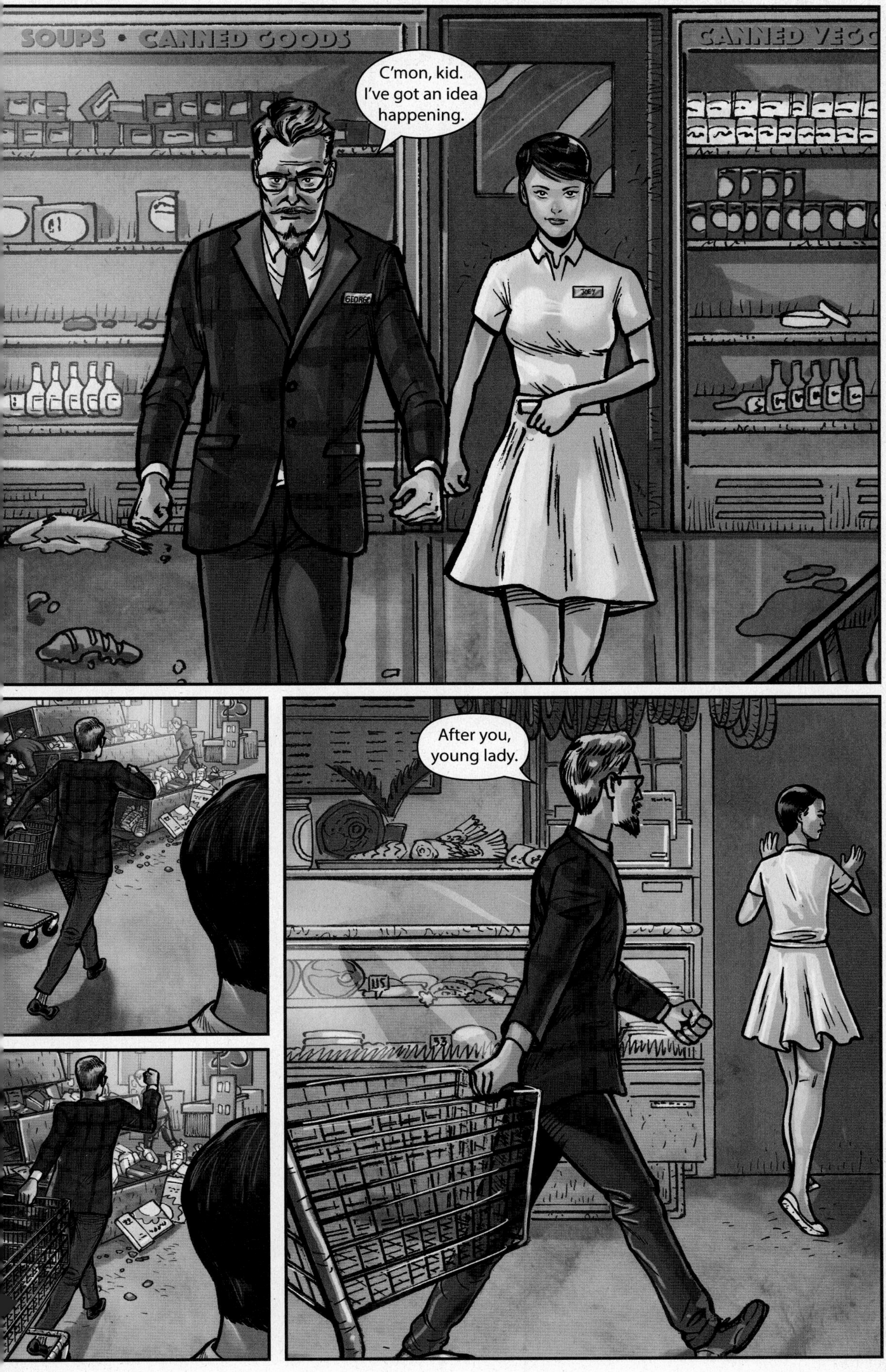
SOUPS • CANNED GOODS
C'mon, kid. I've got an idea happening.
GEORGE
JOEY
After you, young lady.

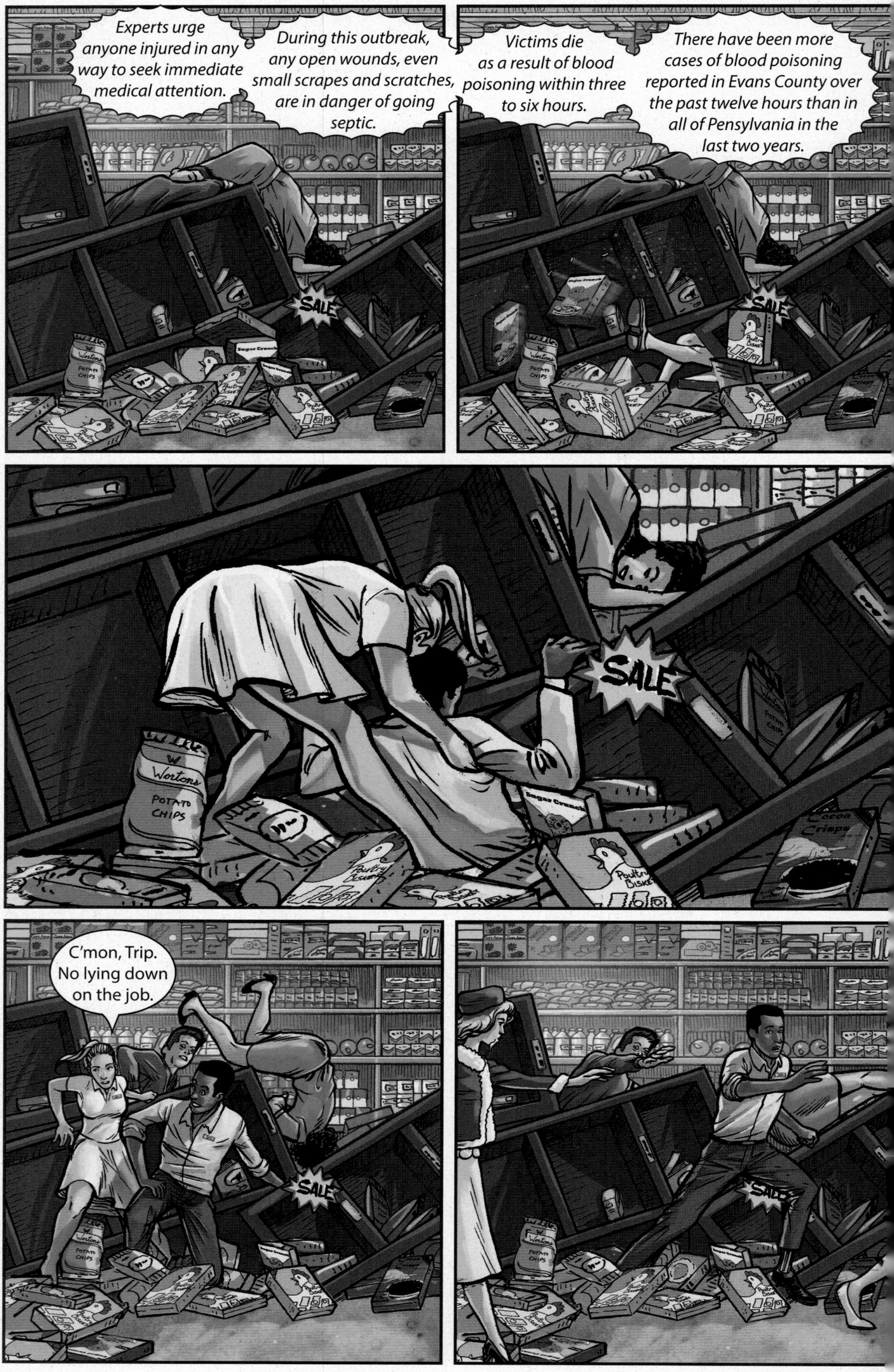
Experts urge anyone injured in any way to seek immediate medical attention.
During this outbreak, any open wounds, even small scrapes and scratches, are in danger of going septic.
SALE
Wortons POTATO CHIPS
Sugar Crunch
Poultry Bisket
Victims die as a result of blood poisoning within three to six hours.
There have been more cases of blood poisoning reported in Evans County over the past twelve hours than in all of Pensylvania in the last two years.
SALE
Sugar Crunch
Poultry Bisket
SALE
Wortons POTATO CHIPS
Sugar Crunch
Poultry Bisket
Cocoa Crisps
C'mon, Trip. No lying down on the job.
SALE
SALE

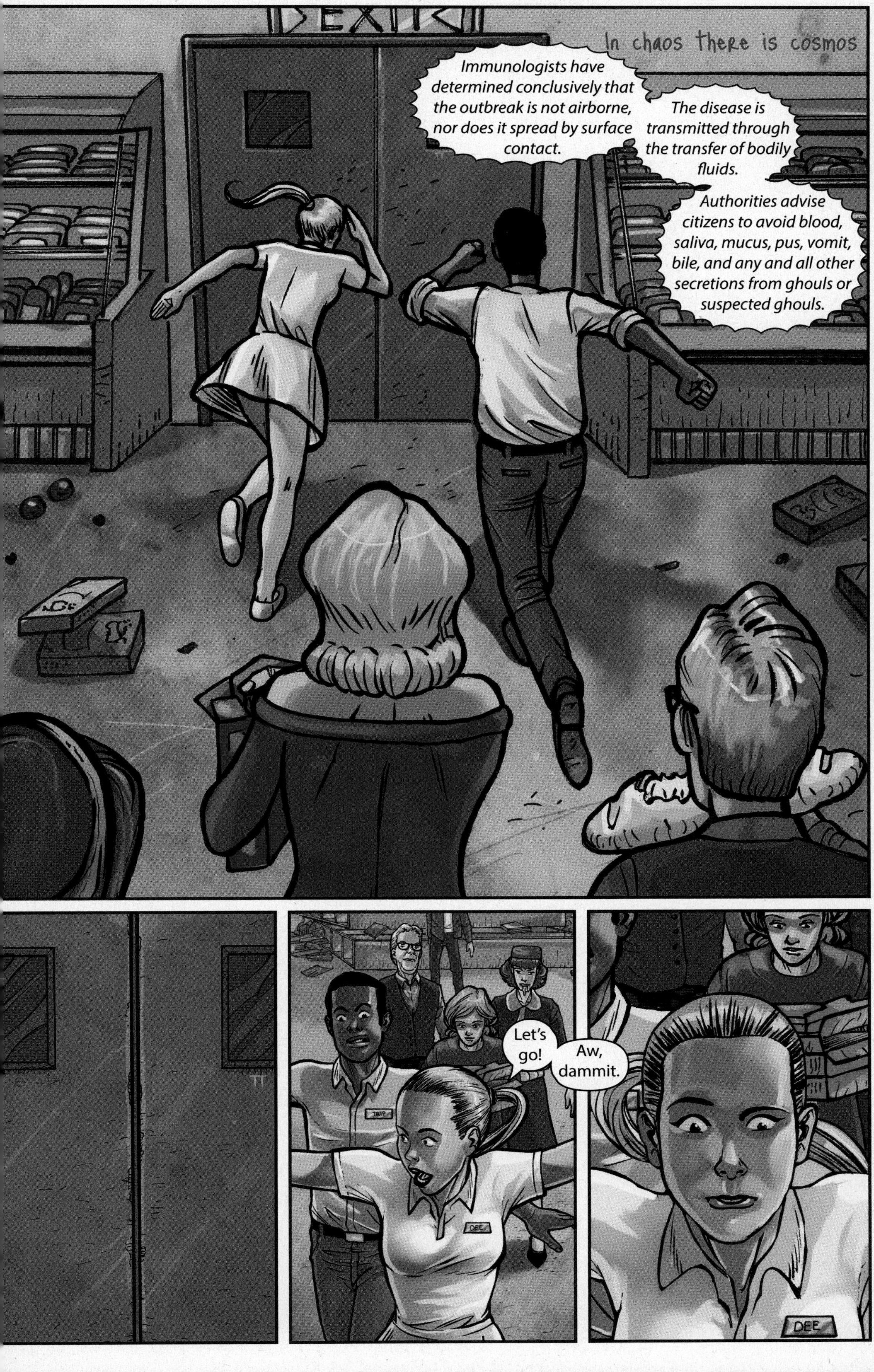
EXIT
In chaos there is cosmos
Immunologists have determined conclusively that the outbreak is not airborne, nor does it spread by surface contact.
The disease is transmitted through the transfer of bodily fluids.
Authorities advise citizens to avoid blood, saliva, mucus, pus, vomit, bile, and any and all other secretions from ghouls or suspected ghouls.
TRIP
Let's go!
Aw, dammit.
DEE
DEE

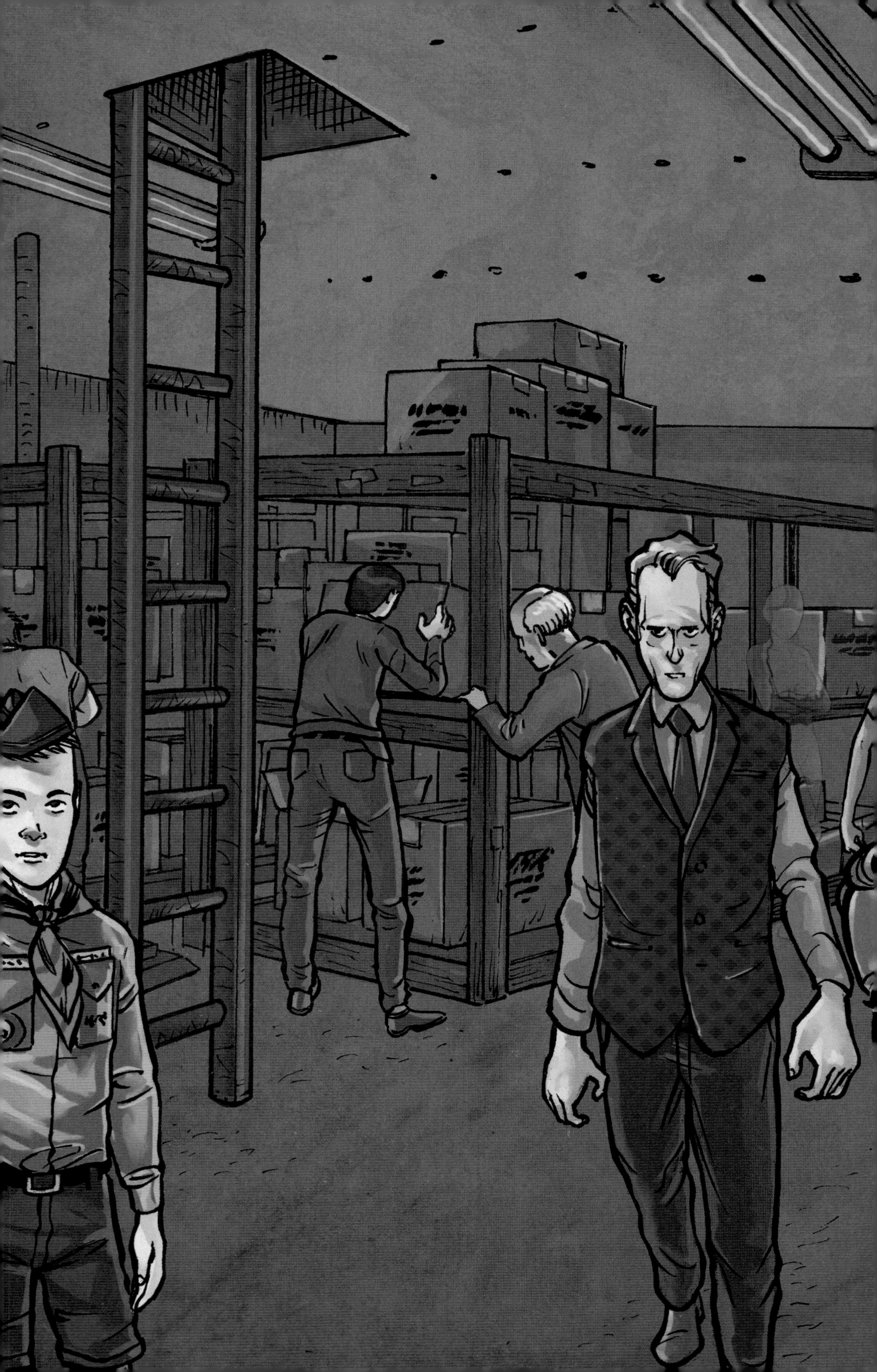

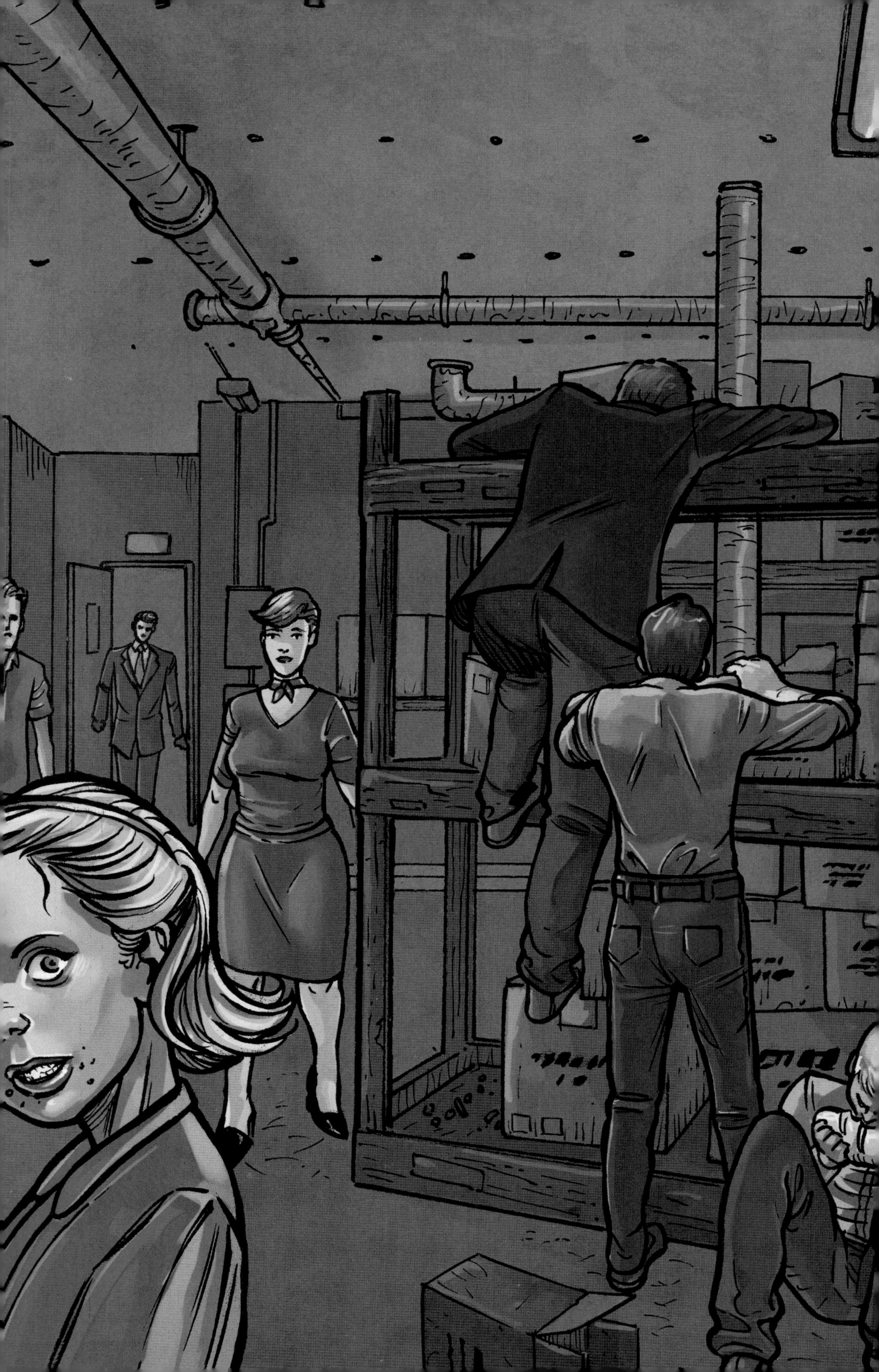

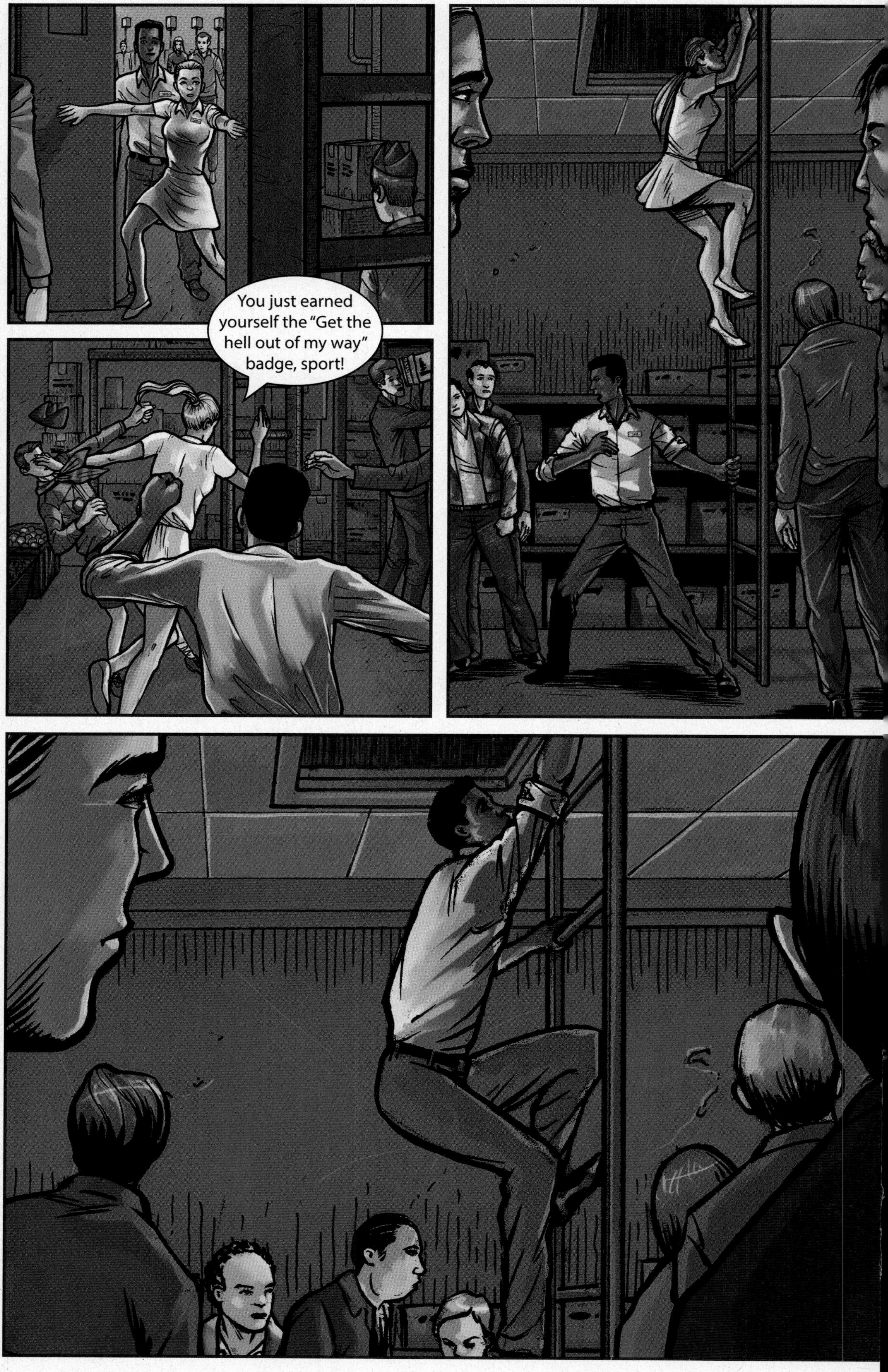
You just earned yourself the "Get the hell out of my way" badge, sport!

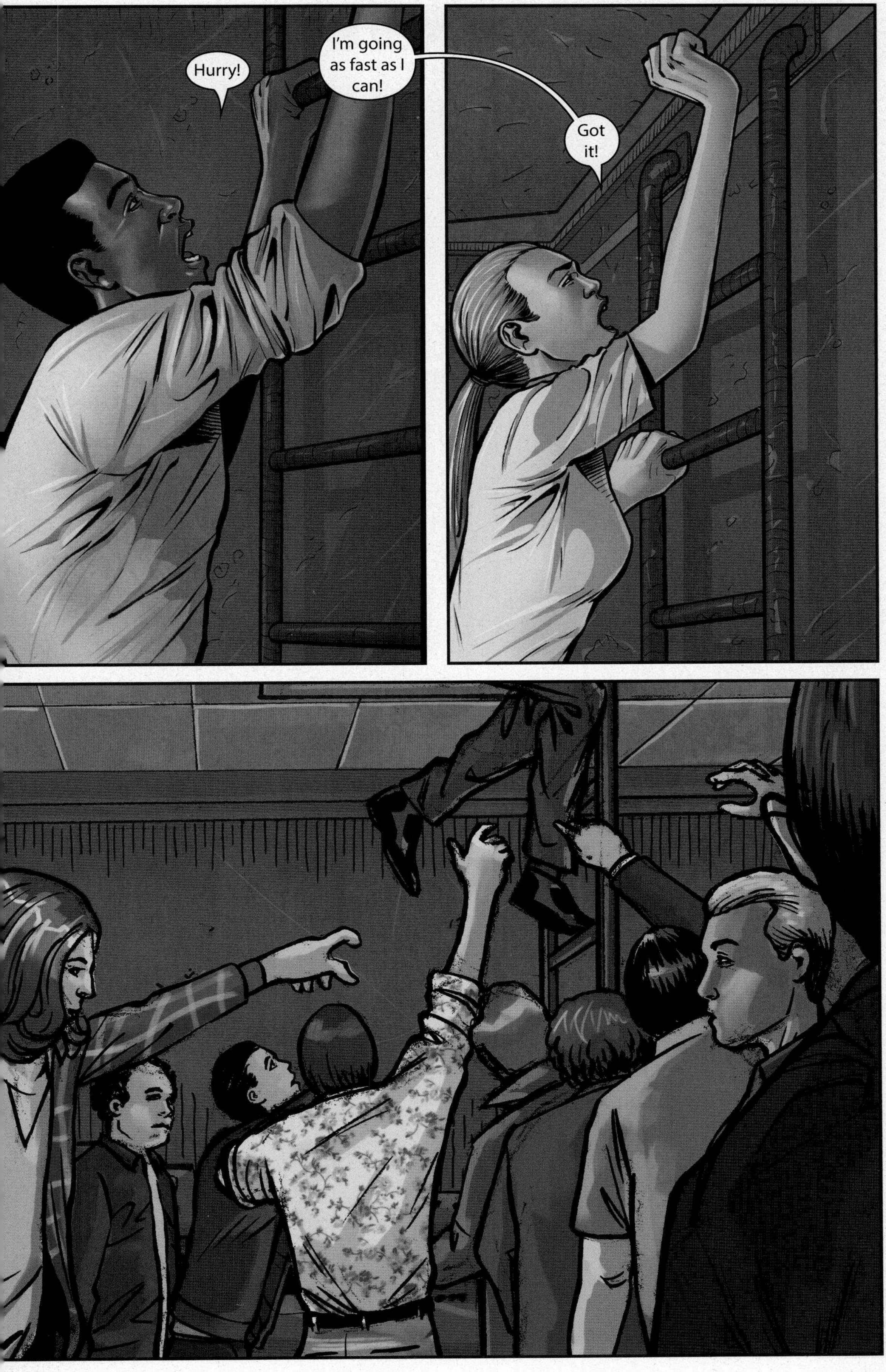
Hurry!
I'm going as fast as I can!
Got it!

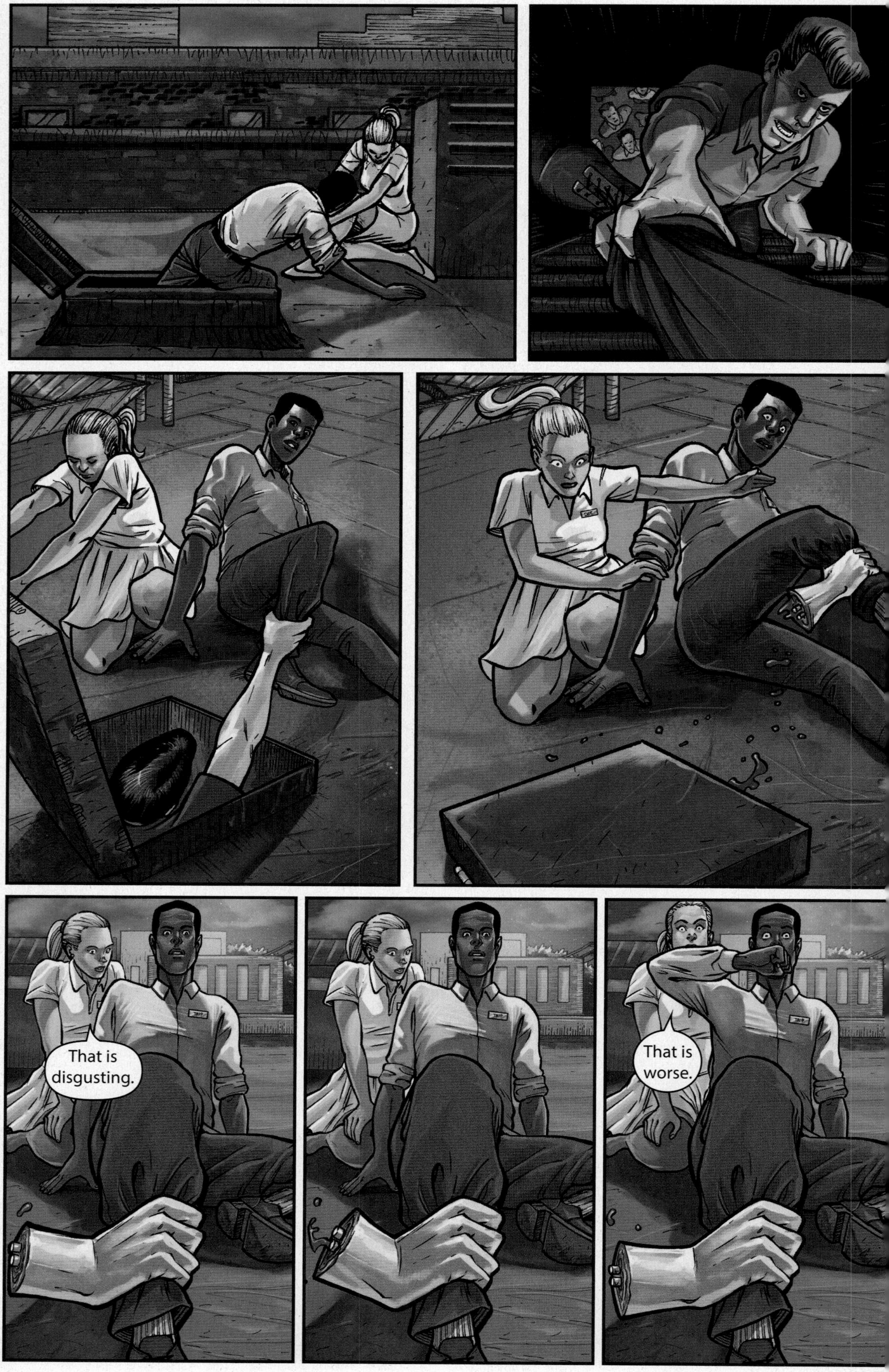
That is disgusting.
That is worse.

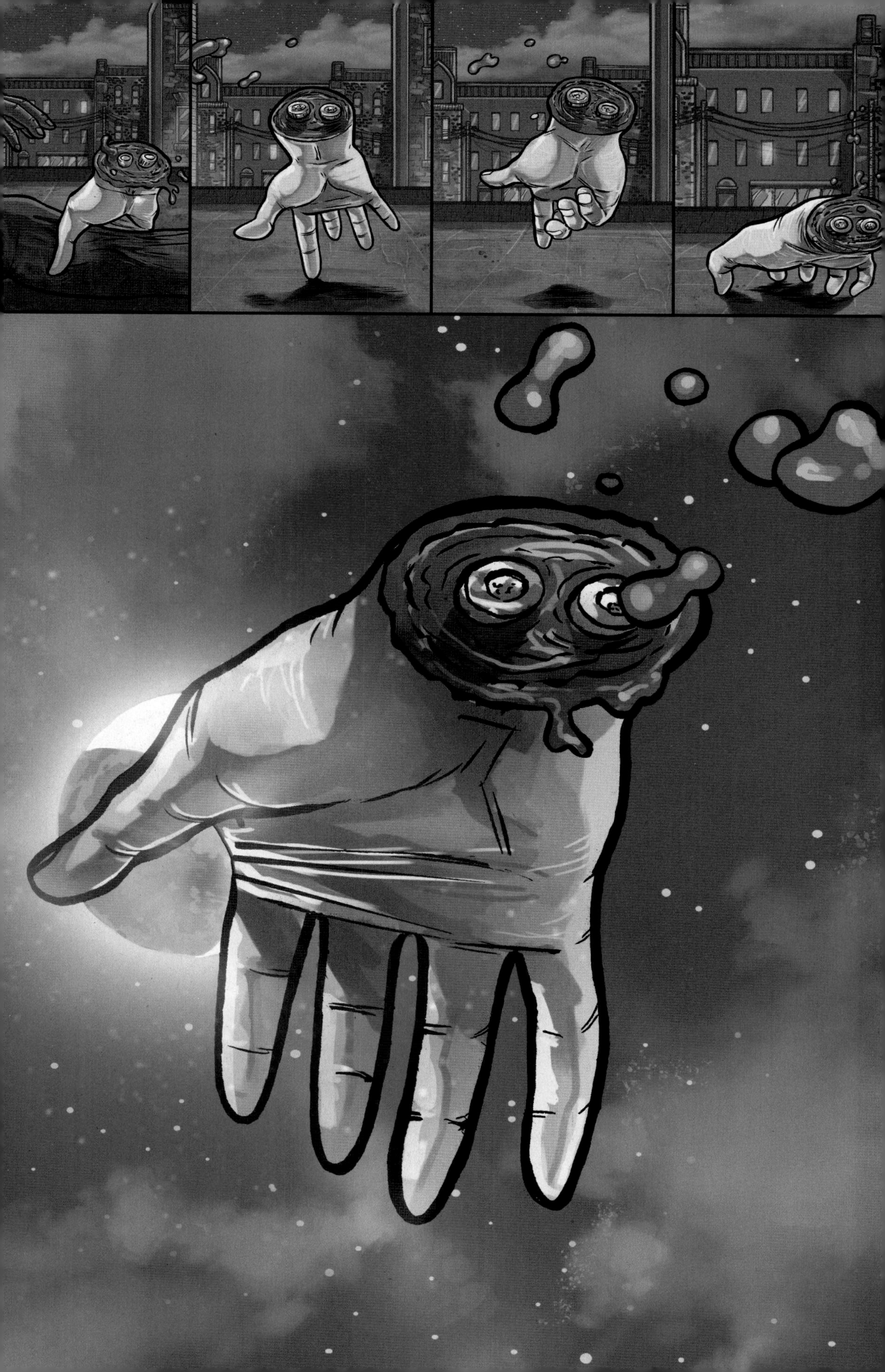

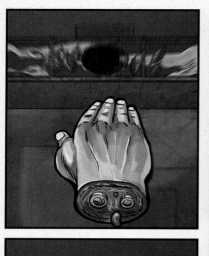

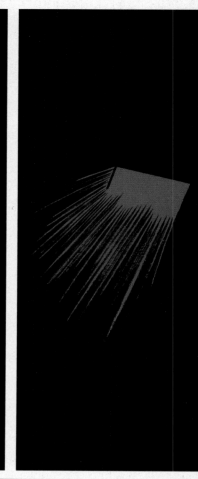

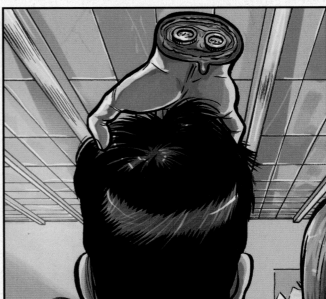
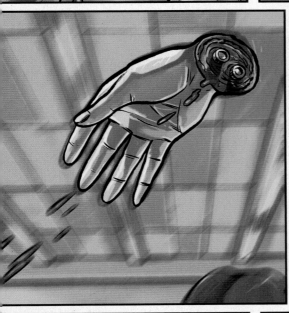

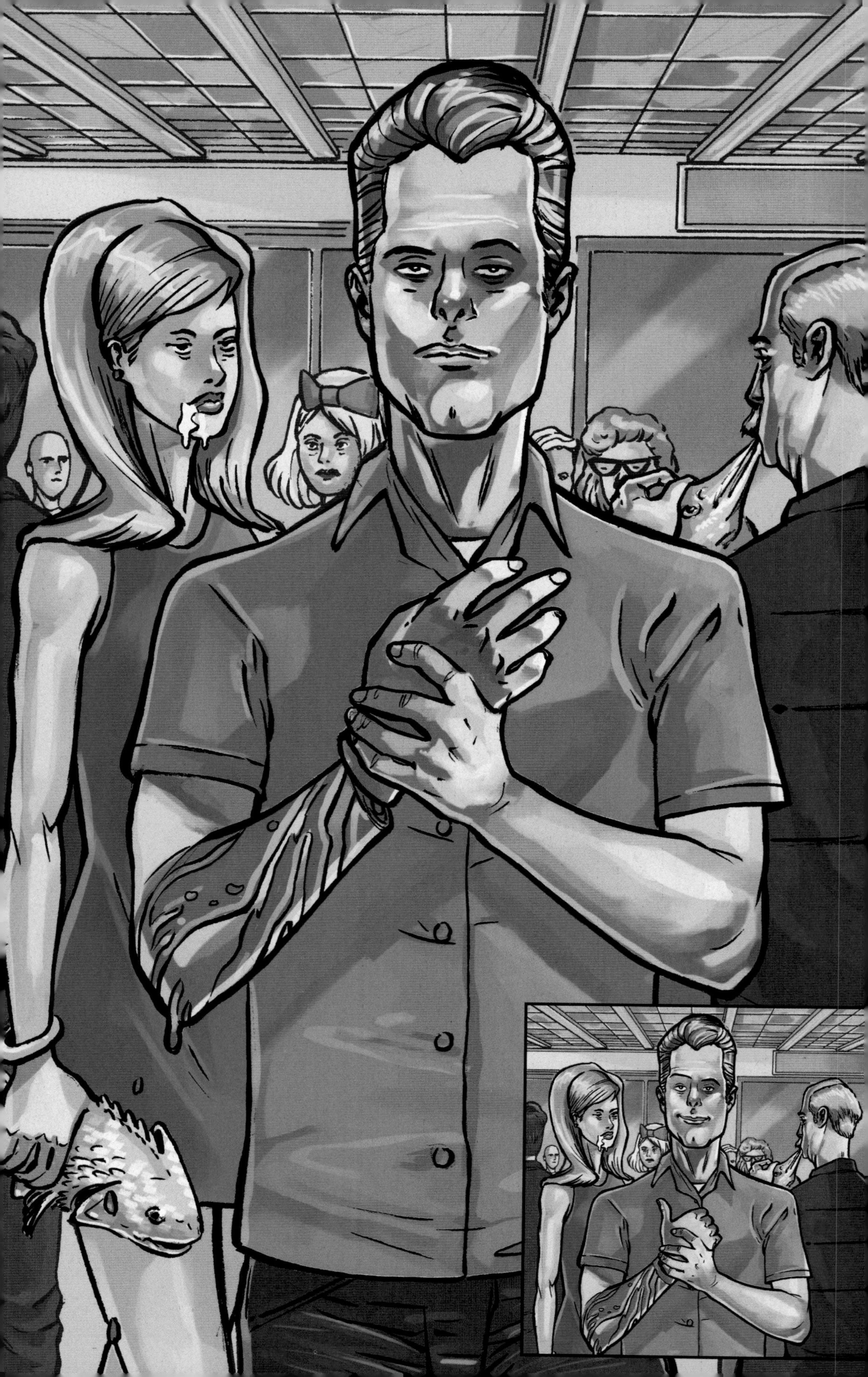

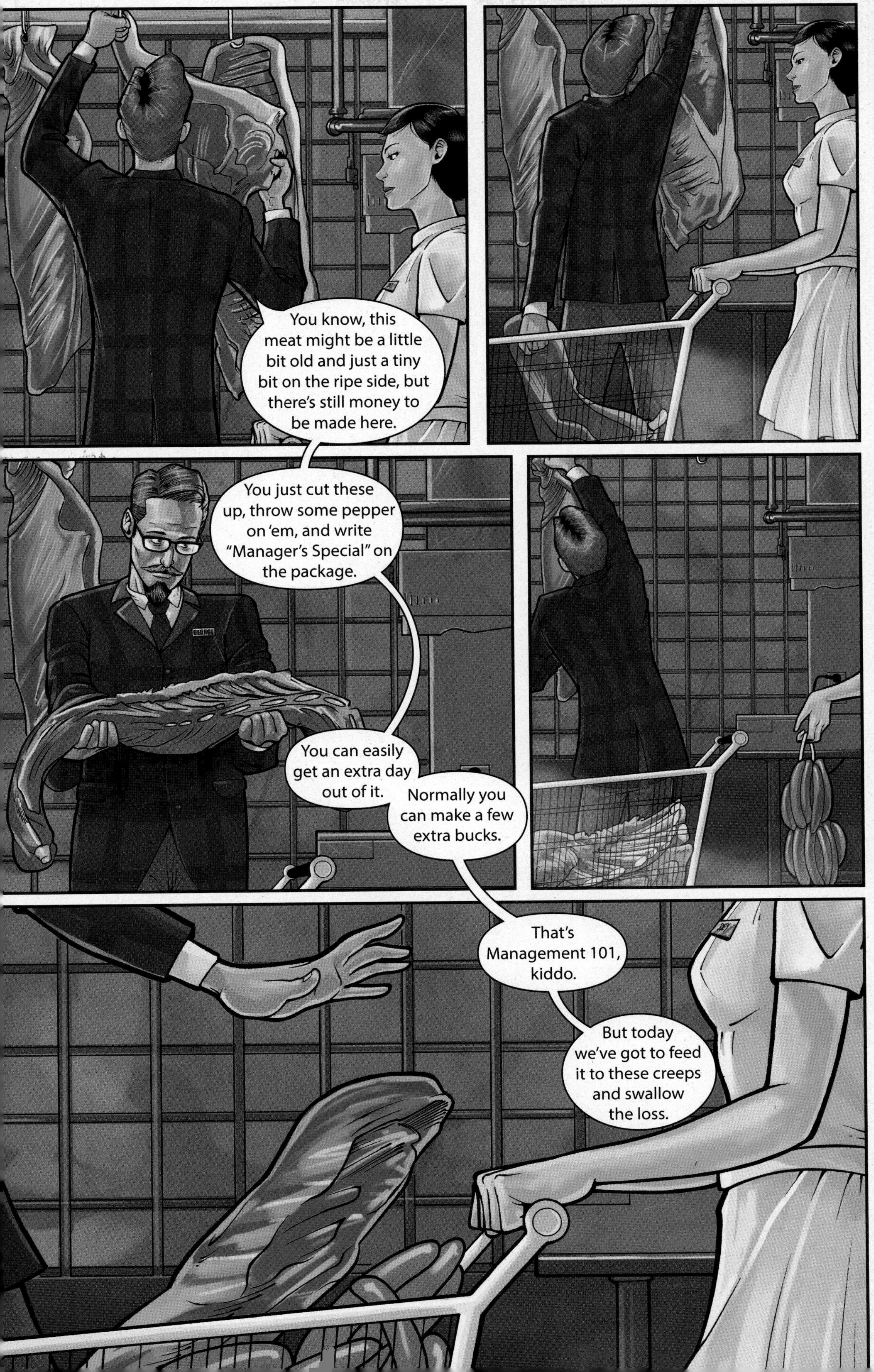

You know, this meat might be a little bit old and just a tiny bit on the ripe side, but there's still money to be made here.
GEORGE
You just cut these up, throw some pepper on 'em, and write "Manager's Special" on the package.
You can easily get an extra day out of it.
Normally you can make a few extra bucks.
That's Management 101, kiddo.
But today we've got to feed it to these creeps and swallow the loss.

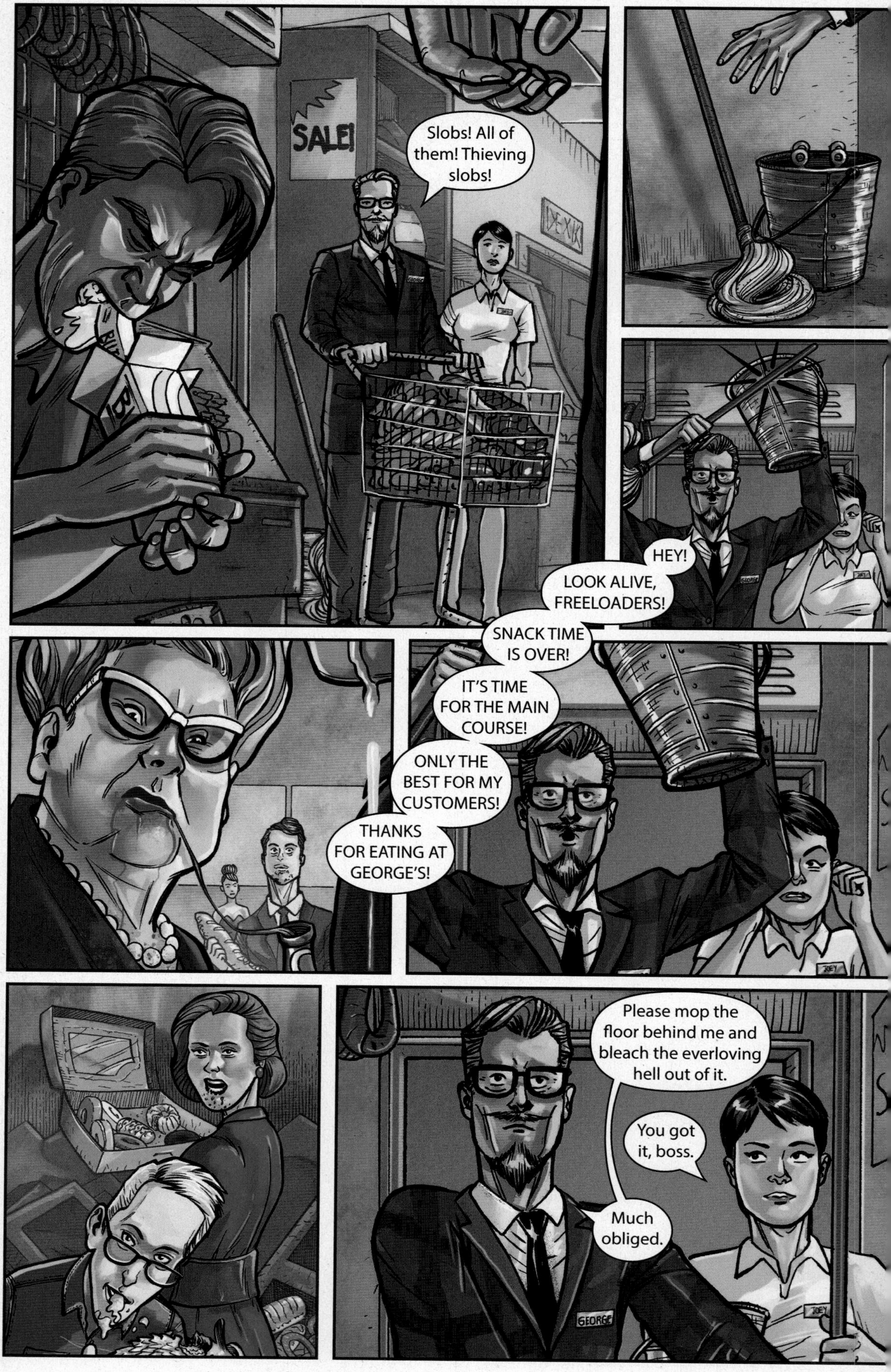
SALE!
Slobs! All of them! Thieving slobs!
HEY!
LOOK ALIVE, FREELOADERS!
SNACK TIME IS OVER!
IT'S TIME FOR THE MAIN COURSE!
ONLY THE BEST FOR MY CUSTOMERS!
THANKS FOR EATING AT GEORGE'S!
Please mop the floor behind me and bleach the everloving hell out of it.
You got it, boss.
Much obliged.
GEORGE
JOEY

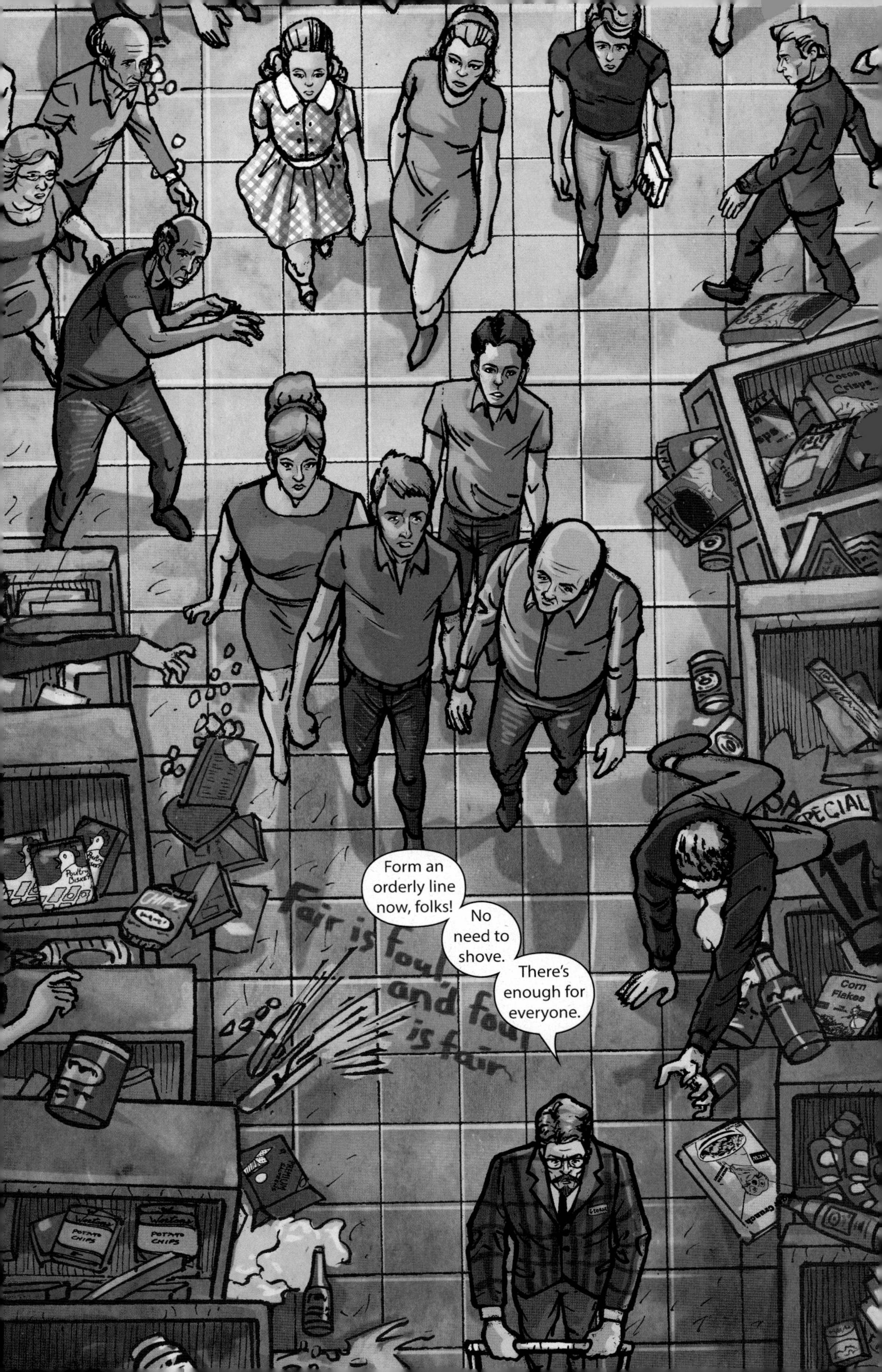
Form an orderly line now, folks!
No need to shove.
There's enough for everyone.
Fair is foul and foul is fair
SPECIAL
Cocoa Crisps
Corn Flakes
Poultry Bisket
Westons POTATO CHIPS
Westons POTATO CHIPS

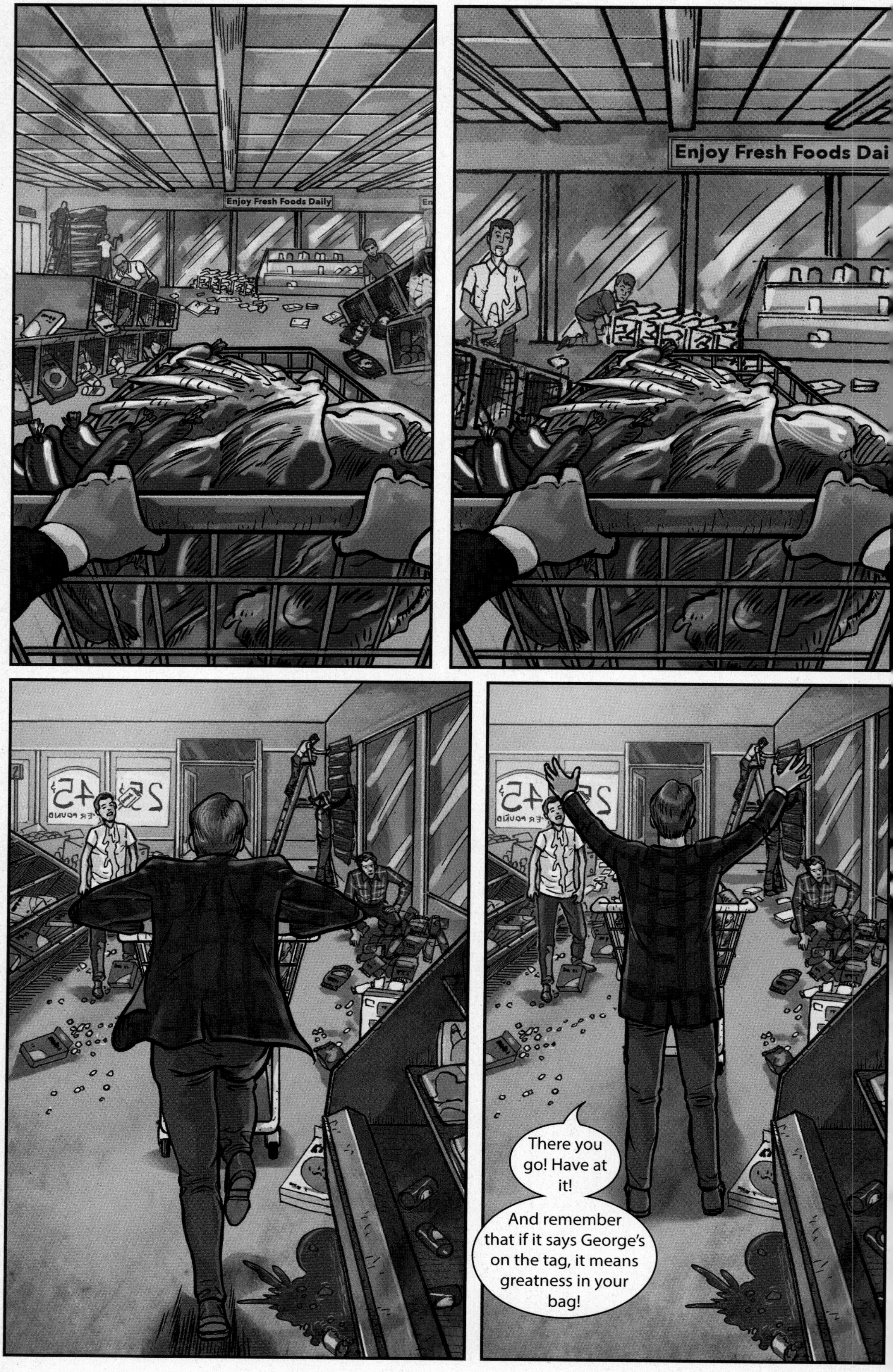
Enjoy Fresh Foods Daily
Enjoy Fresh Foods Dai
There you go! Have at it!
And remember that if it says George's on the tag, it means greatness in your bag!

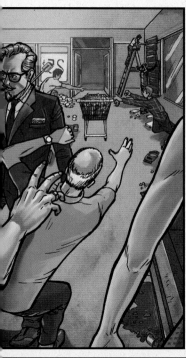

Bye now.

Thanks for coming.

Good riddance.

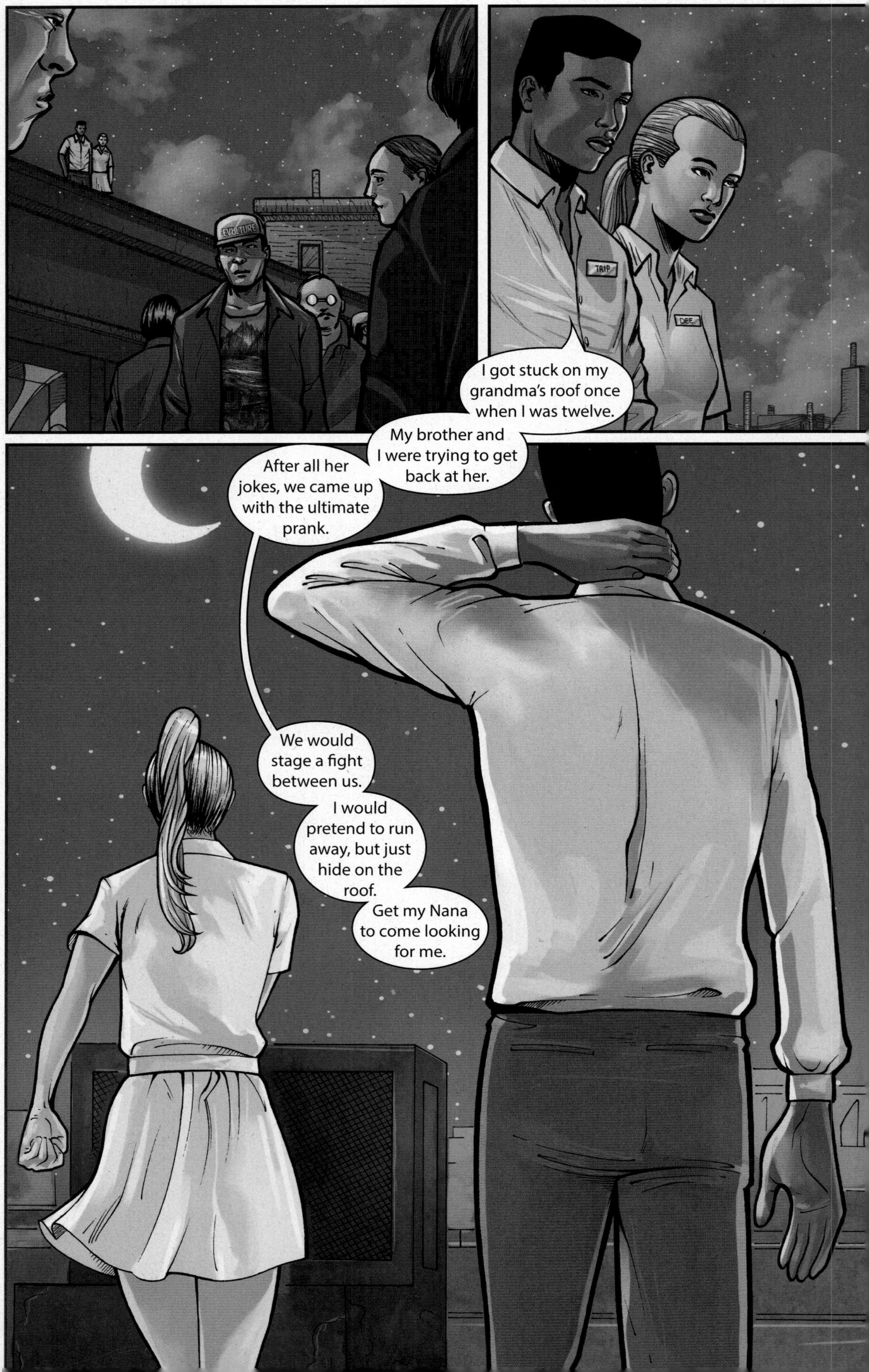
TRIP
DEE
I got stuck on my grandma's roof once when I was twelve.
My brother and I were trying to get back at her.
After all her jokes, we came up with the ultimate prank.
We would stage a fight between us.
I would pretend to run away, but just hide on the roof.
Get my Nana to come looking for me.

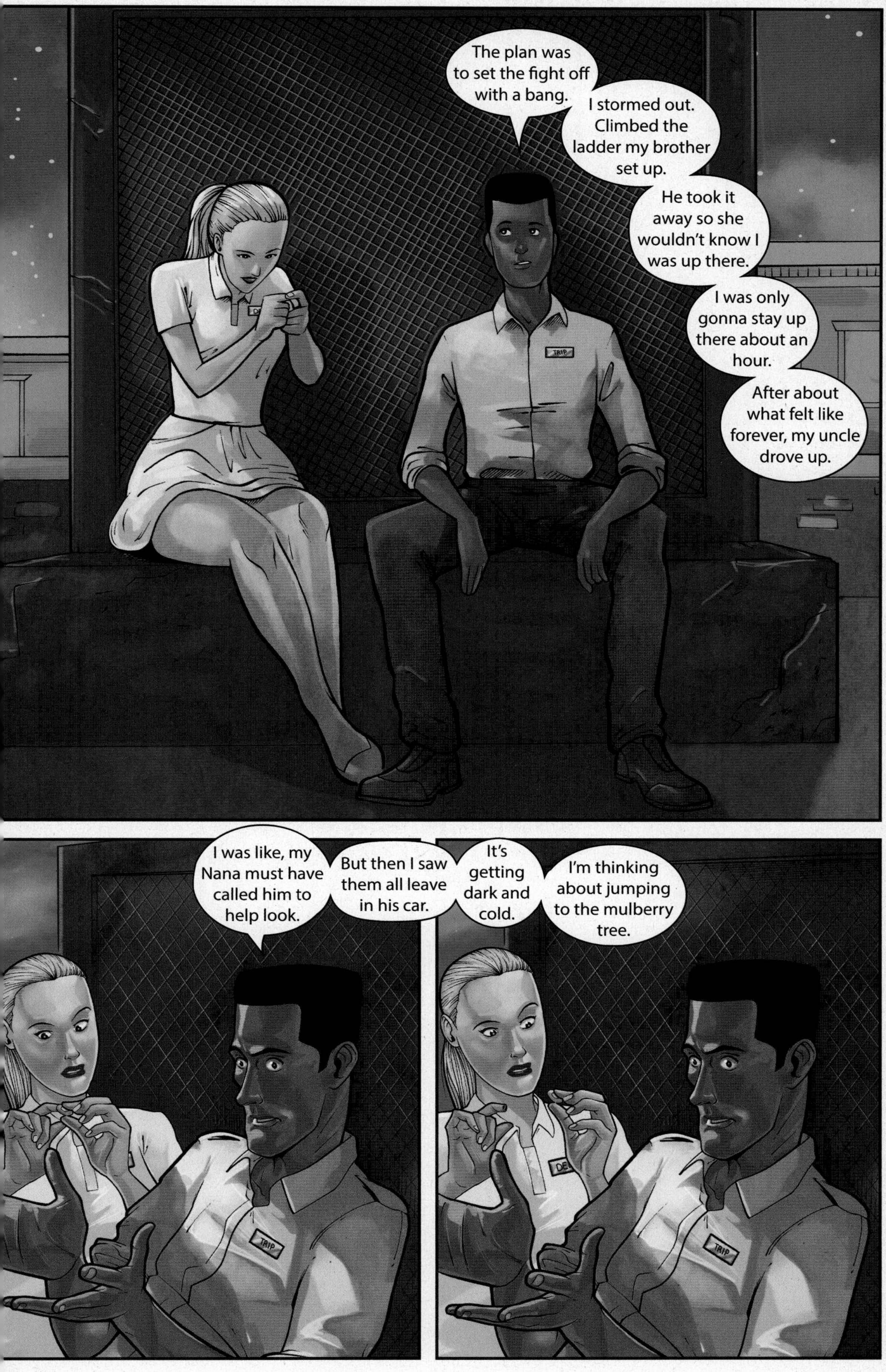

The plan was to set the fight off with a bang.
I stormed out. Climbed the ladder my brother set up.
He took it away so she wouldn't know I was up there.
I was only gonna stay up there about an hour.
After about what felt like forever, my uncle drove up.
TRIP
I was like, my Nana must have called him to help look.
But then I saw them all leave in his car.
TRIP
It's getting dark and cold.
I'm thinking about jumping to the mulberry tree.
DE
TRIP

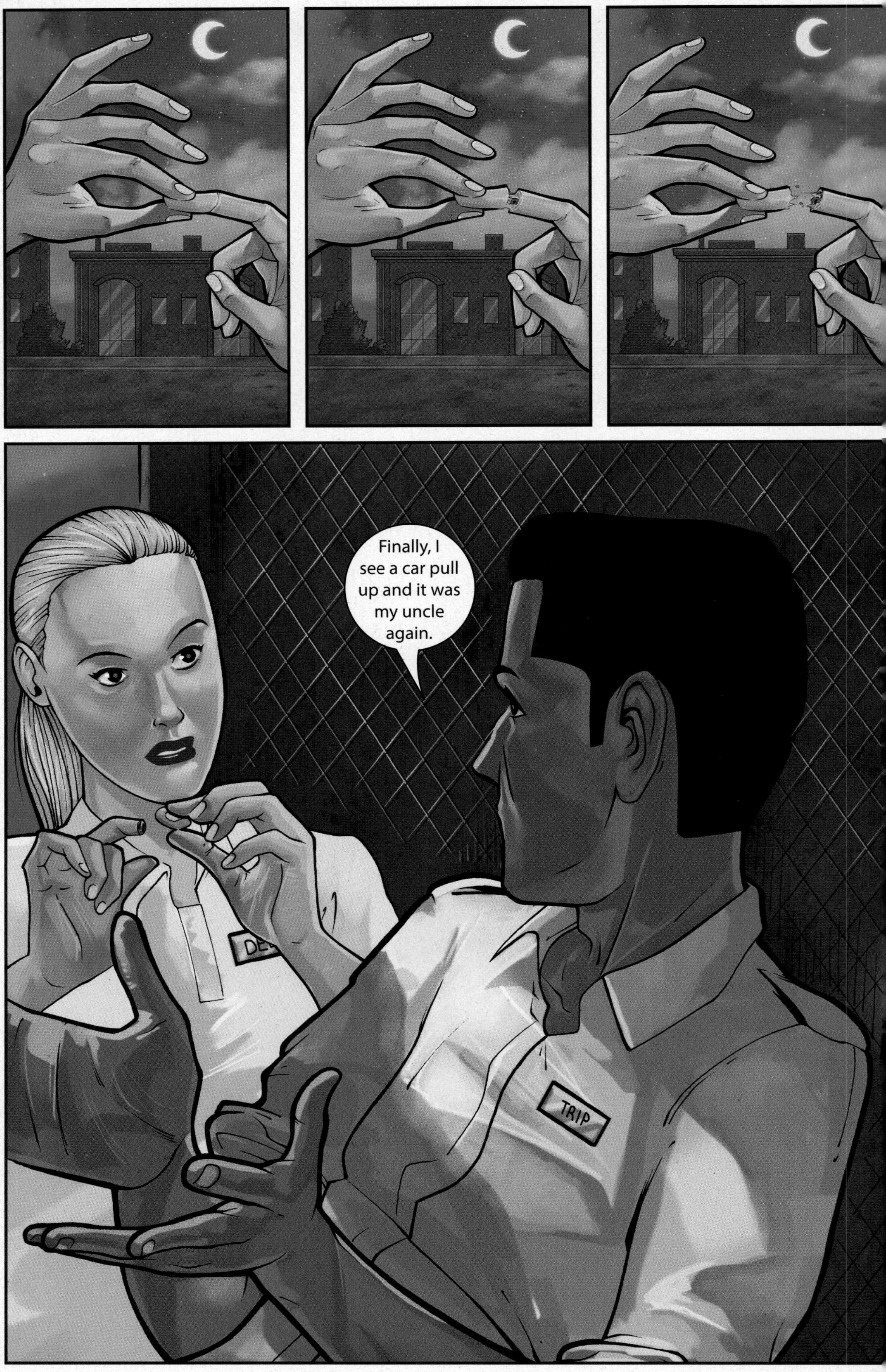
Finally, I see a car pull up and it was my uncle again.
TRIP

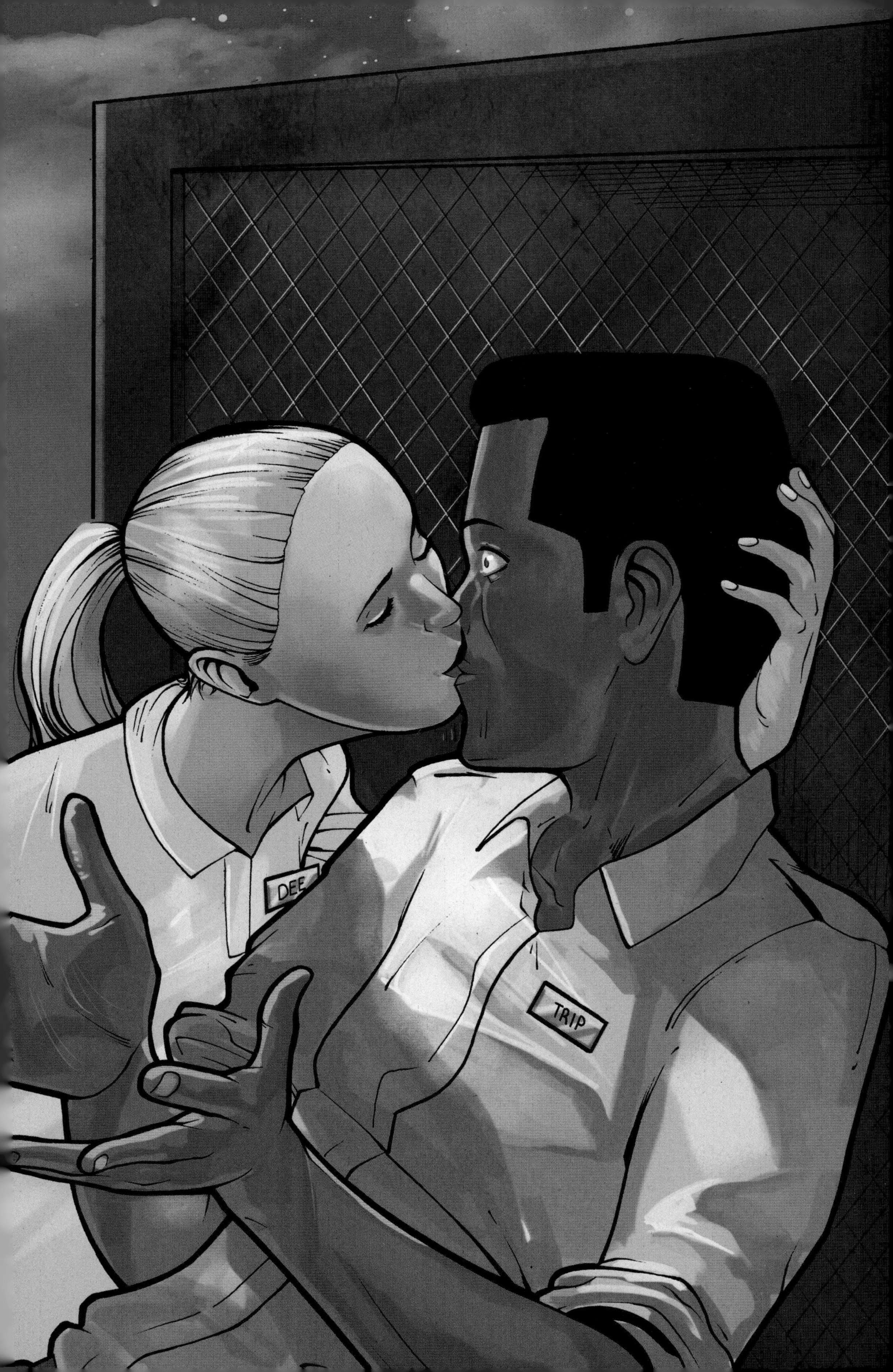
DEE
TRIP

3

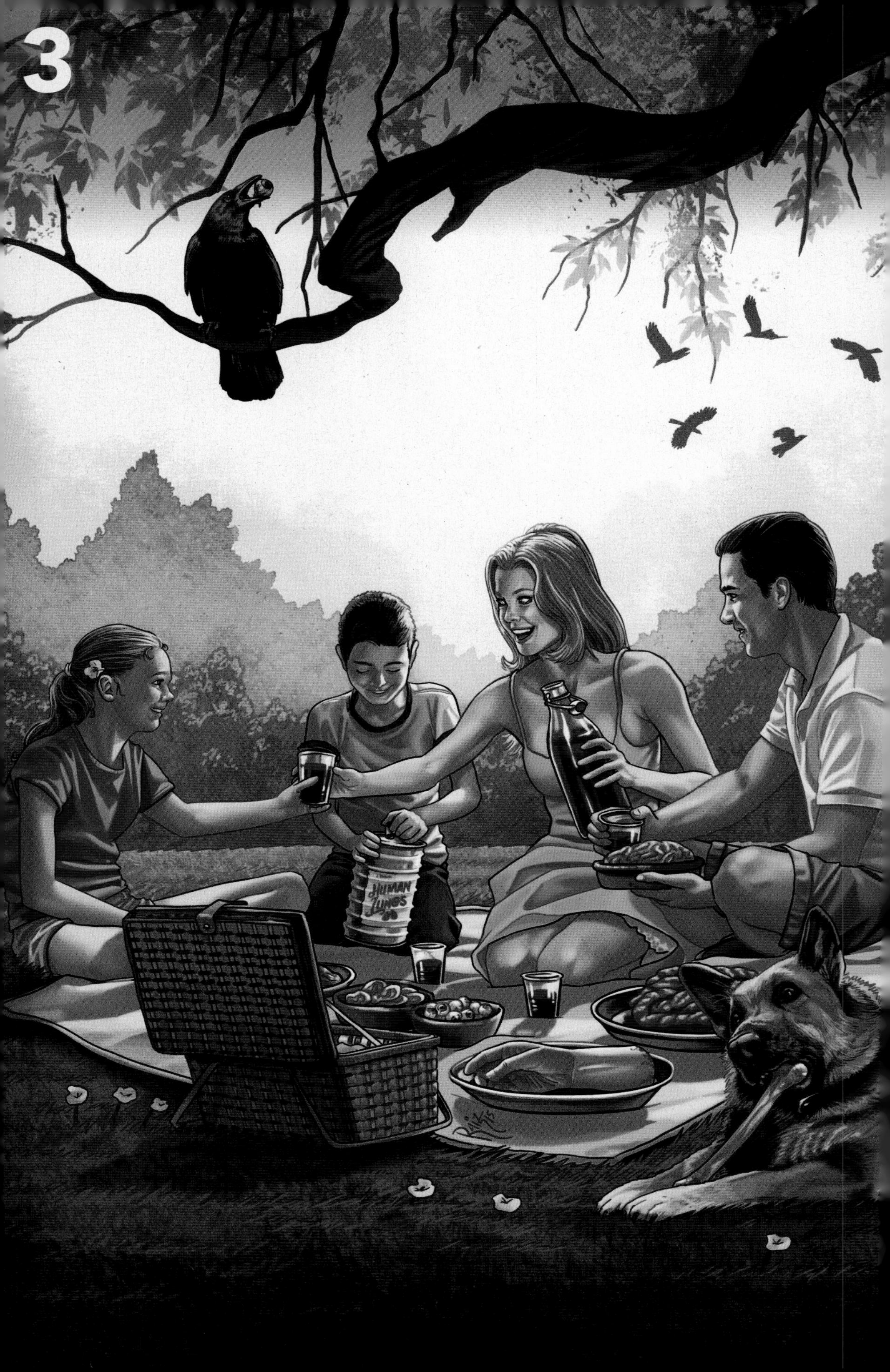
HUMAN
LUNGS

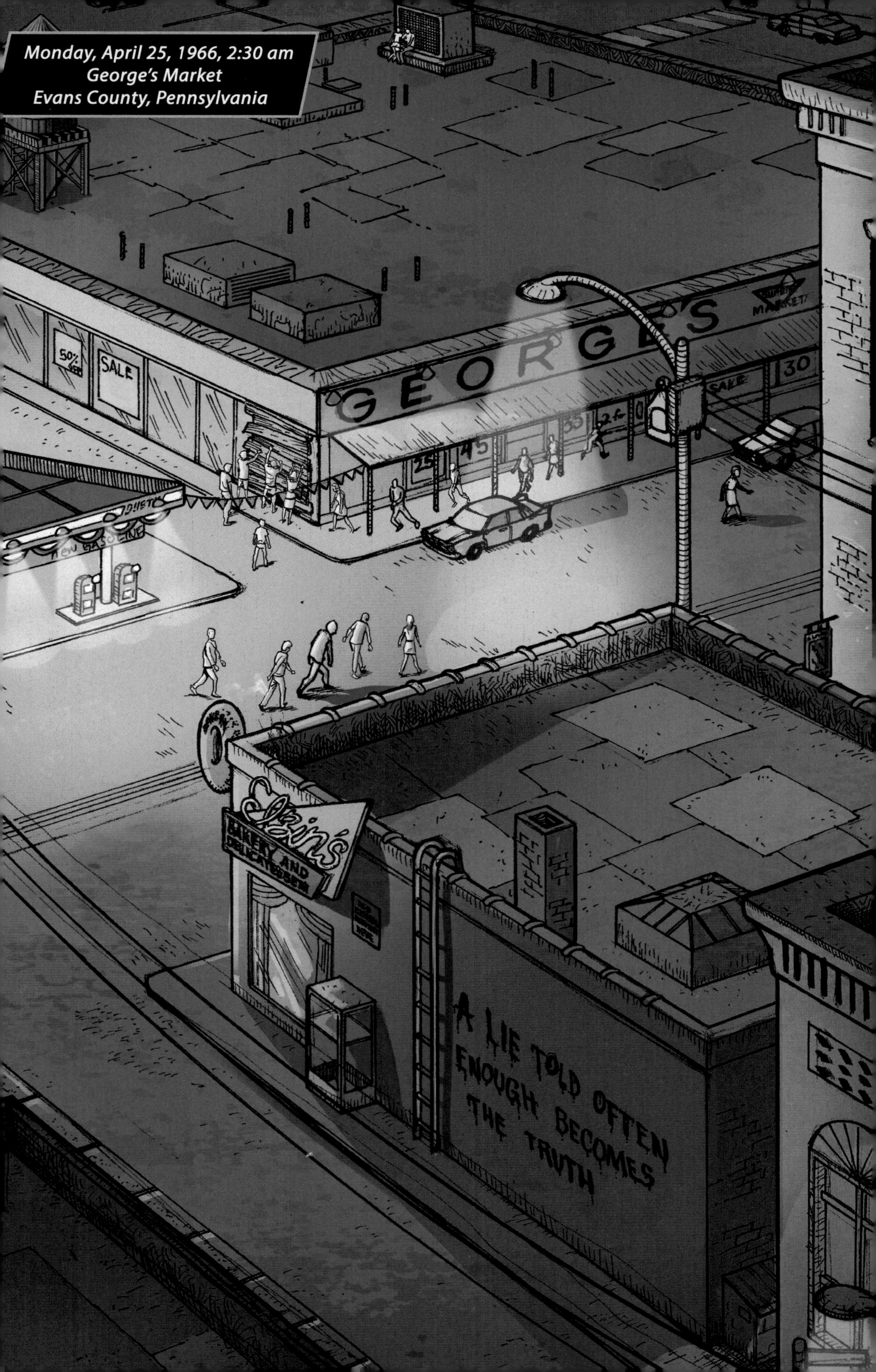
Monday, April 25, 1966, 2:30 am
George's Market
Evans County, Pennsylvania
GEORGE'S
SALE
BAKERY AND DELICATESSEN
A LIE TOLD OFTEN ENOUGH BECOMES THE TRUTH

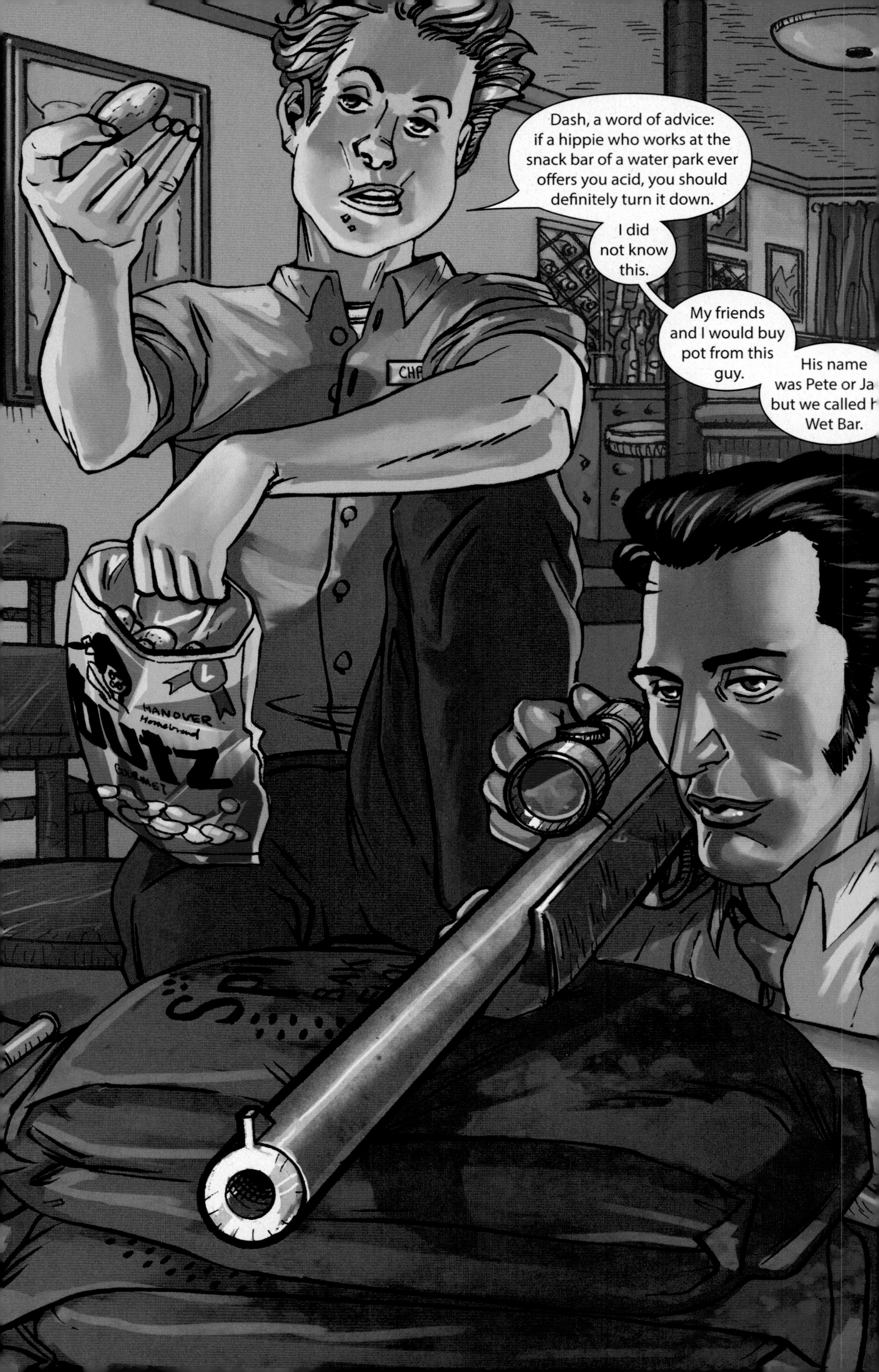
Dash, a word of advice: if a hippie who works at the snack bar of a water park ever offers you acid, you should definitely turn it down.
I did not know this.
My friends and I would buy pot from this guy.
His name was Pete or Ja
but we called h
Wet Bar.
HANOVER Homebrand
UTZ
GOURMET
CH

1960s Job Classifieds

Help Wanted—Female

CLERK TYPIST EXPD
gen'l office duties internat'l co., mdtn, $90-100. Mr. A. H. Olingy TN

CLERK, LITE STENO $95
Catholic Church Org. Hrs 9-4:30
Agency,   John St.

CLERKS $80-85
Retail chain good at figures. Expd
Park Ave South

CLERK TYP/ASST BKPR $85
Charming import ofc ass't. Fee negot.
AGENCY, SPECIALISTS,

CLERKS, NO TYPING, $290
NO FIGURES—NO EXP NEC! HSG!
CO hires today! Boyle Agency

BOOKKEEPER-ASSISTANT
Accounts receivable, general, pleasant surroundings, good pay, benefits. Standard Food Products.

BOOKKEEPER—ASST.
HEAVY EXP   RETAIL CHAIN
35 HOURS   OPPORTUNITY
Apply   B'way, 12th Floor.

CLERKS
HOUSEWIVES
FEE PAID $70-85
DAYS, EVENINGS OR NITES
MAN Agency   Broadway
Cortldt or Fulton sta. 8-6 daily, 9-1 Sat.

GAL FRIDAY
Salary open. Some knl bkkpg, typing, filing, etc. 1 girl ofc. Brooklyn. 788-8000
GAL FRI   FEE PD $95
Good typist. Figure Facility.
Unusually interesting organization.
AGENCY   E. 48th

GAL FRIDAY $70-80
Knowl typing & lite modeling. Excel oppty for brite gal. Mademoiselle Furs, 7th Ave, NYC. 3rd Floor.

GAL FRI, NO STEN, FEE PD, $90
"SWANK MEN'S CLUB"   (3) AGENCIES
5 AVE   W 42   Bway

GAL FRIDAY
General office work, good typing, good with figures. Miss Garr, AL 5-4400.

COLLEGE GRADUATES

COLLEGE grad trainee for mkt research. Famous intl. co. seeks figure oriented gals to learn analyst work. Future. Top benefits. Fee refunded. To $95.
E 42 St. (Lex)

COLL GRAD   80-85
ENGLISH MAJOR
Train Publishing Asst Ed/Editor
Agency   5th Ave 41st St

COLLEGE GRADS, Any Major, $90-110
——TRAVEL AGENCY——
Intel+Sls exp or pslty—exciting career
Agency,   5th Ave 41 St.

Coll Grad, Home Eco Maj
FEE PAID $475
Test kitchen of well known company
Position Secur Agency,   Maiden La.

COLL GRAD $5,200
THINKING NOT TYPING
Co trains business methods. Any Major
Agency   5th Ave. 41 St.

Coll Psych Secty $100 Fee Pd
Some coll. oppty assist consultant. Marketing dept. Managerial psy group. 9-5.
AGENCY, SPECIALISTS,   E 42.

Help Wanted—Male

ELECTRONICS
FIELD ENGINEERS TECHNICIANS AND WRITERS

Immediate openings overseas and stateside for the following categories. Minimum of 3 years experience required.

GROUND COMMUNICATIONS

GROUND NAVAIDS

DIGITAL COMPUTER

SHIPBOARD ELECTRONICS

HEAVY GROUND RADAR

GROUND TELEMETRY

PRECISION TEST EQUIPMENT

DIESEL-ELECTRIC POWER (OVERSEAS ONLY)

DIGITAL WRITERS

ELECTRONIC SUPPLY

INSTALLATION CRAFTSMEN

MACHINISTS
EXPERIMENTAL MACHINISTS

Excellent Company-Paid Benefits

Good Working Conditions

Congenial Atmosphere

All around machinists for modern model shops at our Syosset facility. Must be capable of setting up and operating all lathes, millers, grinder and jig borers for close tolerance work. Knowledge of measuring instruments and equipment necessary.

AIRLINE NAVIGATORS
FAA LICENSED
Pacific flying, Oakland based. Write or call Saturn Airways Inc. PO Box 26, Oakland International Airport,   Oakland, California. Telephone ( )   562-2719.

AIRLINE $75-$100
TRAINEES
NO EXP. CO TRAINS. RESV
Agency   E 42 St
AGENCY   B'way
(NEAR WALL STREET)
AIRLINE   IMMEDIATE
EXCLUSIVE WITH OUR AGENCY
AGENTS
AIRLINE OPPORTUNITIES AGENCY
Hillside Ave Jamaica   3666

ACCOUNTANTS
SEMI-SENIORS
National CPA Firm has a number of openings for men with 2-4 years of good audit and tax experience. Permanent positions for qualified men. Please submit all essential information preliminary to an interview. Replies held in confidence. PO Box Bowling Green Station NY. NY. 1004.

AEROSPACE
Apollo/ Saturn V Openings New York Interviews, February 21 through 26

The   Space Division has immediate openings for engineers, management staff and technicians on the NASA Apollo/Saturn V program. Assignments are at Cape Kennedy, Huntsville, New Orleans and the Mississippi Test Facility at Bay St. Louis, Miss.

Senior Computer Operator
Immediate long term temporary positions available for work in modern Data Processing installation on I.B.M. 360. Should have 360 experience plus minimum 2-3 years heavy computer operational experience (1401 - 1410) with tape "on-line" background. Programming knowledge helpful.

COLLEGE GRADUATES

COLLEGE GRAD
$5200-$6000 + CO CAR
Fine old establ Co. offers immed career oppty ofc mgt trng prog for ambitious & sincere man. If you are recent college grad & draft deferred, this job is yours. Sal $5200-6000 start. Co car, fee paid by Co. Call Joe Martin. Snelling & Snelling Agency,   Court St, Bklyn. UL 5-5100

COLL GRADS FEE PD. $57-6500
MANAGEMENT
Train in all phases of admin., start methods planning dept, any major.
Agency,   5th Ave., 41 St.

COLL GRAD — STAFF MGR TRNG
WITH NATL CO IN AUTOMOTIVE FIELD. ROTATION TRNG LEADS TO HIGH LEVEL EXEC SPOT WITHIN 1 YR. $6,000. PART FEE REIMB.
AGENCY,   W. 44

COLL GRADS "NO EXP NEC" $6-8000
PROGRAMMING
Analytical mind? — Puzzle solver?
Free testing.   Agency   W 40

COLL GRADS Fee Refunded $5700-$6500
EXEC MANAGEMENT
Trnee spot all phases admin; work with Co Pres-any major-lead to $12M.
AGENCY   5 Av Rm

COLL GRAD $100
LIBERAL ARTS
Co. trains correspondent. No typing.
Agency   5th Ave 41st St

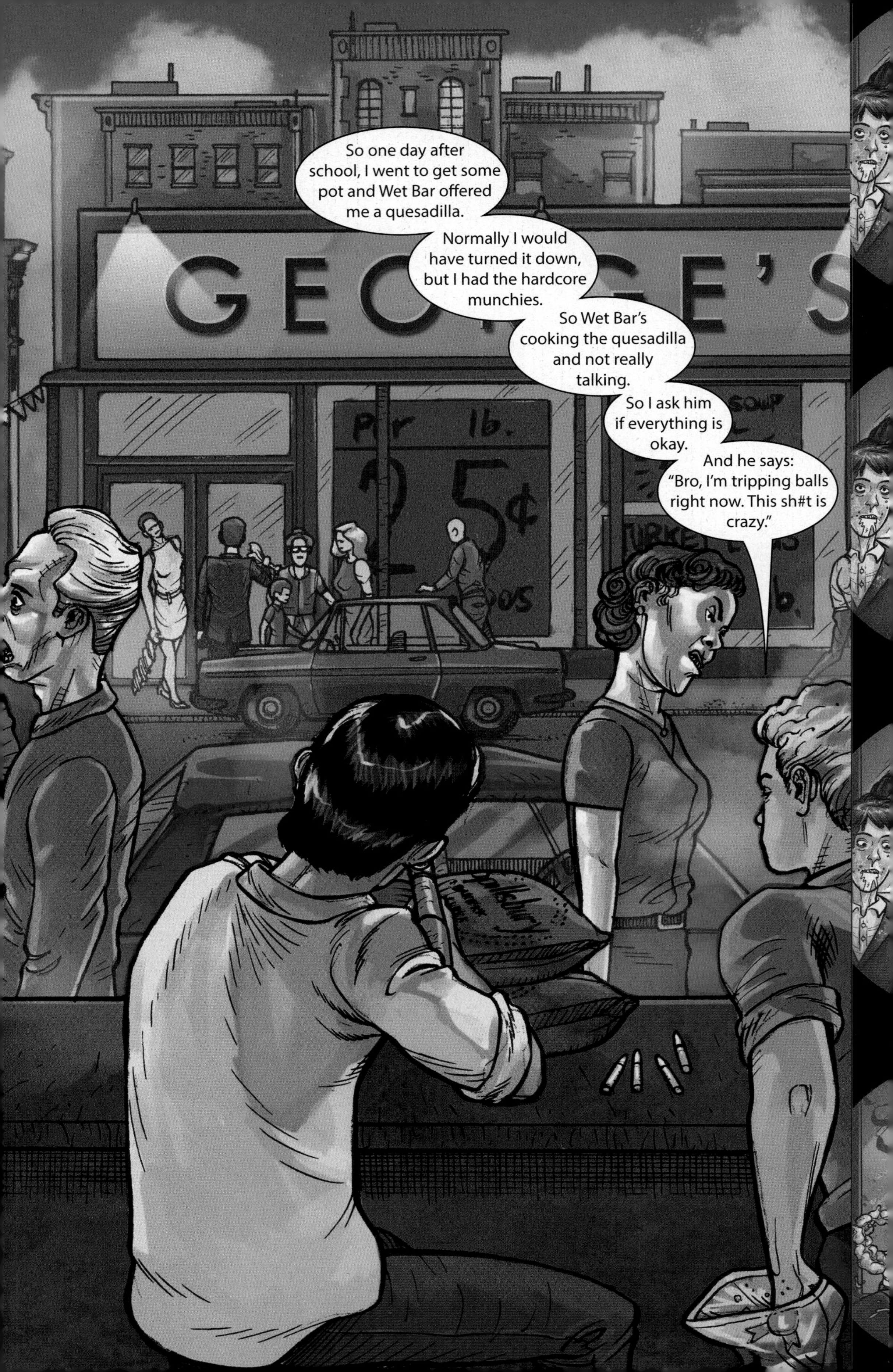
So one day after school, I went to get some pot and Wet Bar offered me a quesadilla.
Normally I would have turned it down, but I had the hardcore munchies.
So Wet Bar's cooking the quesadilla and not really talking.
So I ask him if everything is okay.
And he says: "Bro, I'm tripping balls right now. This sh#t is crazy."

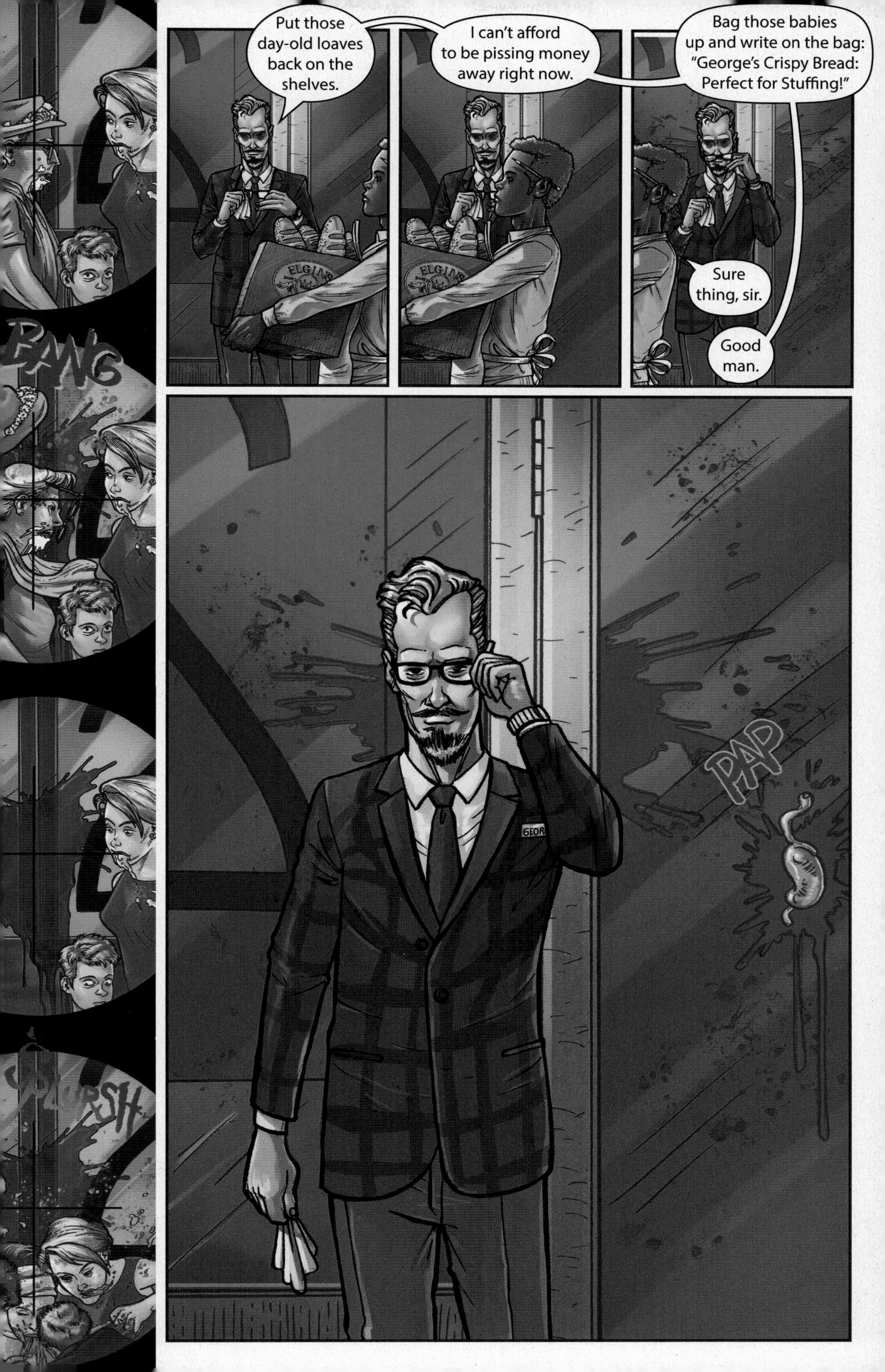
Put those day-old loaves back on the shelves.
I can't afford to be pissing money away right now.
Bag those babies up and write on the bag: "George's Crispy Bread: Perfect for Stuffing!"
Sure thing, sir.
Good man.
BANG
SPLURSH
PAP

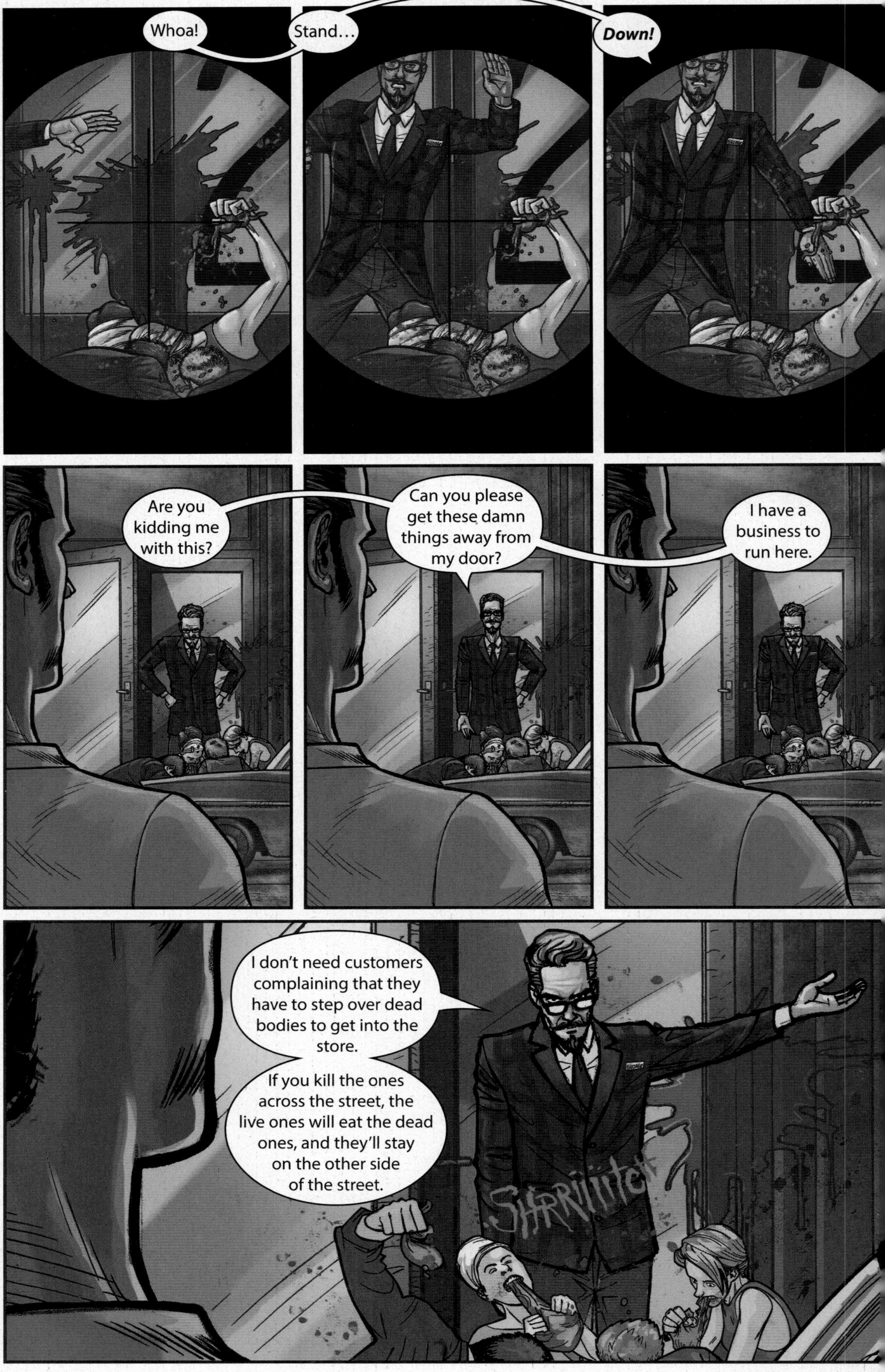
Whoa!
Stand…
Down!
Are you kidding me with this?
Can you please get these damn things away from my door?
I have a business to run here.
I don't need customers complaining that they have to step over dead bodies to get into the store.
If you kill the ones across the street, the live ones will eat the dead ones, and they'll stay on the other side of the street.
SHRRIIIITCH

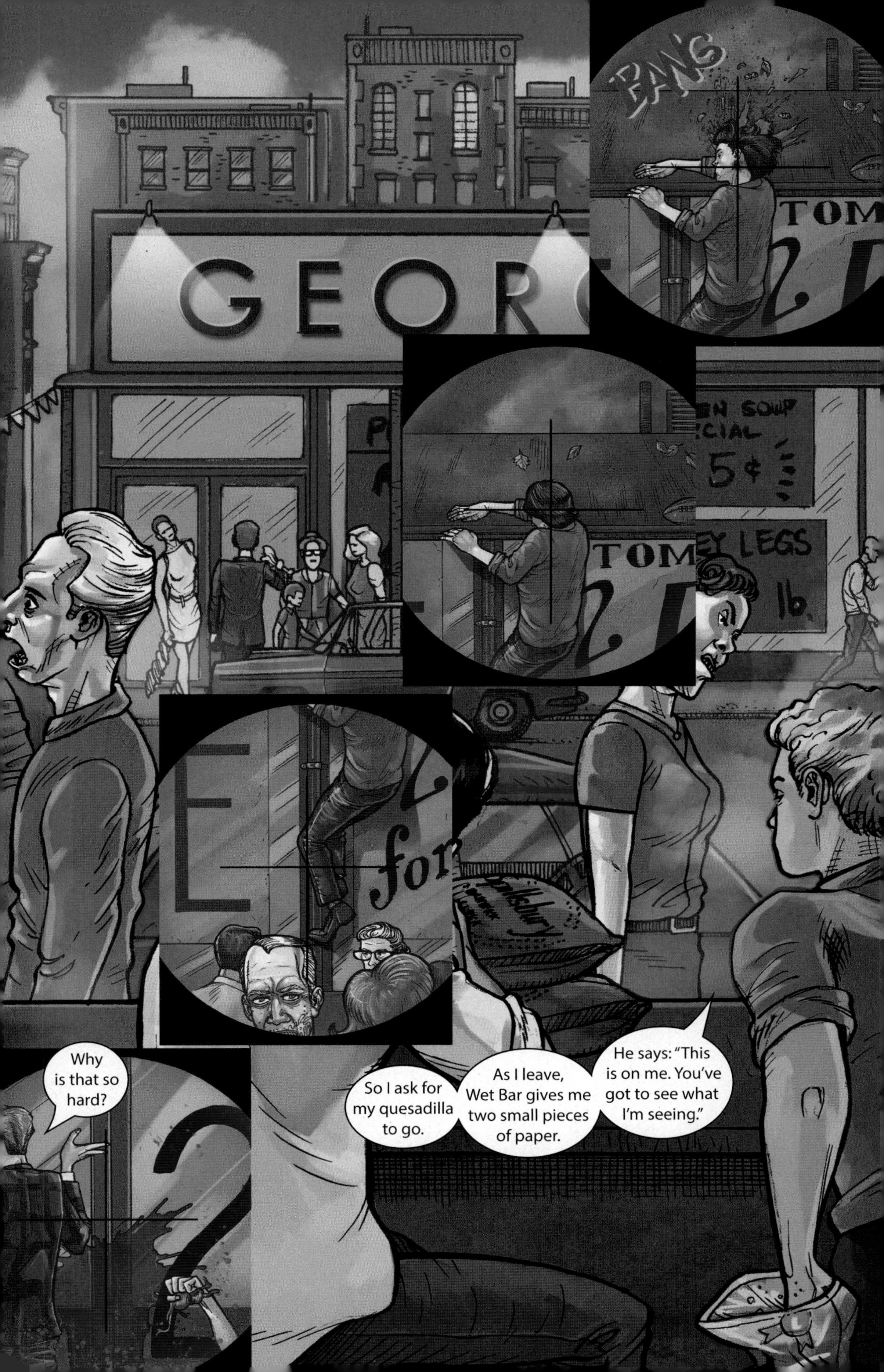
GEOR
BANG
TOM
EN SOUP
CIAL
5¢
EY LEGS
lb.
for
Why is that so hard?
So I ask for my quesadilla to go.
As I leave, Wet Bar gives me two small pieces of paper.
He says: "This is on me. You've got to see what I'm seeing."

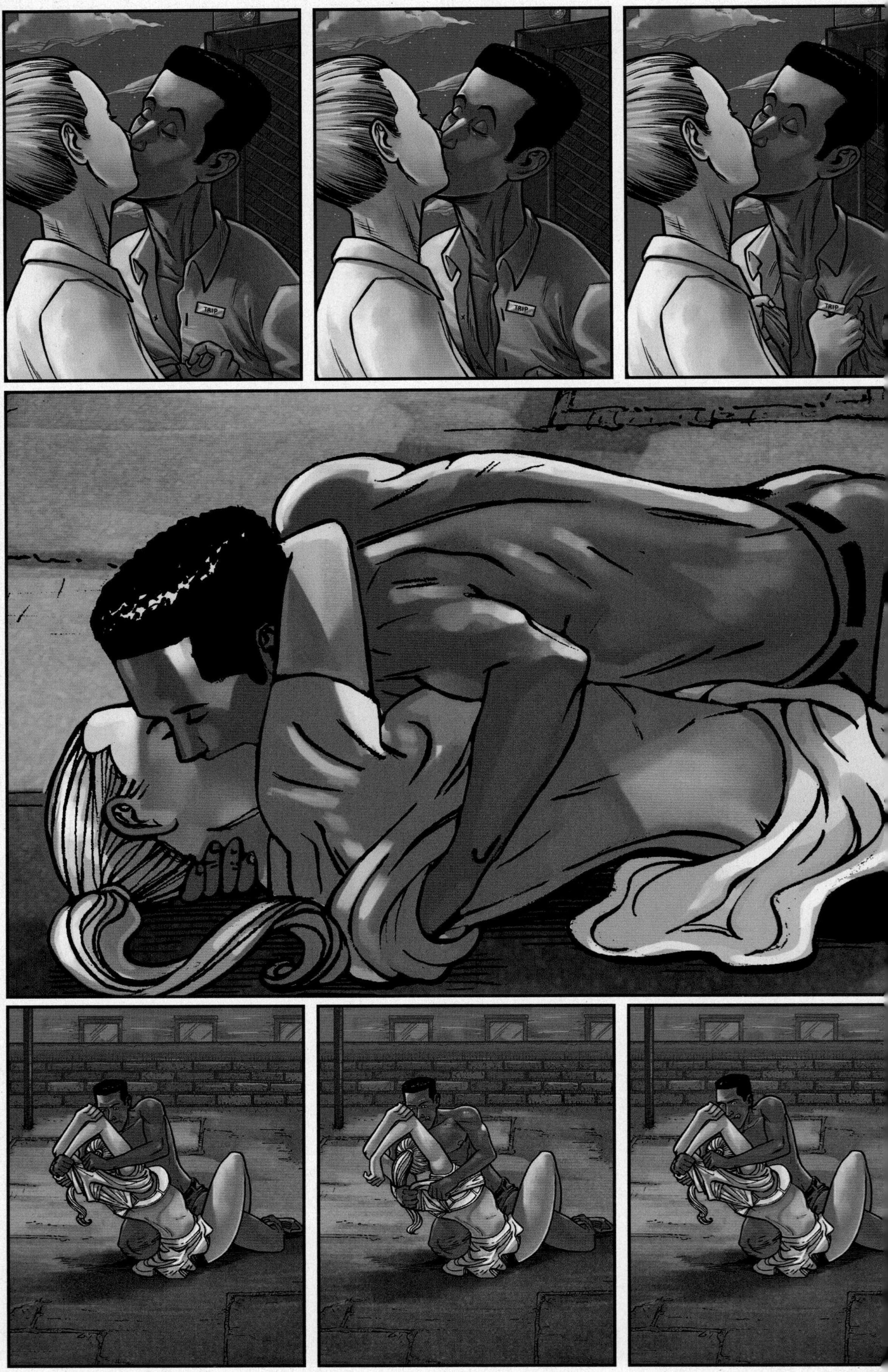
TRIP
TRIP
TRIP

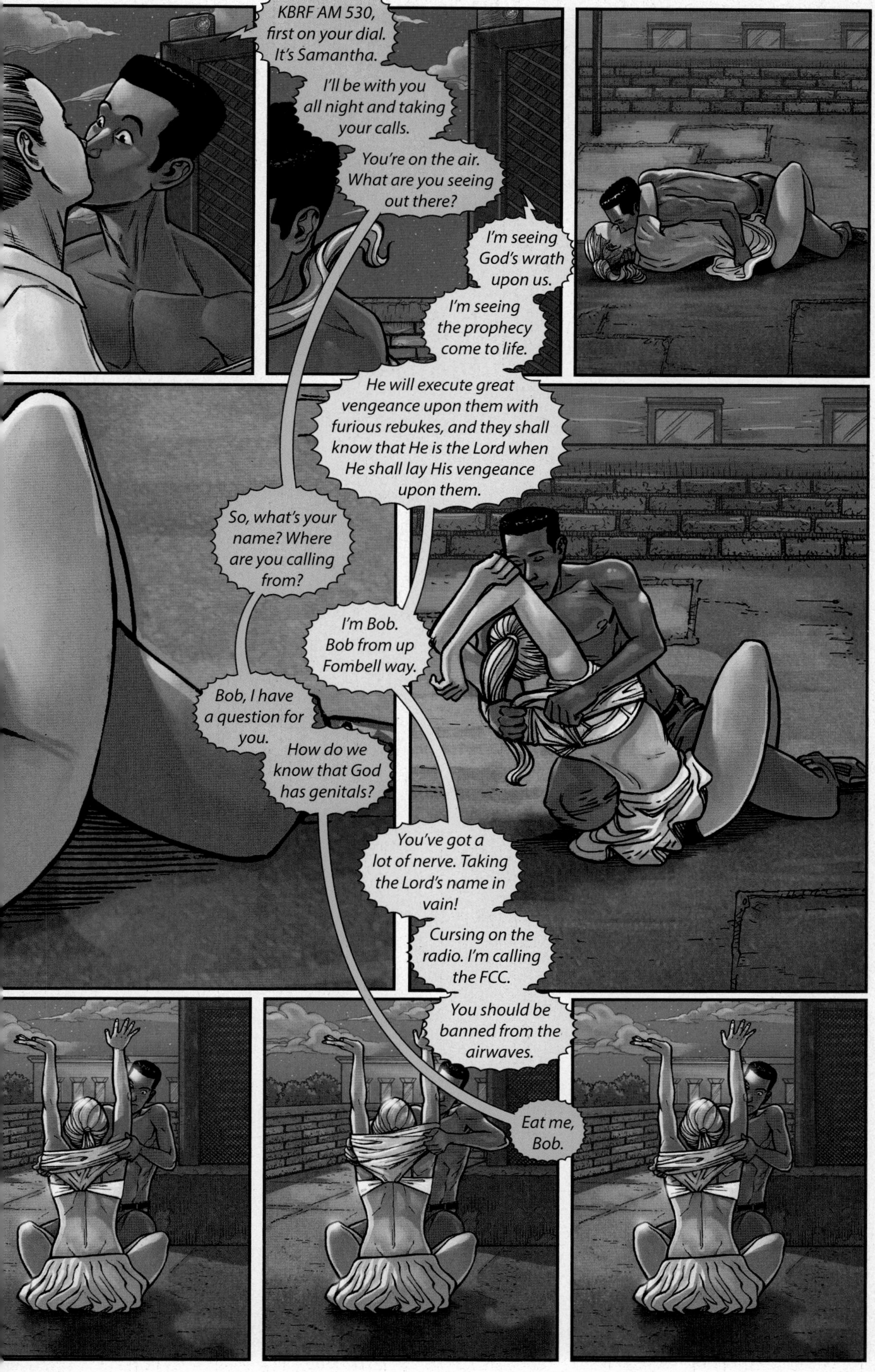
KBRF AM 530, first on your dial. It's Samantha.
I'll be with you all night and taking your calls.
You're on the air. What are you seeing out there?
I'm seeing God's wrath upon us.
I'm seeing the prophecy come to life.
He will execute great vengeance upon them with furious rebukes, and they shall know that He is the Lord when He shall lay His vengeance upon them.
So, what's your name? Where are you calling from?
I'm Bob. Bob from up Fombell way.
Bob, I have a question for you.
How do we know that God has genitals?
You've got a lot of nerve. Taking the Lord's name in vain!
Cursing on the radio. I'm calling the FCC.
You should be banned from the airwaves.
Eat me, Bob.

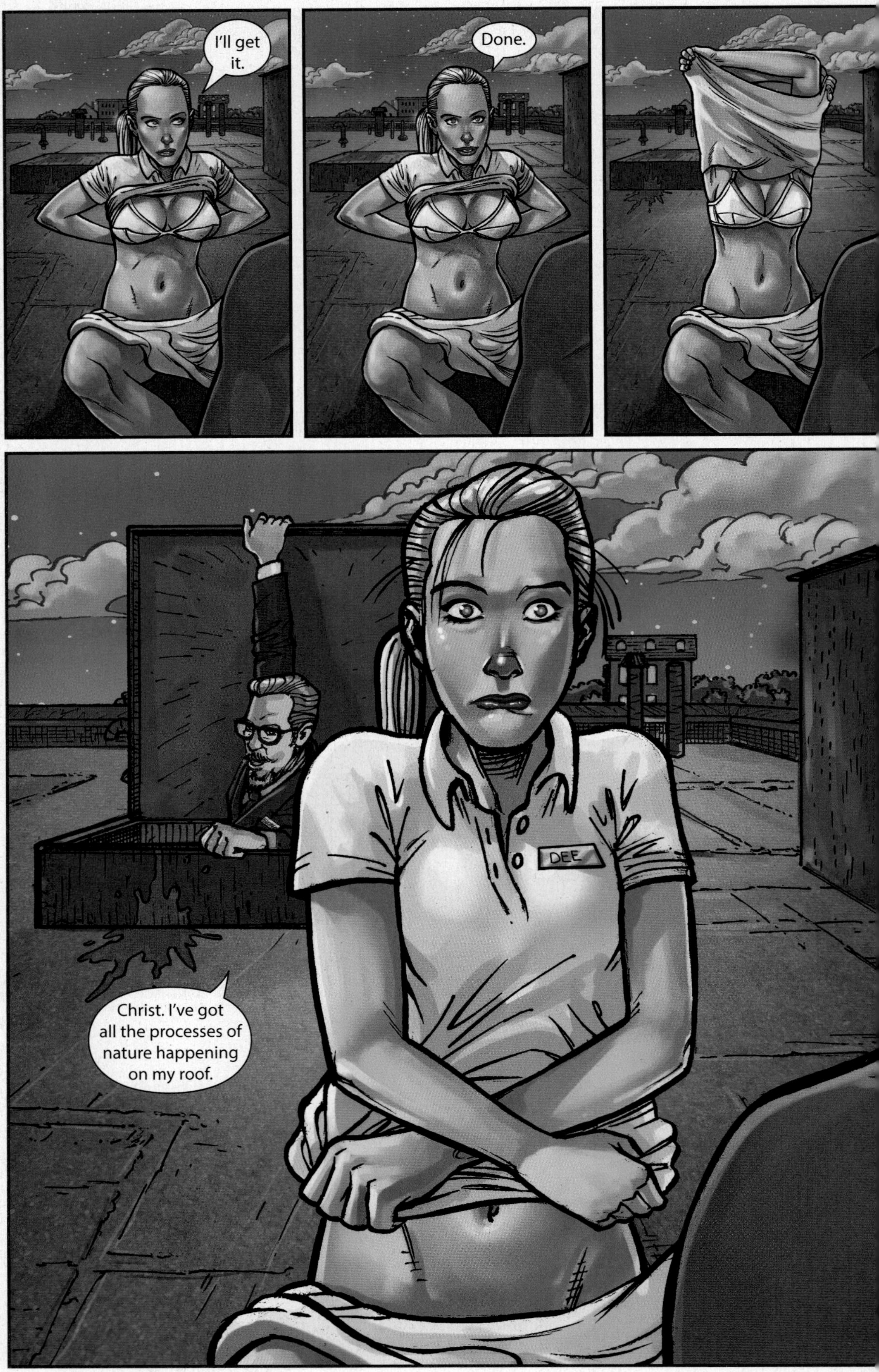
I'll get it.
Done.
DEE
Christ. I've got all the processes of nature happening on my roof.

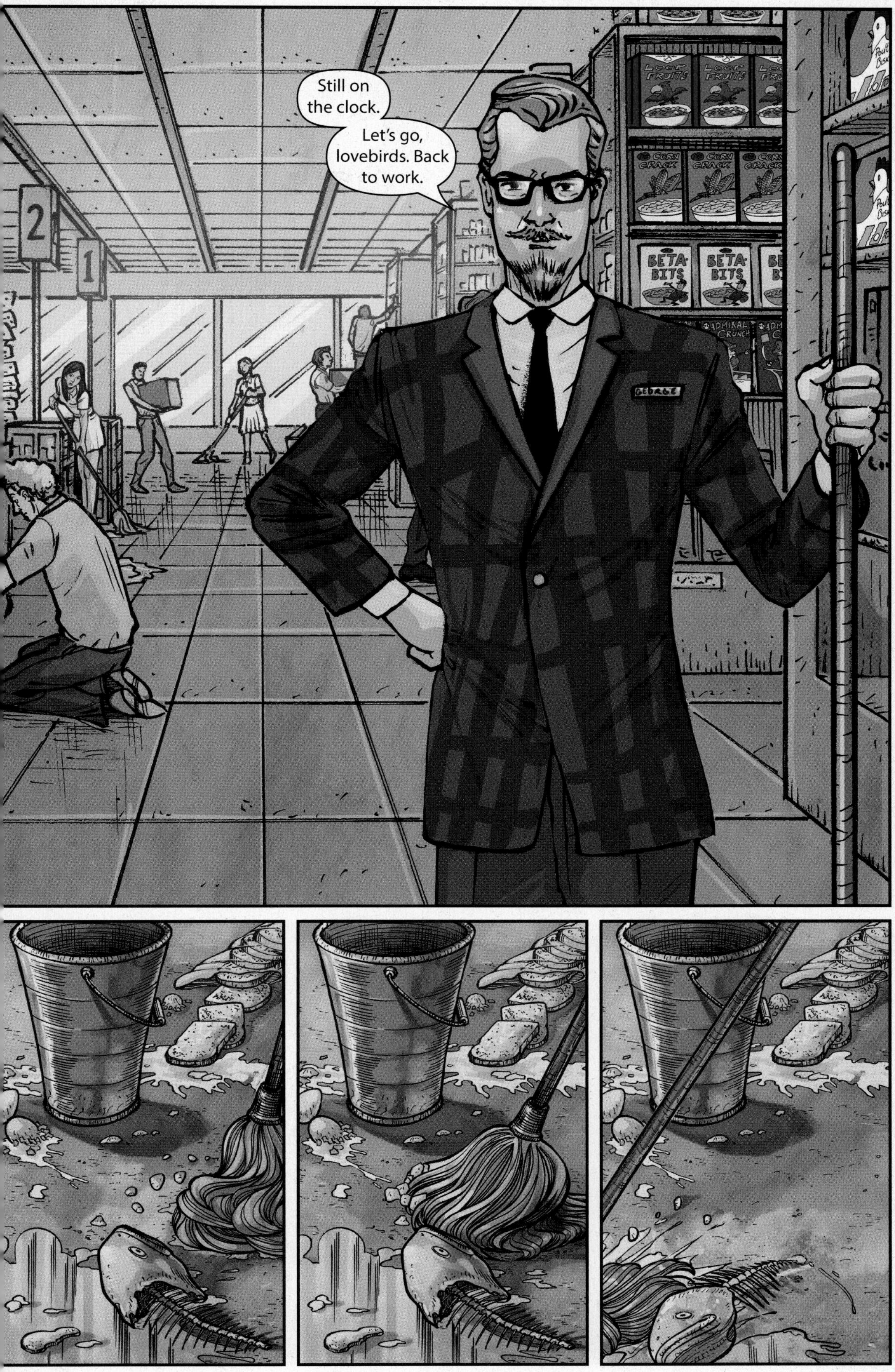
Still on the clock.
Let's go, lovebirds. Back to work.
2
1
LOOP FRUITS
CORN CRACK
BETA-BITS
ADMIRAL CRUNCH
GEORGE

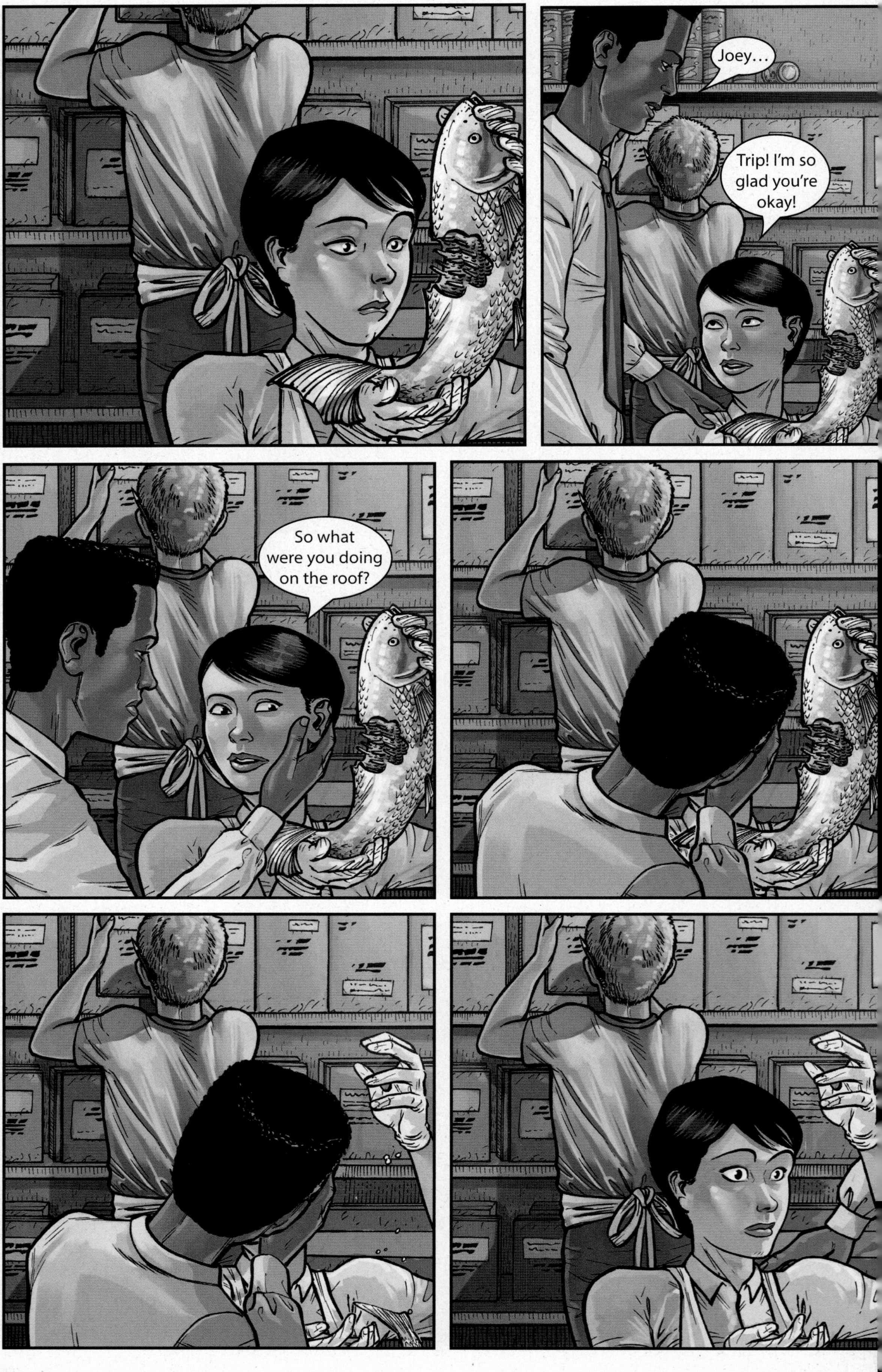
Joey…
Trip! I'm so glad you're okay!
So what were you doing on the roof?

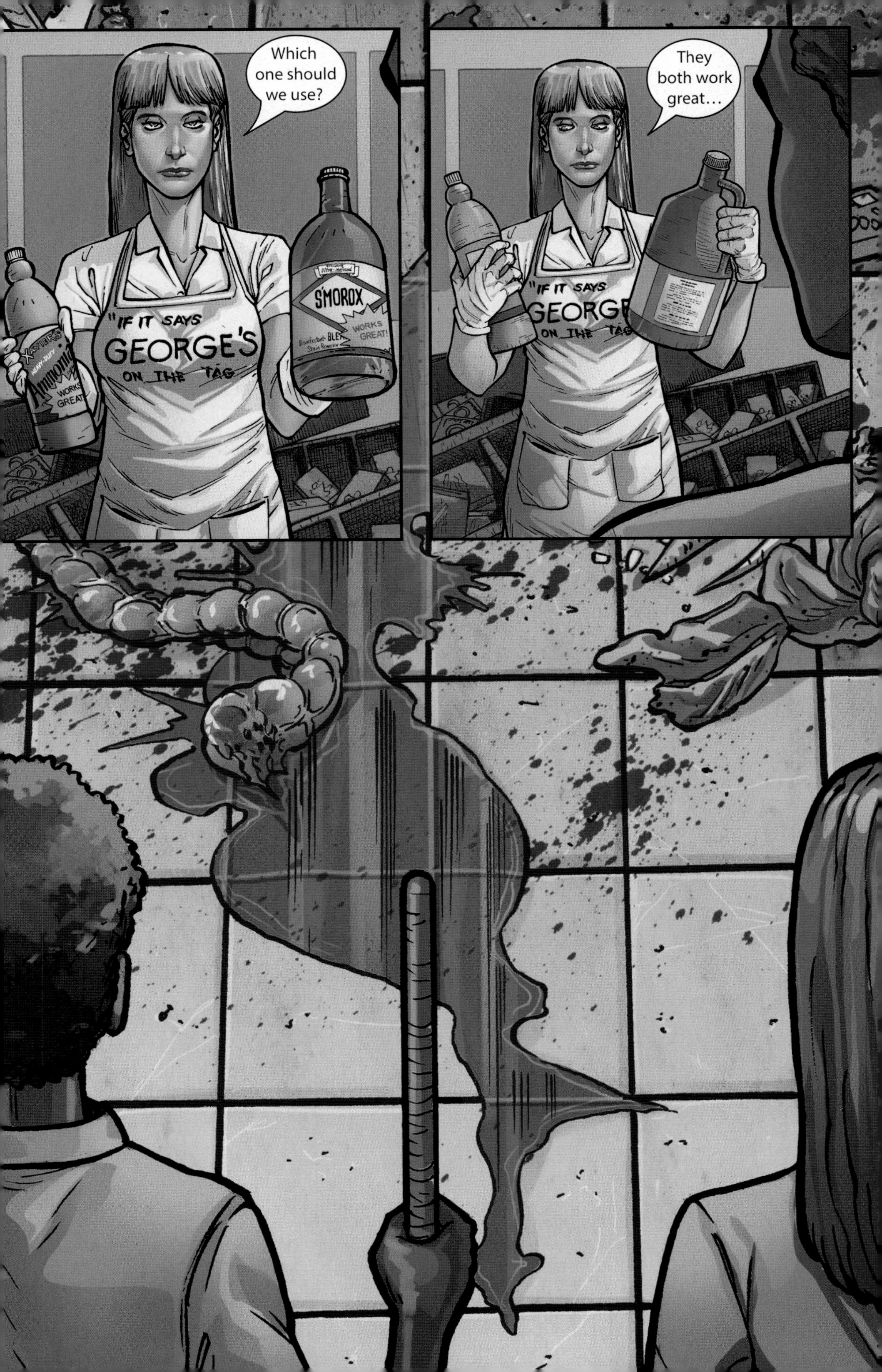
Which one should we use?
"IF IT SAYS GEORGE'S ON THE TAG
Ammonia
WORKS GREAT
S'MOROX
WORKS GREAT!
They both work great…

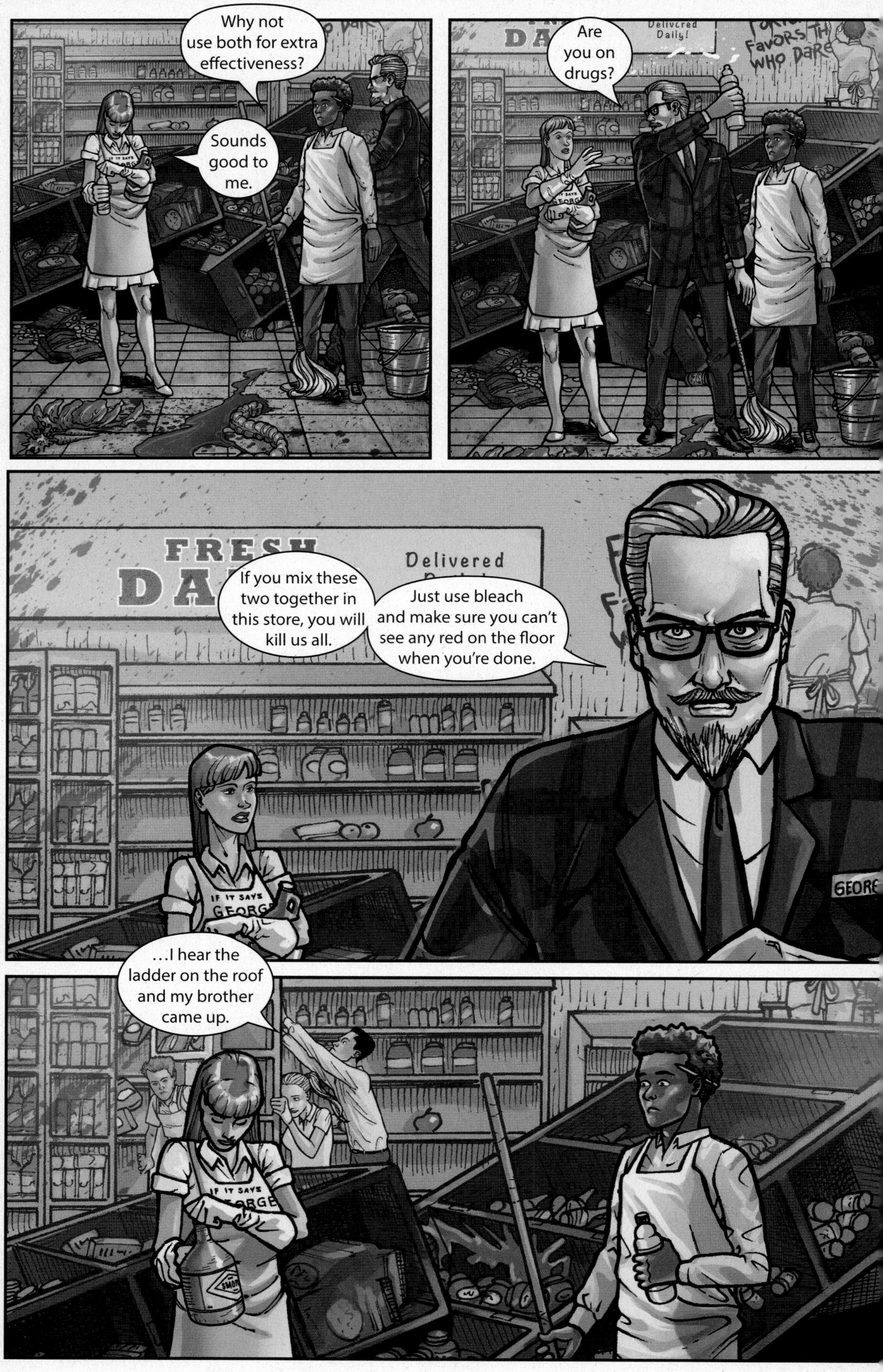
Why not use both for extra effectiveness?
Sounds good to me.
Are you on drugs?
If you mix these two together in this store, you will kill us all.
Just use bleach and make sure you can't see any red on the floor when you're done.
...I hear the ladder on the roof and my brother came up.

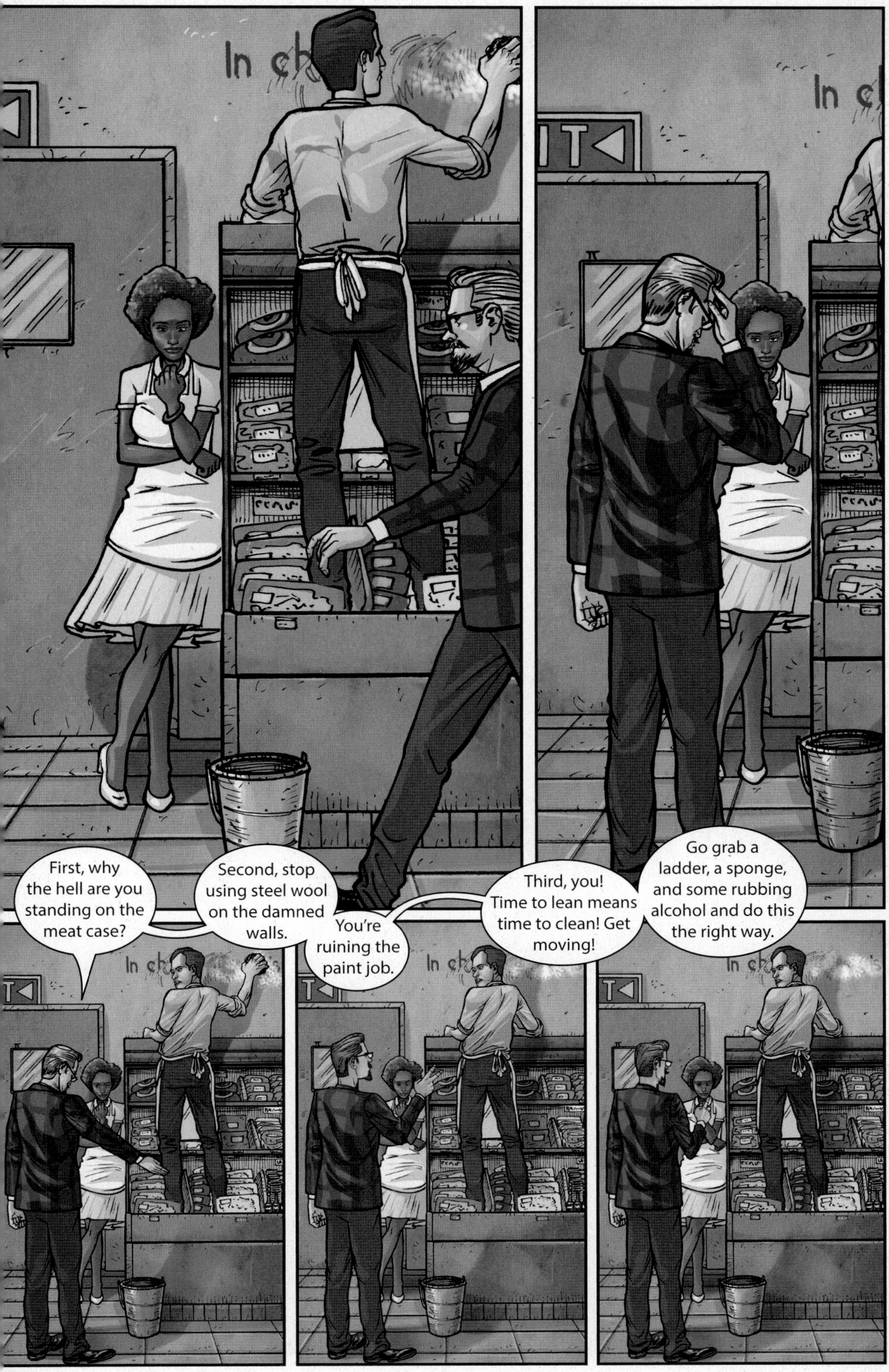
In ch
In ch
First, why the hell are you standing on the meat case?
Second, stop using steel wool on the damned walls.
You're ruining the paint job.
Third, you! Time to lean means time to clean! Get moving!
Go grab a ladder, a sponge, and some rubbing alcohol and do this the right way.

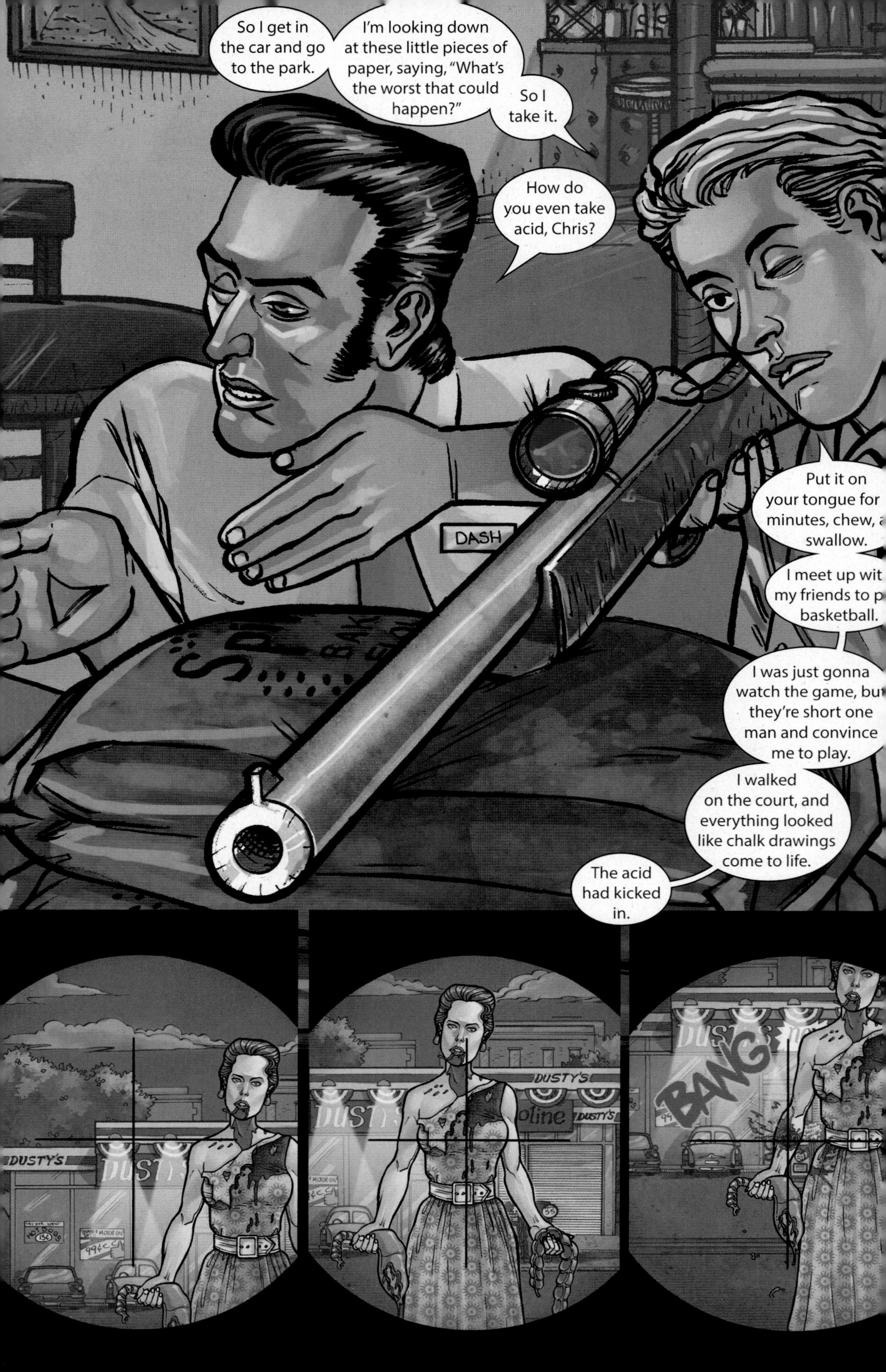
So I get in the car and go to the park.
I'm looking down at these little pieces of paper, saying, "What's the worst that could happen?"
So I take it.
How do you even take acid, Chris?
Put it on your tongue for minutes, chew, swallow.
I meet up wit my friends to p basketball.
I was just gonna watch the game, bu they're short one man and convince me to play.
I walked on the court, and everything looked like chalk drawings come to life.
The acid had kicked in.
DASH
DUSTY'S
DUSTY'S
DUSTY'S
BANG

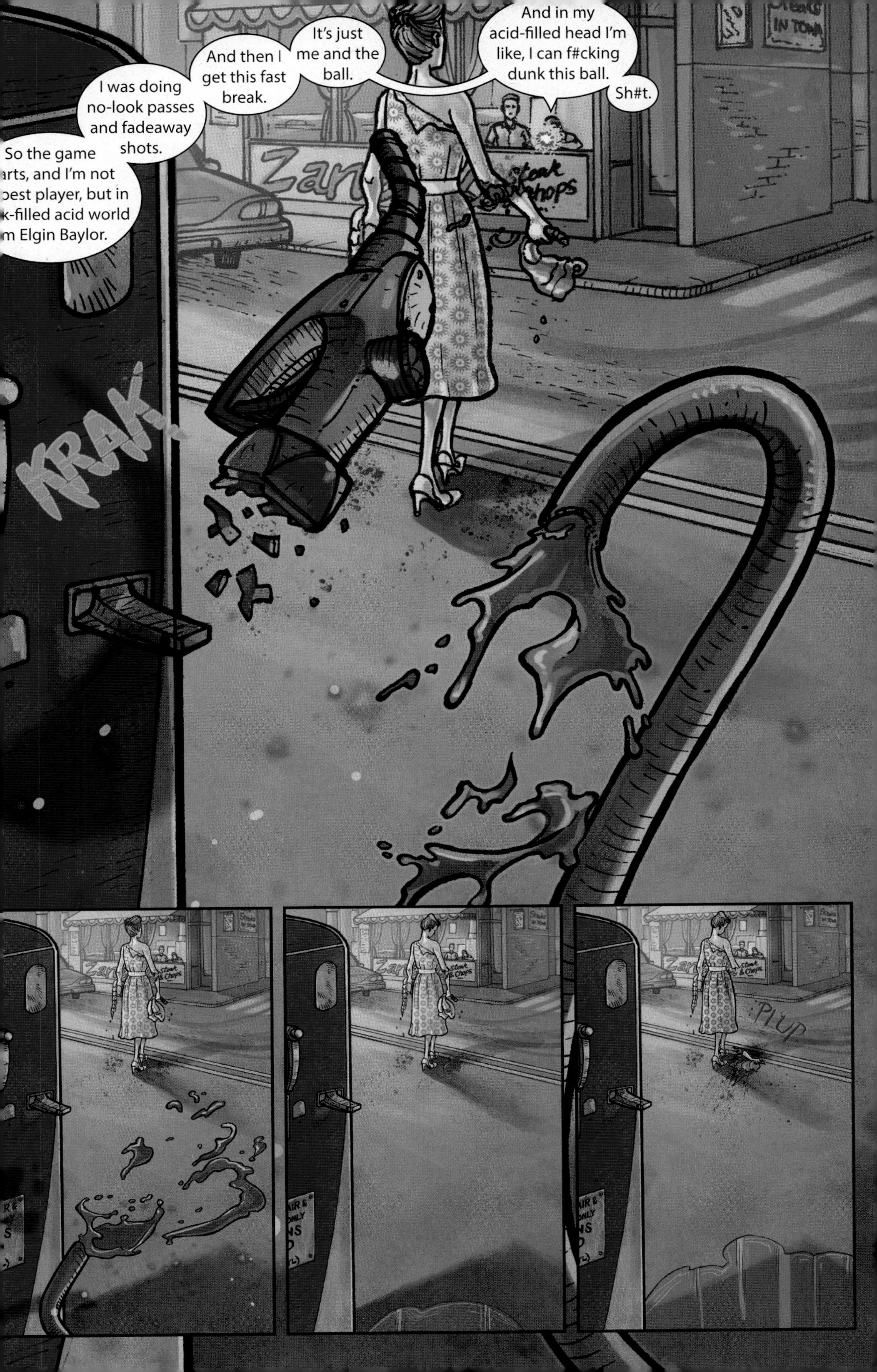
So the game
arts, and I'm not
best player, but in
k-filled acid world
m Elgin Baylor.
I was doing no-look passes and fadeaway shots.
And then I get this fast break.
It's just me and the ball.
And in my acid-filled head I'm like, I can f#cking dunk this ball.
Sh#t.
KRAK...
PLUP

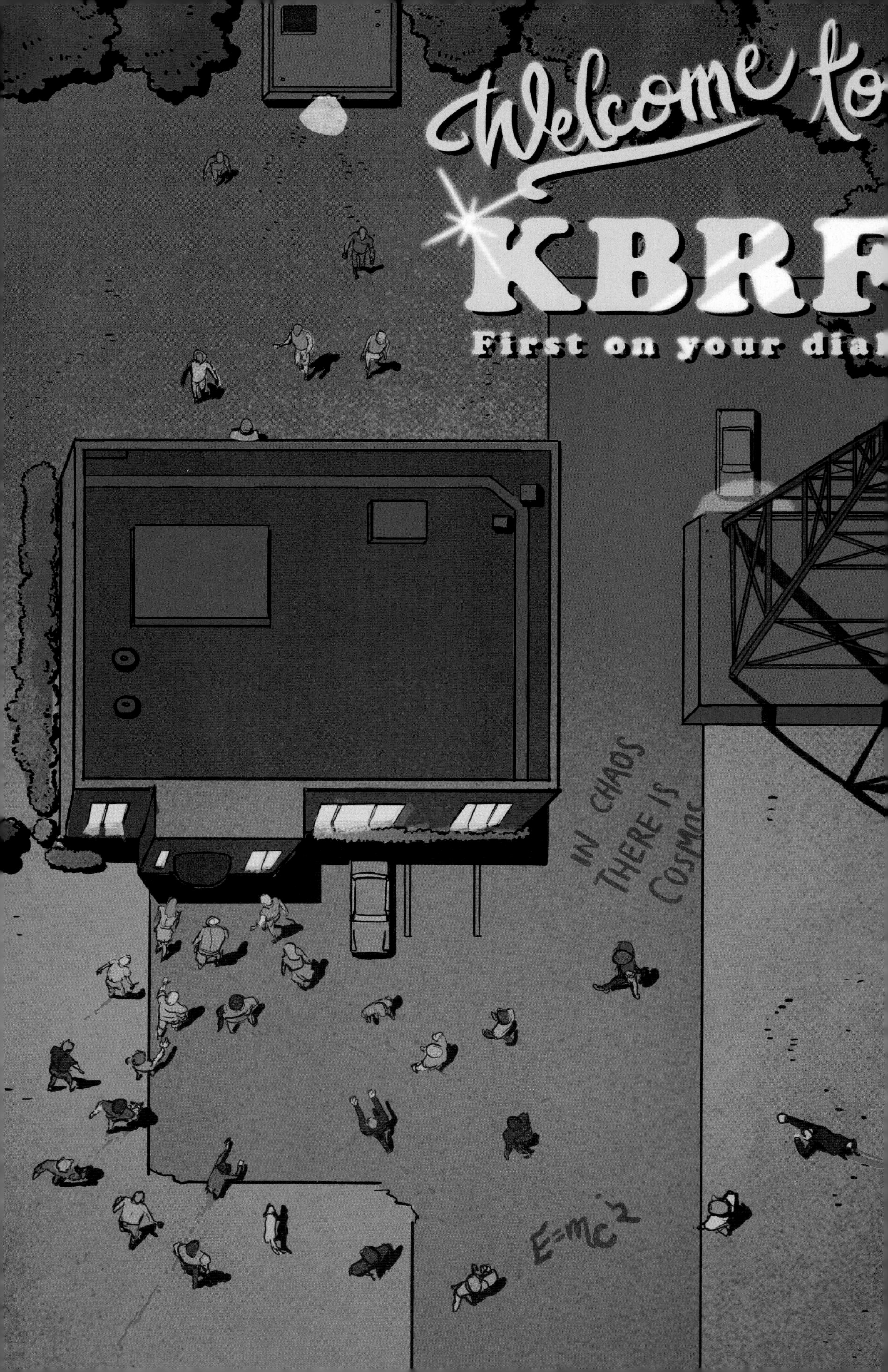
Welcome to
KBRF
First on your dial
IN CHAOS THERE IS COSMOS
E=mc2

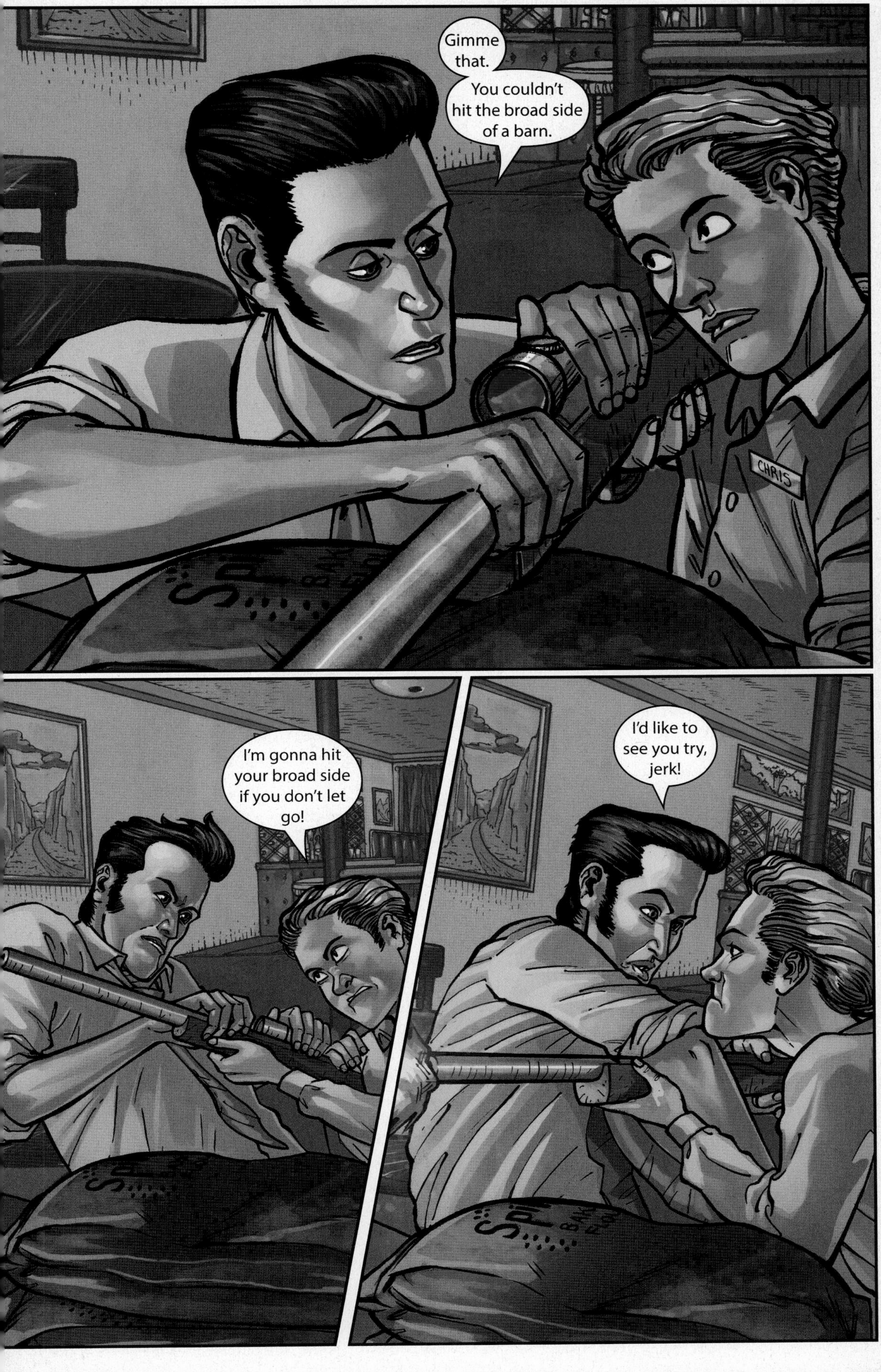
Gimme that.
You couldn't hit the broad side of a barn.
CHRIS
I'm gonna hit your broad side if you don't let go!
I'd like to see you try, jerk!

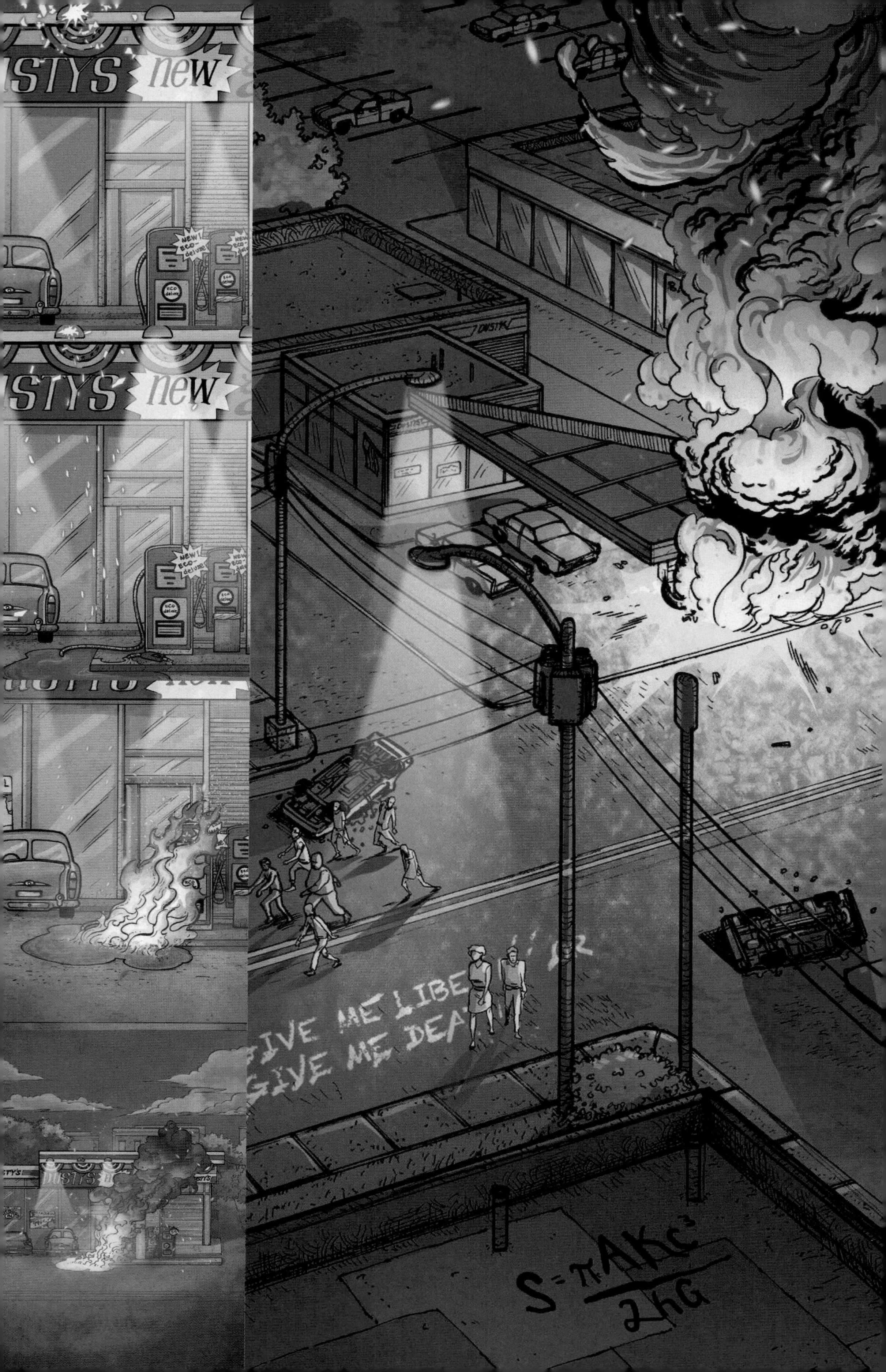
STYS
new
NEW! ECO-deluxe
ECO deluxe
GIVE ME LIBE
GIVE ME DEA
$S = \frac{\pi A K c^3}{2 h G}$

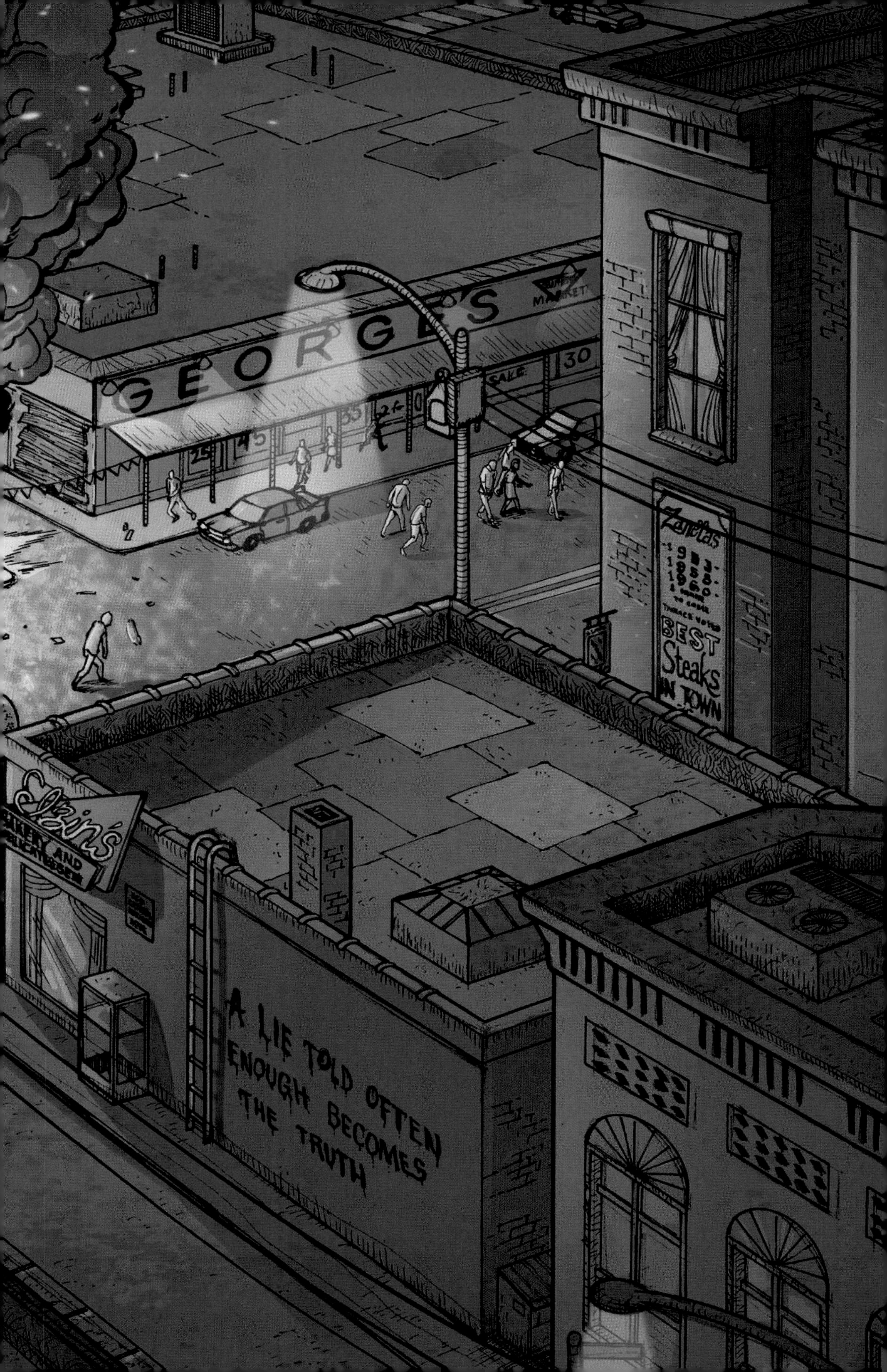
GEORGE'S
SALE
30
BEST
Steaks
IN TOWN
A LIE TOLD OFTEN
ENOUGH BECOMES
THE TRUTH

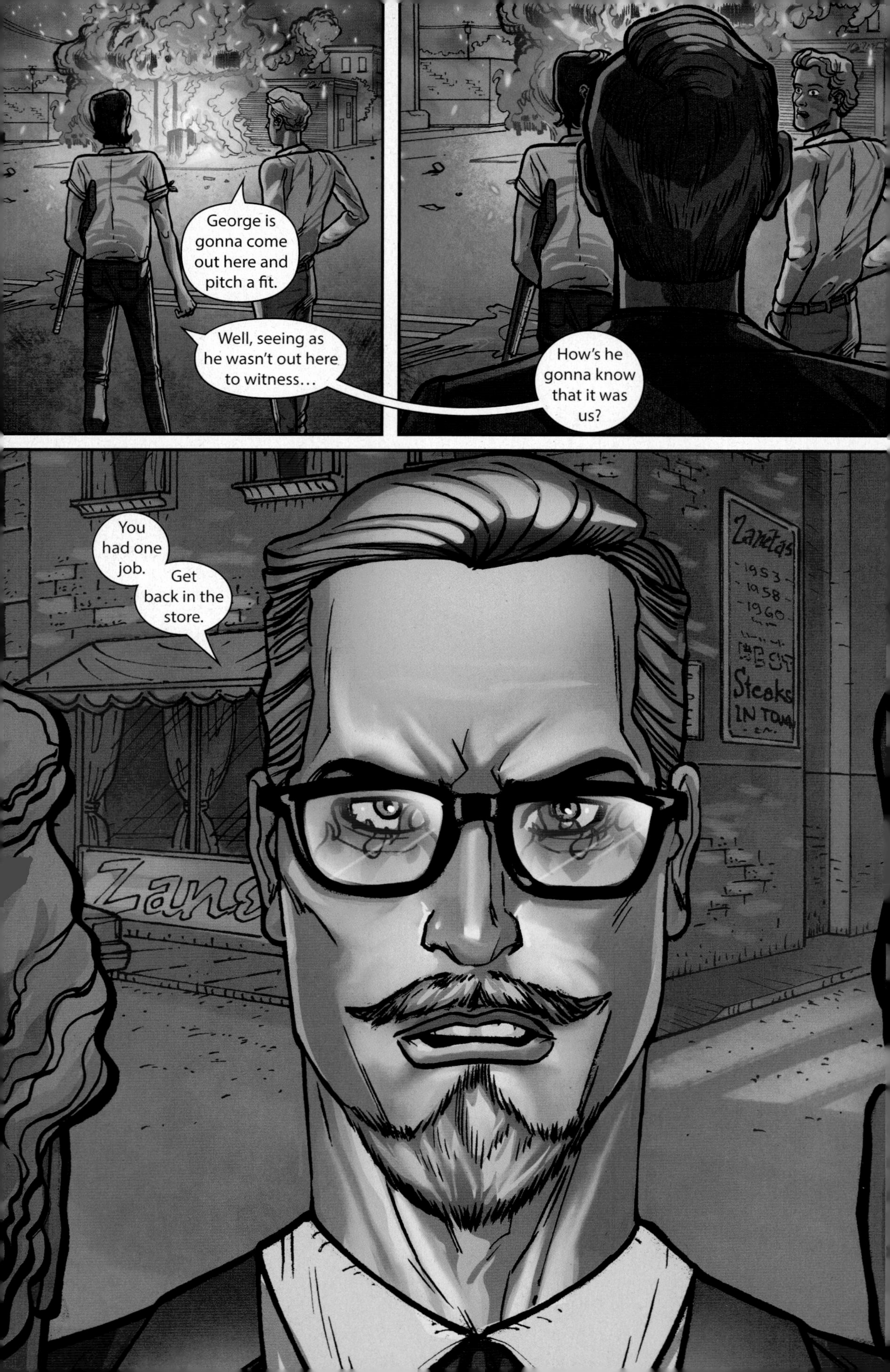
George is gonna come out here and pitch a fit.
Well, seeing as he wasn't out here to witness…
How's he gonna know that it was us?
You had one job.
Get back in the store.
Zanetas
1953
1958
1960
Steaks
IN TOWN
Zan

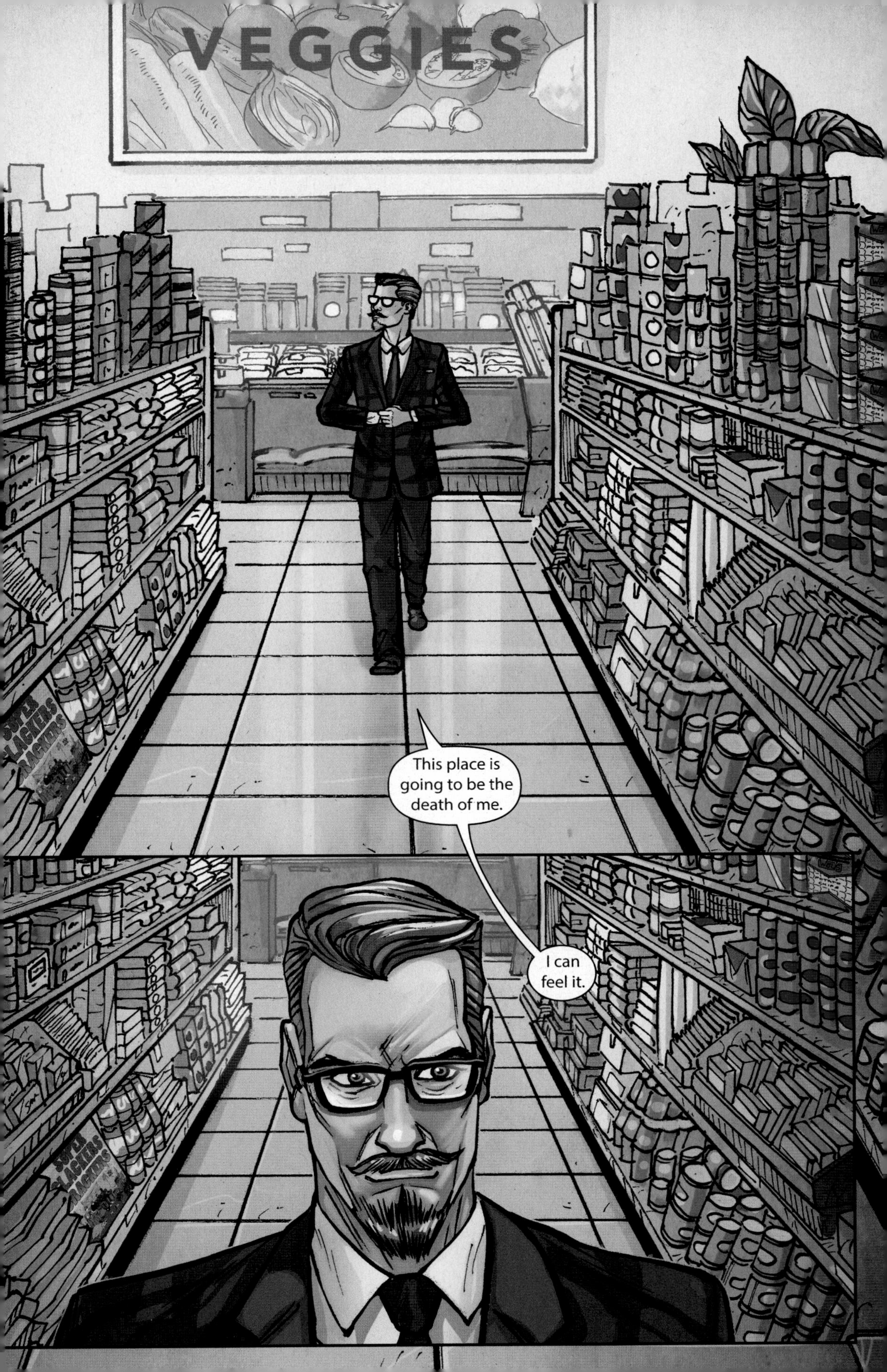
VEGGIES
This place is going to be the death of me.
I can feel it.

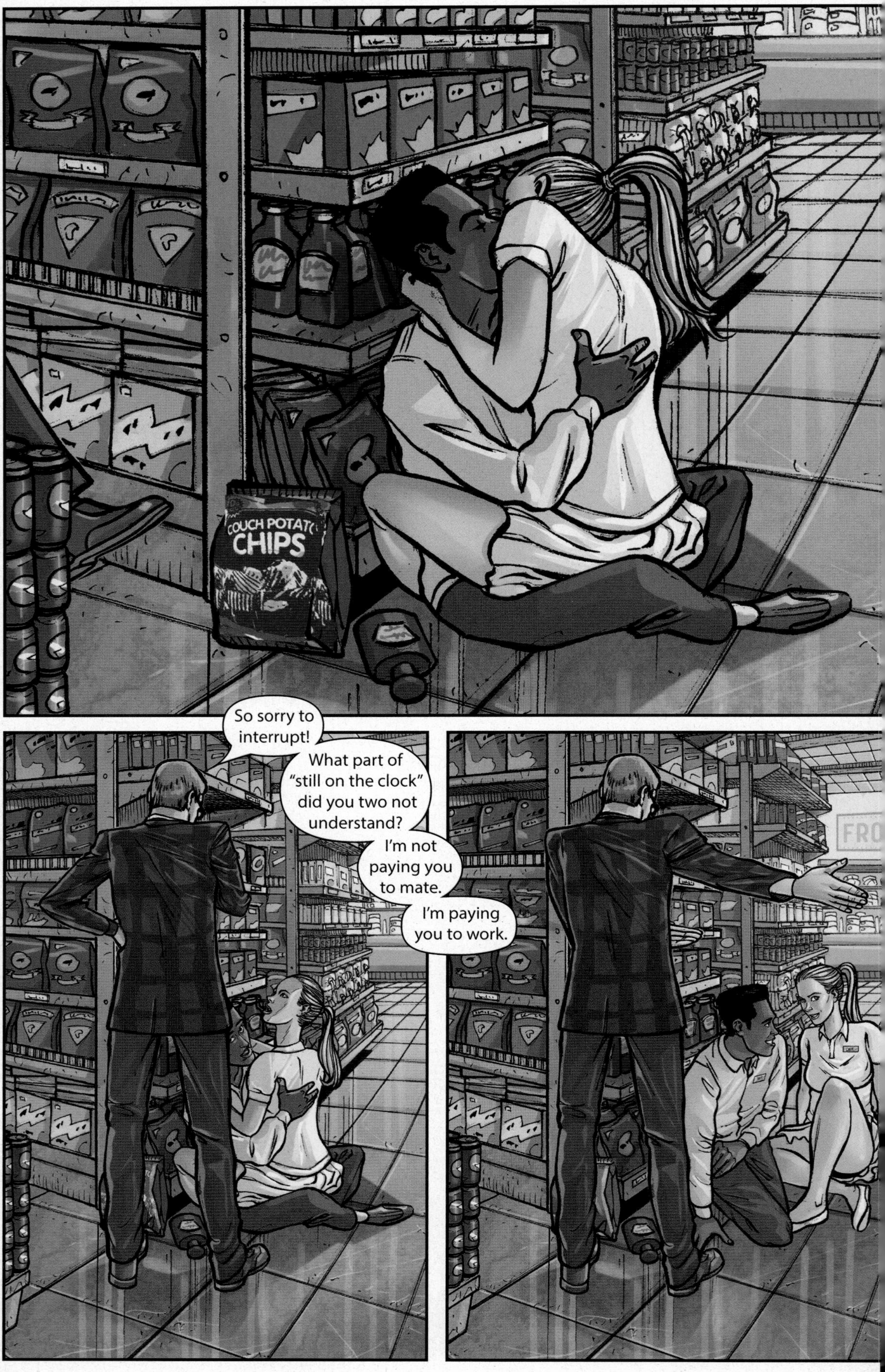
COUCH POTATO
CHIPS
So sorry to interrupt!
What part of "still on the clock" did you two not understand?
I'm not paying you to mate.
I'm paying you to work.

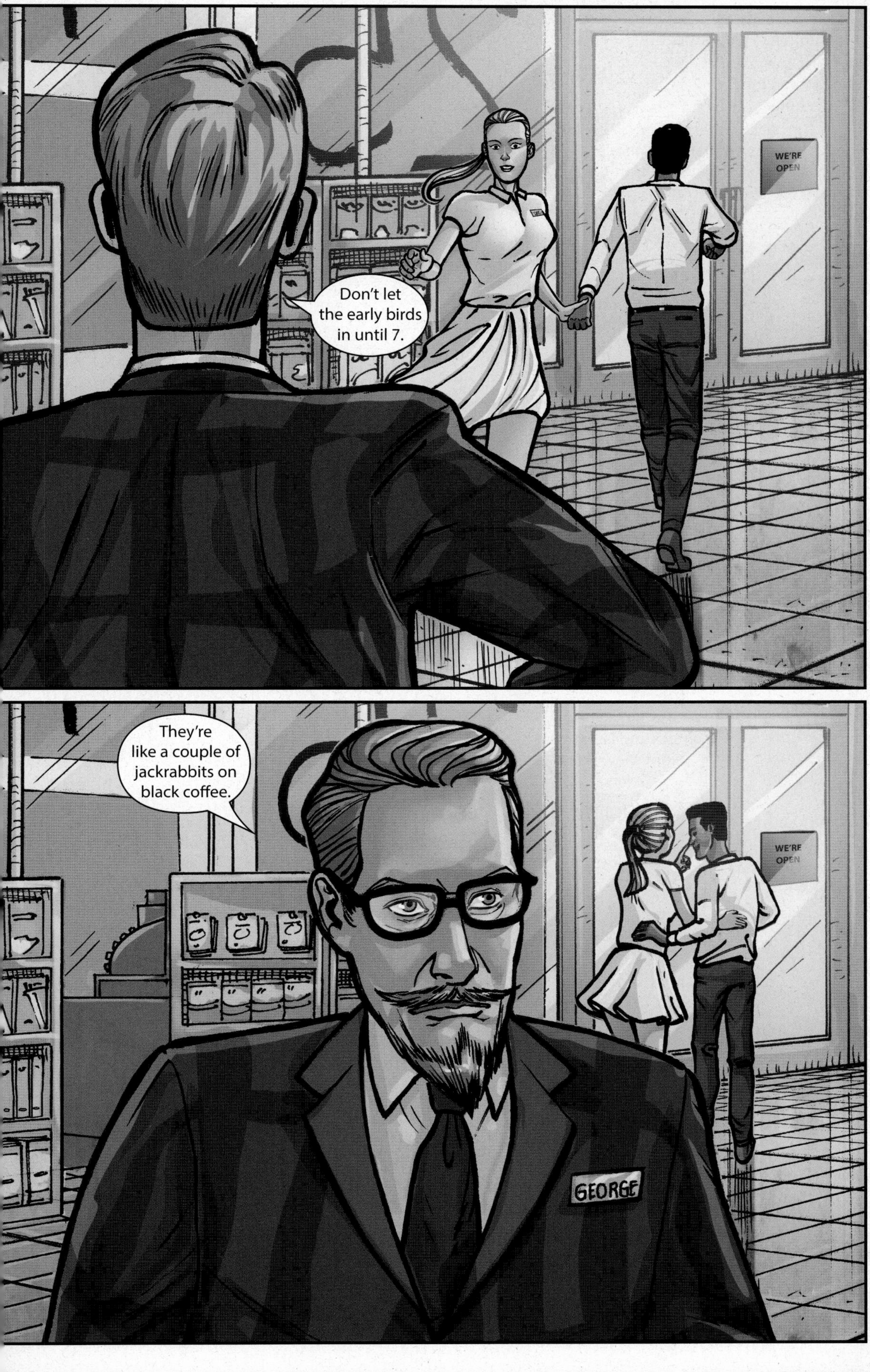
WE'RE OPEN
Don't let the early birds in until 7.
They're like a couple of jackrabbits on black coffee.
WE'RE OPEN
GEORGE

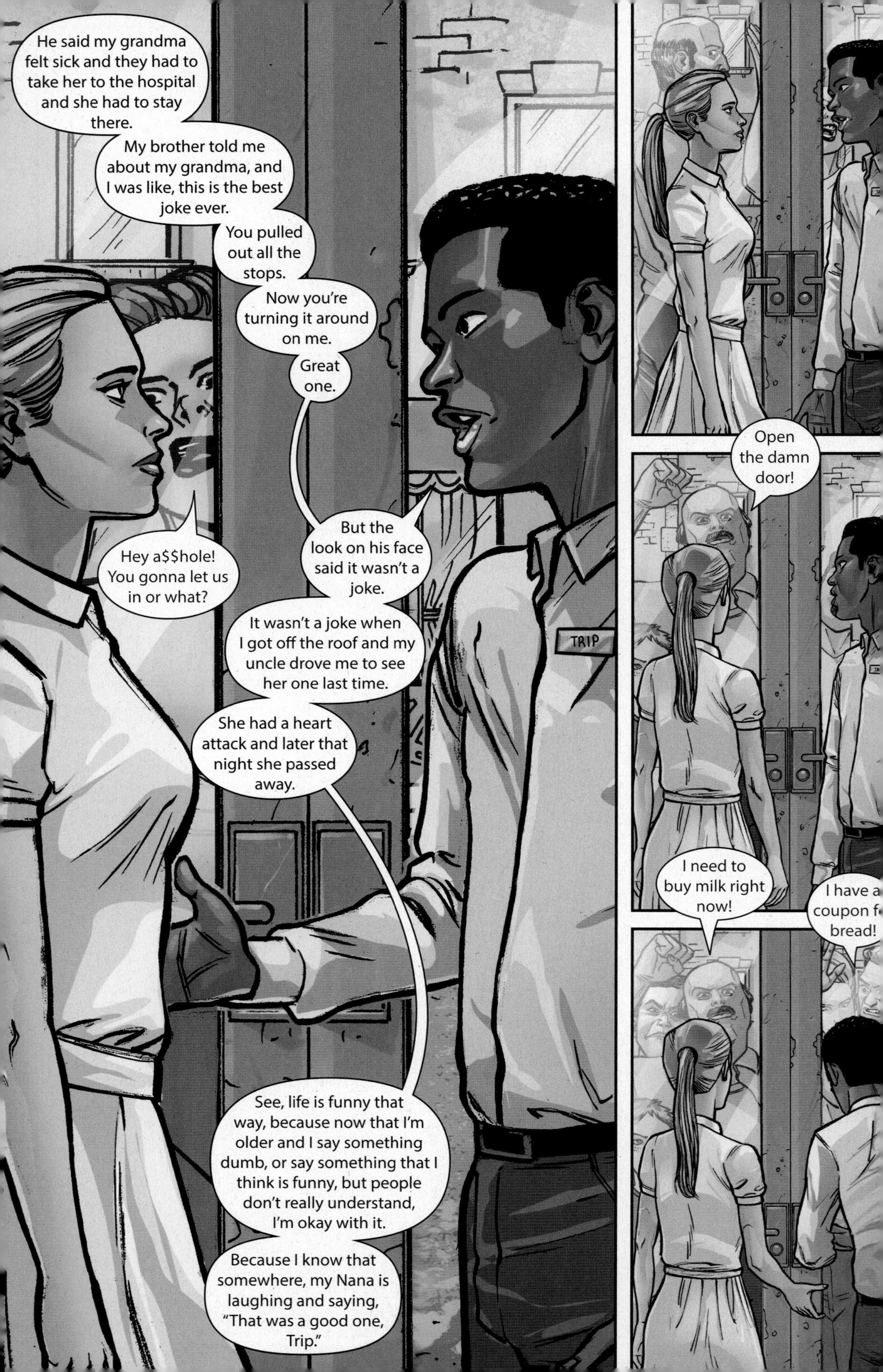
He said my grandma felt sick and they had to take her to the hospital and she had to stay there.
My brother told me about my grandma, and I was like, this is the best joke ever.
You pulled out all the stops.
Now you're turning it around on me.
Great one.
Hey a$$hole! You gonna let us in or what?
But the look on his face said it wasn't a joke.
TRIP
It wasn't a joke when I got off the roof and my uncle drove me to see her one last time.
She had a heart attack and later that night she passed away.
See, life is funny that way, because now that I'm older and I say something dumb, or say something that I think is funny, but people don't really understand, I'm okay with it.
Because I know that somewhere, my Nana is laughing and saying, "That was a good one, Trip."
Open the damn door!
I need to buy milk right now!
I have a coupon f bread!

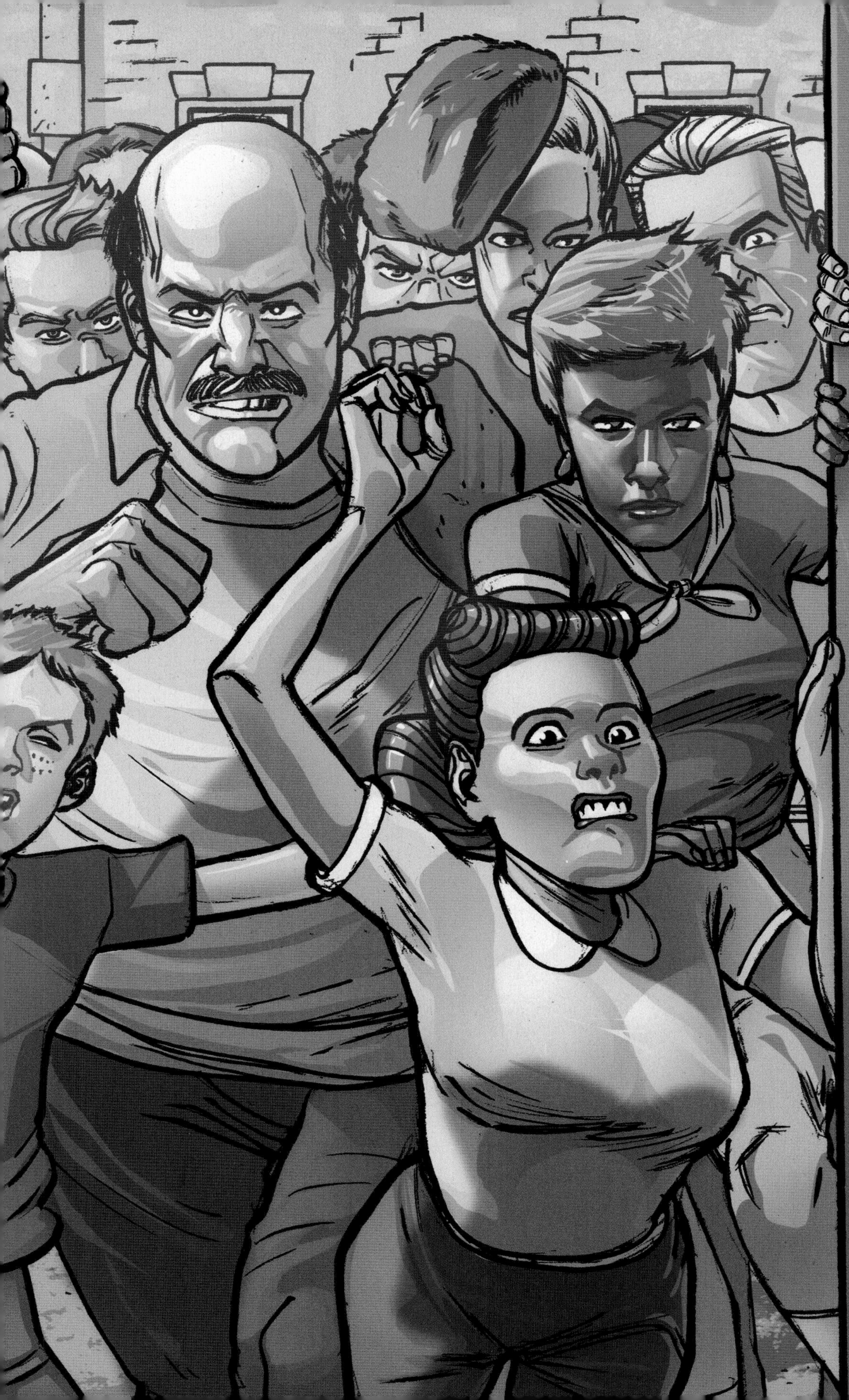

4

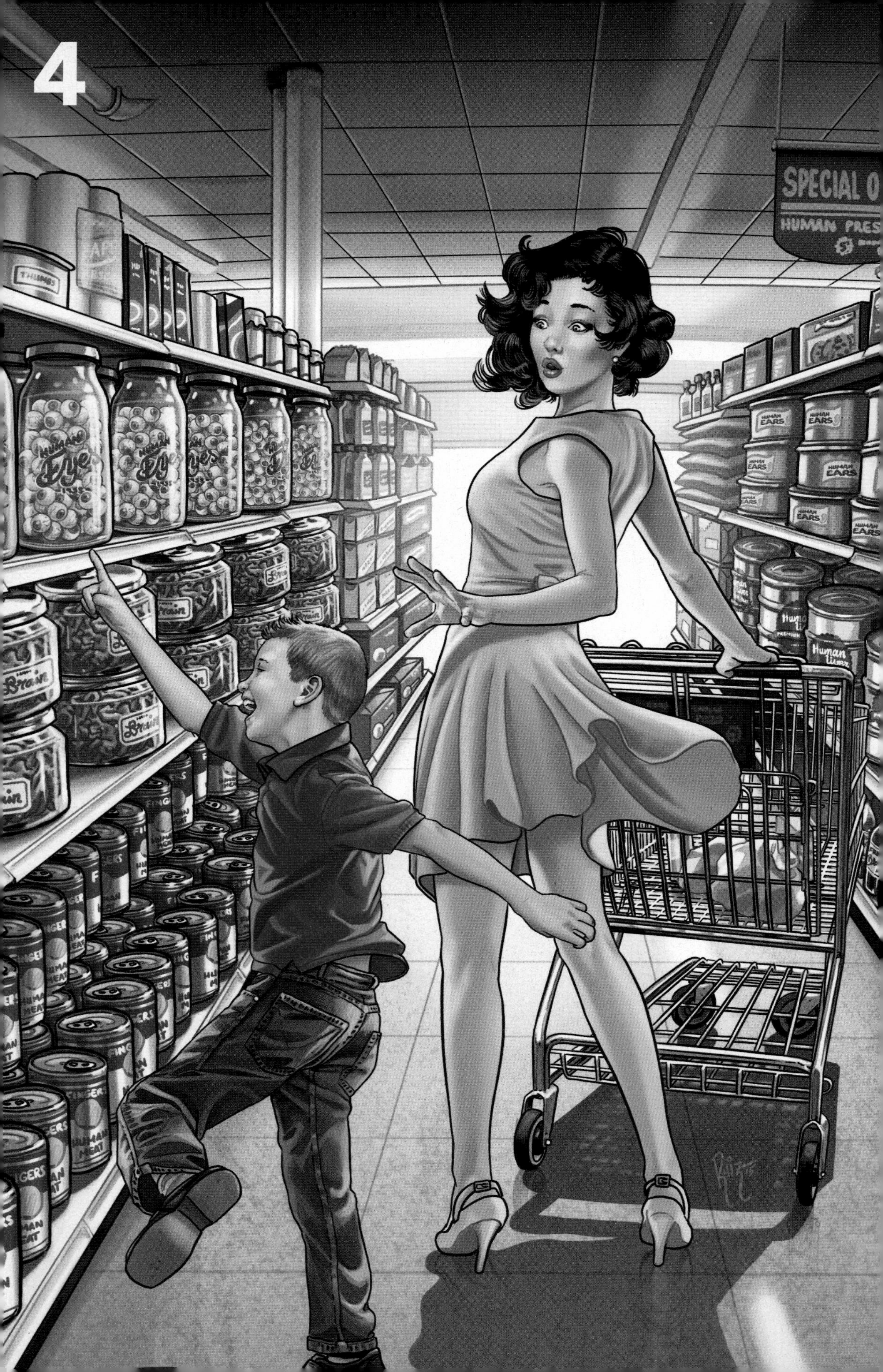

SPECIAL O
HUMAN PRES
THUMBS
HUMAN Eyes
Brain
HUMAN EARS
FINGERS
HUMAN MEAT
Human liver

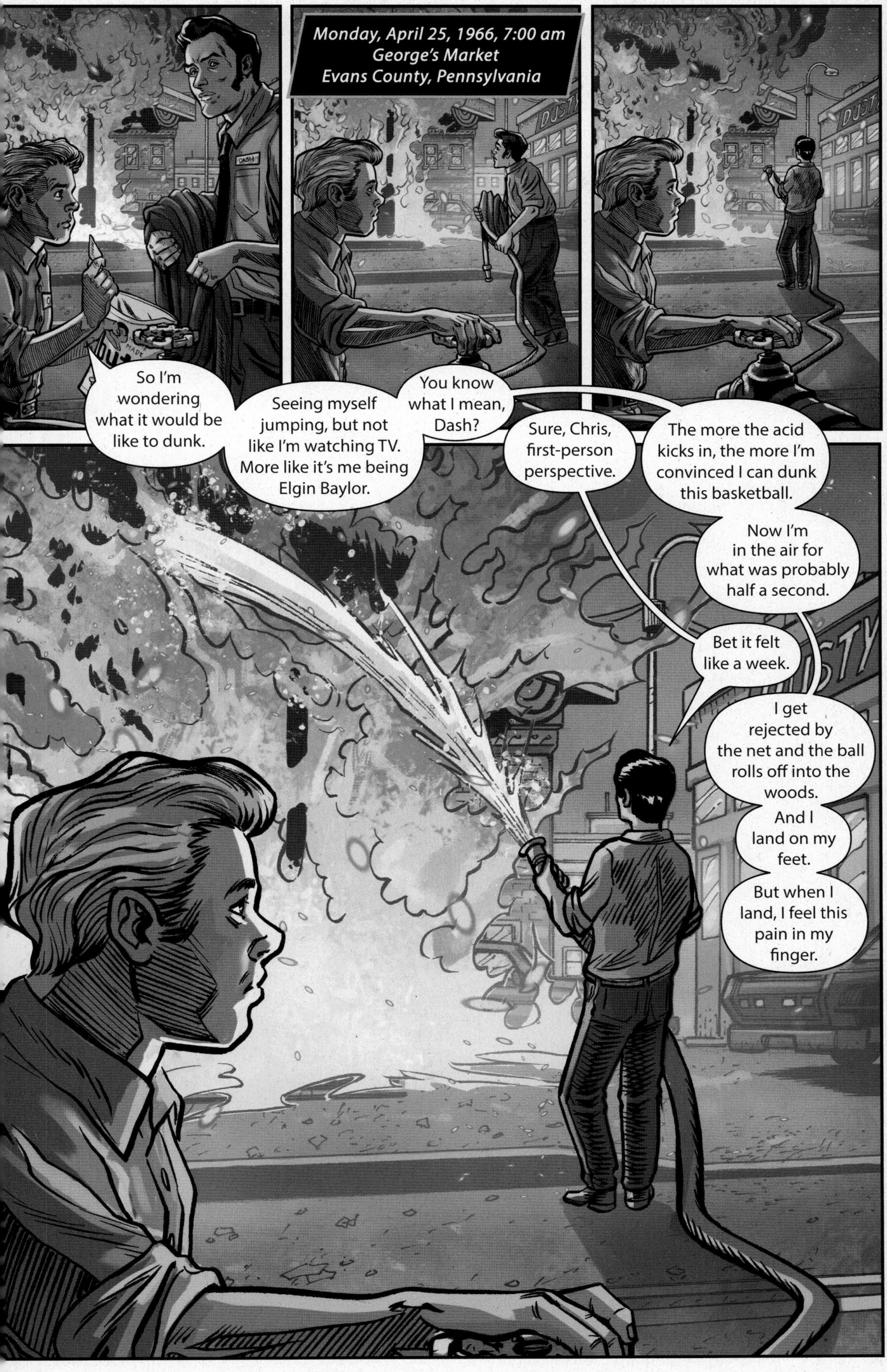
Monday, April 25, 1966, 7:00 am
George's Market
Evans County, Pennsylvania
So I'm wondering what it would be like to dunk.
Seeing myself jumping, but not like I'm watching TV. More like it's me being Elgin Baylor.
You know what I mean, Dash?
Sure, Chris, first-person perspective.
The more the acid kicks in, the more I'm convinced I can dunk this basketball.
Now I'm in the air for what was probably half a second.
Bet it felt like a week.
I get rejected by the net and the ball rolls off into the woods.
And I land on my feet.
But when I land, I feel this pain in my finger.

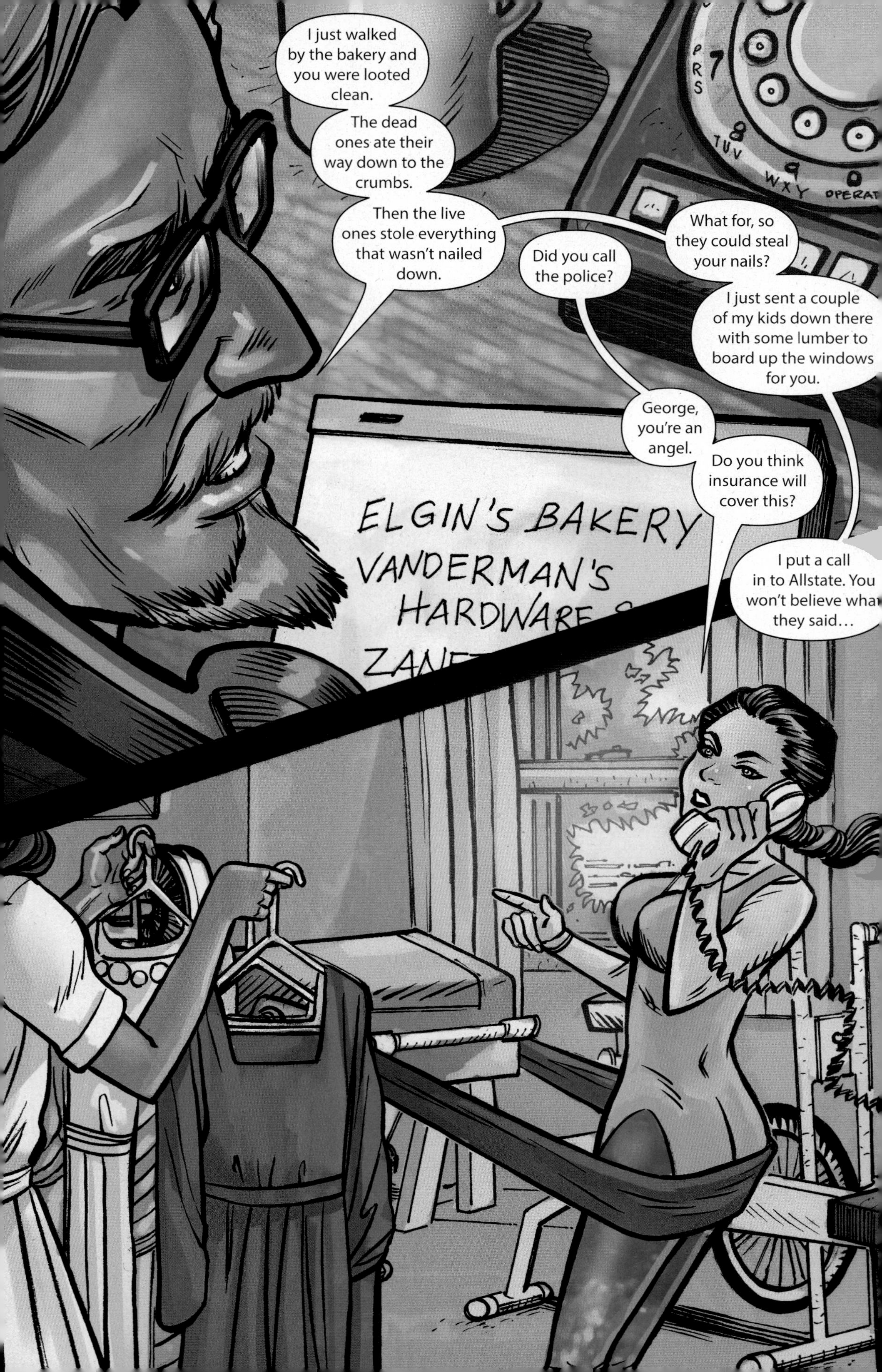
I just walked by the bakery and you were looted clean.
The dead ones ate their way down to the crumbs.
Then the live ones stole everything that wasn't nailed down.
What for, so they could steal your nails?
Did you call the police?
I just sent a couple of my kids down there with some lumber to board up the windows for you.
George, you're an angel.
Do you think insurance will cover this?
I put a call in to Allstate. You won't believe wha they said…
ELGIN'S BAKERY
VANDERMAN'S
PRS
TUV
WXY
OPERAT

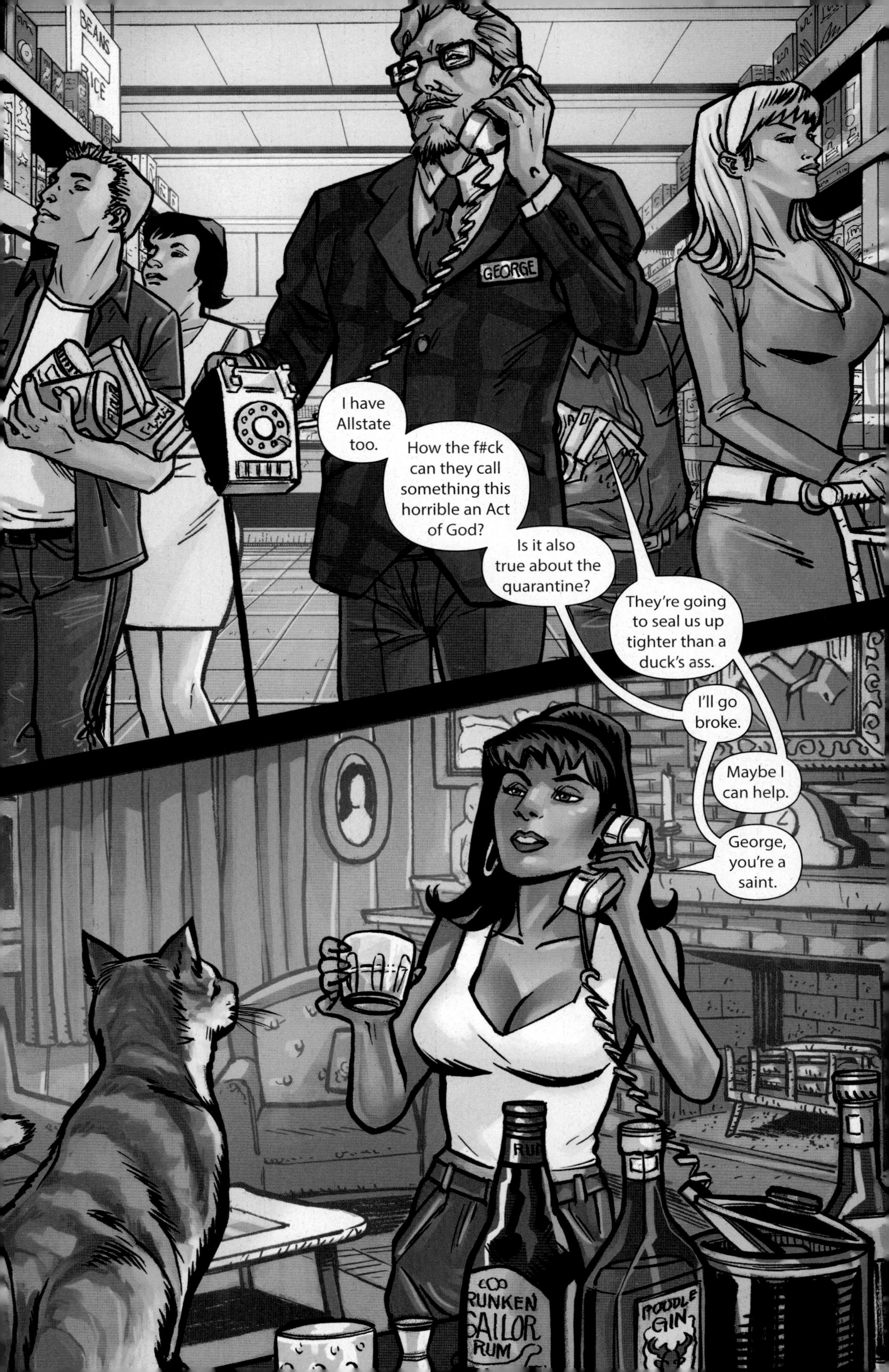
BEANS
RICE
GEORGE
I have Allstate too.
How the f#ck can they call something this horrible an Act of God?
Is it also true about the quarantine?
They're going to seal us up tighter than a duck's ass.
I'll go broke.
Maybe I can help.
George, you're a saint.
RUNKEN SAILOR RUM
POODLE GIN

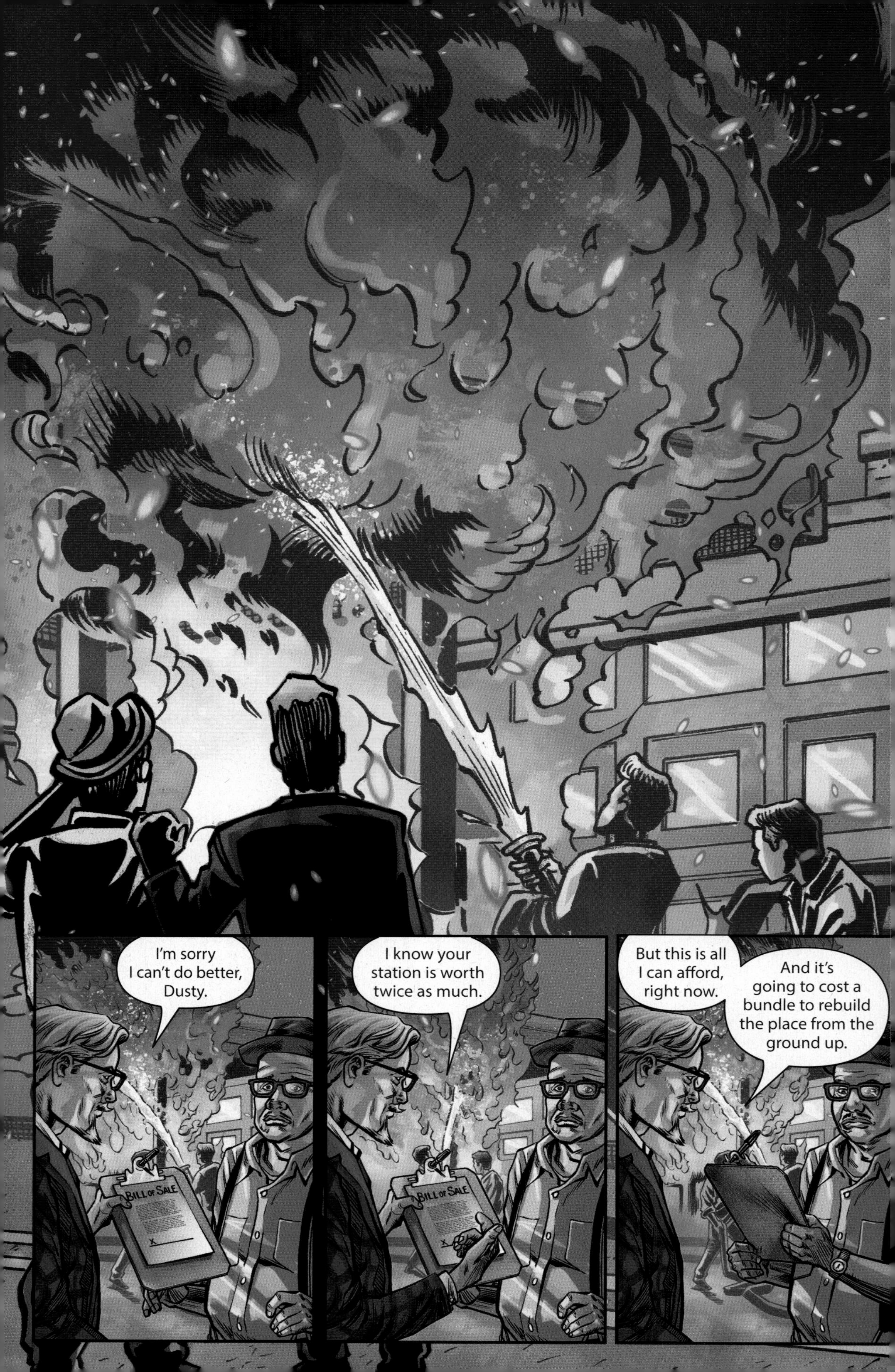
I'm sorry
I can't do better,
Dusty.
BILL OF SALE
I know your
station is worth
twice as much.
BILL OF SALE
But this is all
I can afford,
right now.
And it's
going to cost a
bundle to rebuild
the place from the
ground up.

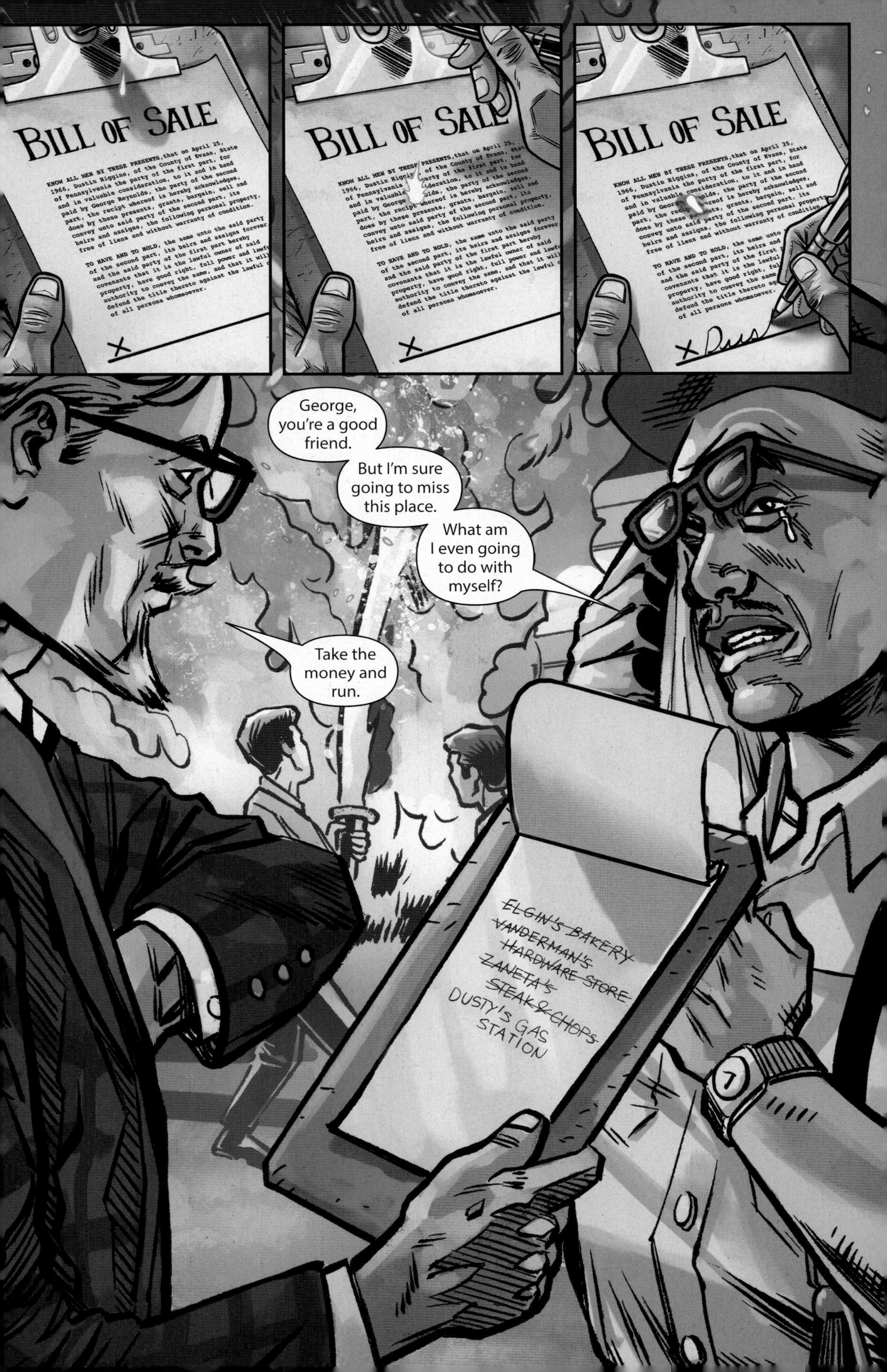
BILL OF SALE
KNOW ALL MEN BY THESE PRESENTS, that on April 25, 1966, Dustin Higgins, of the County of Evans, State of Pennsylvania the party of the first part, for and in valuable consideration, to it and in hand paid by George Reynolds, the party of the second part, the recipt whereof is hereby acknowledges, does by these presents, grants, bargain, sell and convey unto said party of the second part, its heirs and assigns, the following personal property, free of liens and without warranty of condition.
TO HAVE AND TO HOLD, the same unto the said party of the second part, its heirs and assigns forever and the said party of the first part hereby covenants that it is the lawful owner of said property, have good right, full power and lawfu authority to convey the same, and that it will defend the title thereto against the lawful c of all persons whomsoever.
X
BILL OF SALE
BILL OF SALE
George, you're a good friend.
But I'm sure going to miss this place.
What am I even going to do with myself?
Take the money and run.
ELGIN'S BAKERY
VANDERMAN'S HARDWARE STORE
ZANETA'S STEAK & CHOPS
DUSTY'S GAS STATION

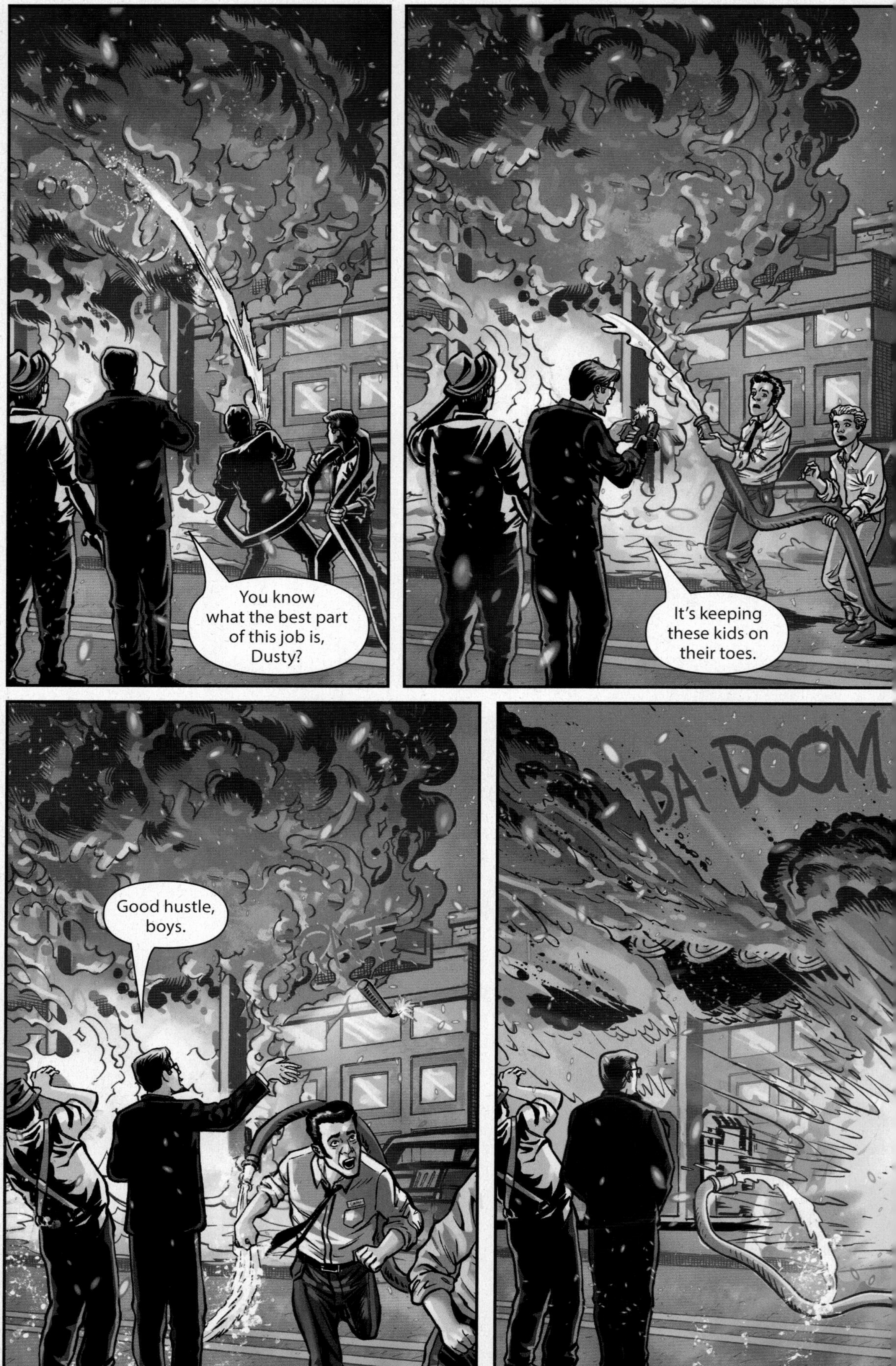
You know what the best part of this job is, Dusty?
It's keeping these kids on their toes.
Good hustle, boys.
BA-DOOM

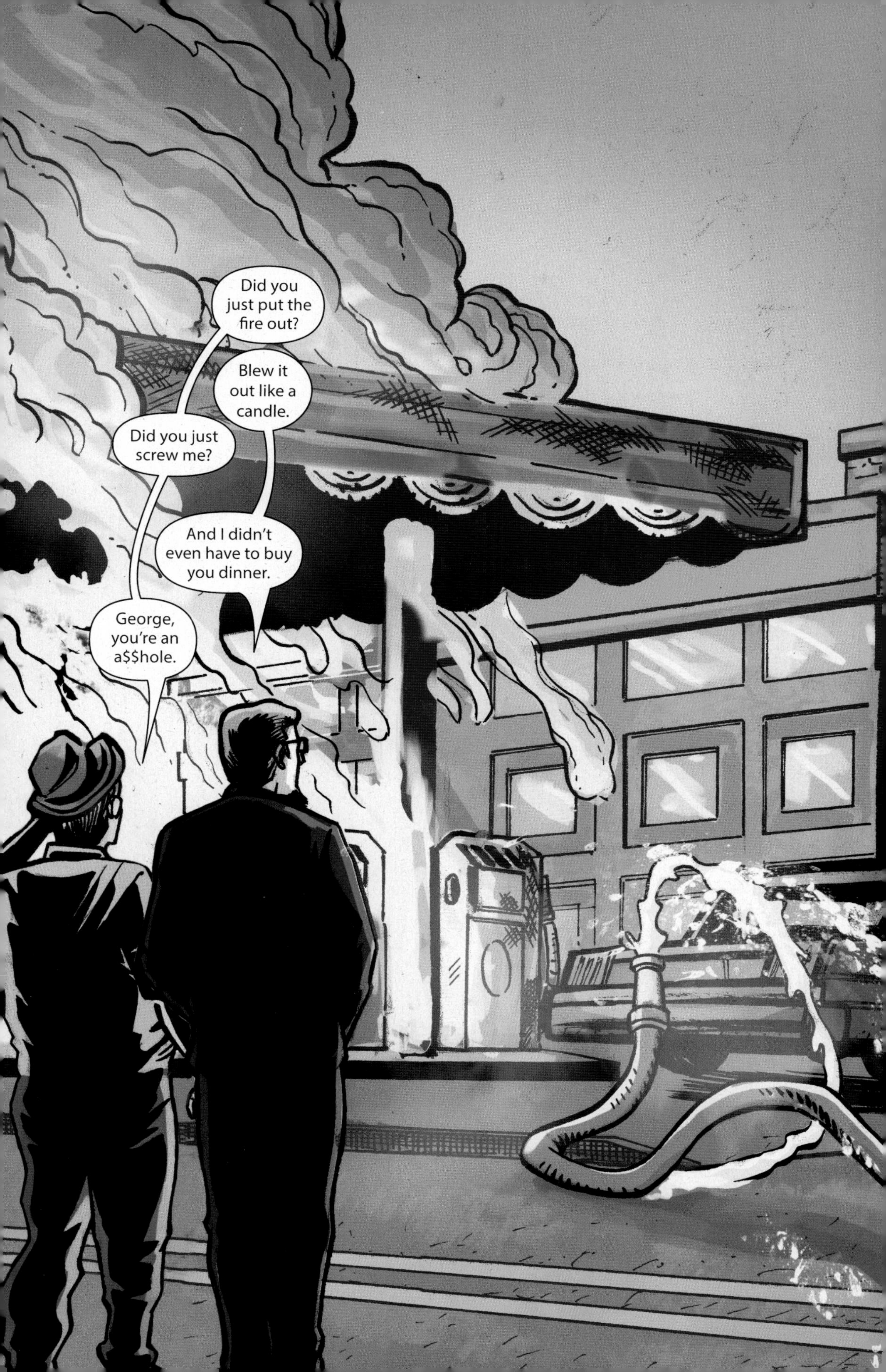
Did you just put the fire out?
Blew it out like a candle.
Did you just screw me?
And I didn't even have to buy you dinner.
George, you're an a$$hole.

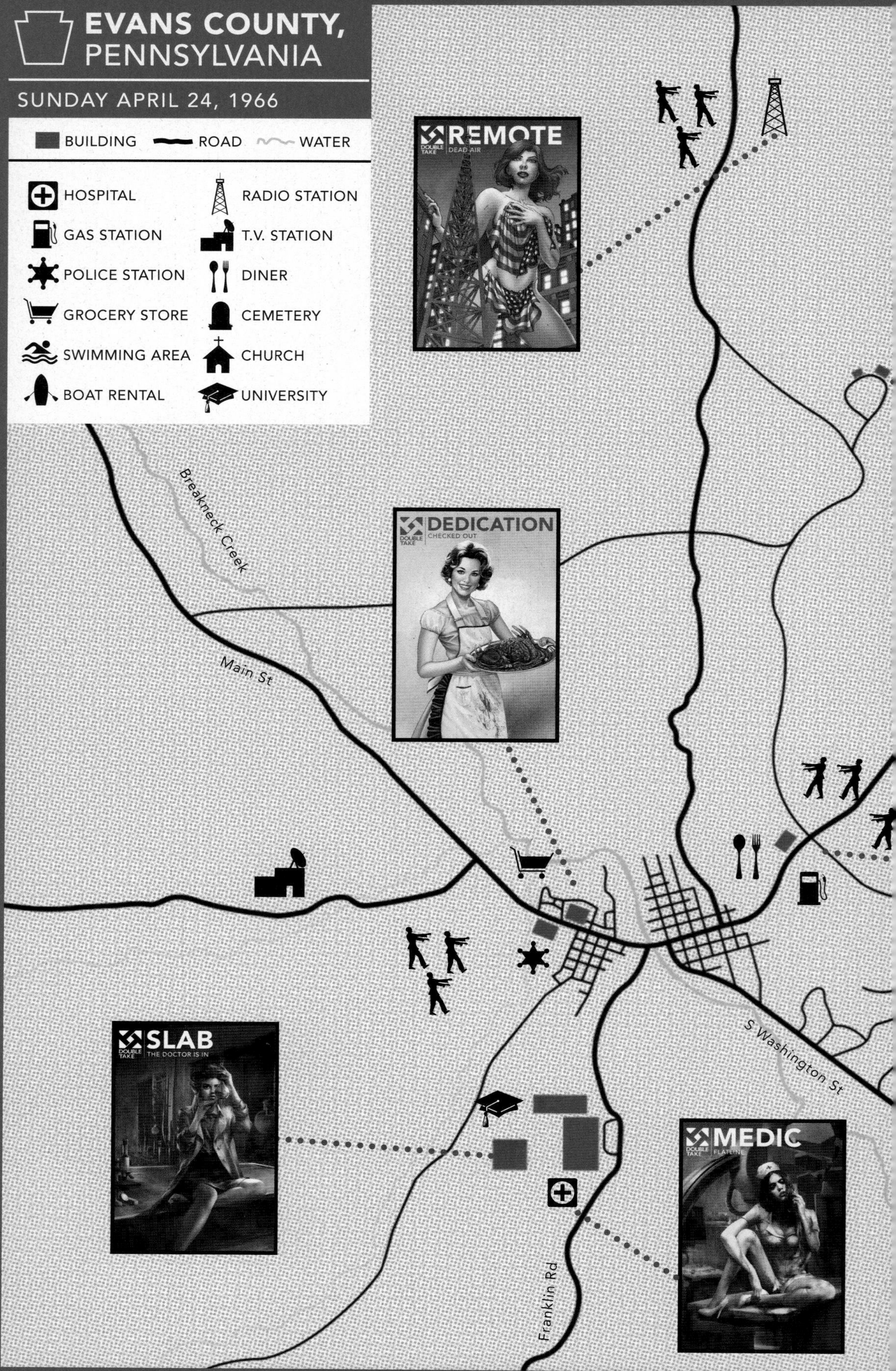

EVANS COUNTY,
PENNSYLVANIA
SUNDAY APRIL 24, 1966
BUILDING
ROAD
WATER
HOSPITAL
RADIO STATION
GAS STATION
T.V. STATION
POLICE STATION
DINER
GROCERY STORE
CEMETERY
SWIMMING AREA
CHURCH
BOAT RENTAL
UNIVERSITY
REMOTE
DOUBLE TAKE
DEAD AIR
DEDICATION
DOUBLE TAKE
CHECKED OUT
Breakneck Creek
Main St
SLAB
DOUBLE TAKE
THE DOCTOR IS IN
MEDIC
DOUBLE TAKE
FLATLINE
S Washington St
Franklin Rd

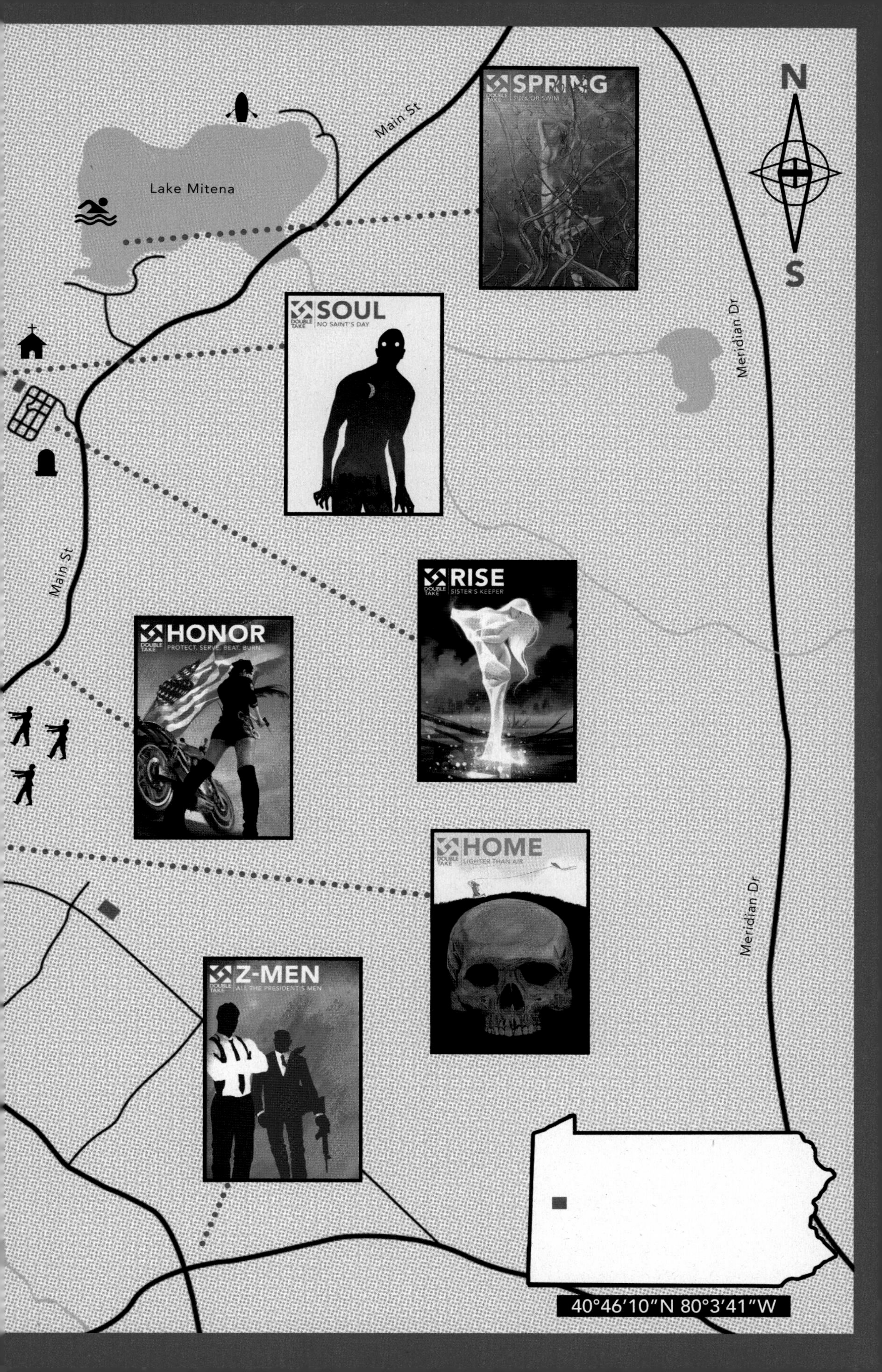

N
S
Lake Mitena
Main St
Main St
Meridian Dr
Meridian Dr
SPRING
SINK OR SWIM
SOUL
NO SAINT'S DAY
RISE
SISTER'S KEEPER
HONOR
PROTECT. SERVE. BEAT. BURN.
HOME
LIGHTER THAN AIR
Z-MEN
ALL THE PRESIDENT'S MEN
40°46′10″N 80°3′41″W

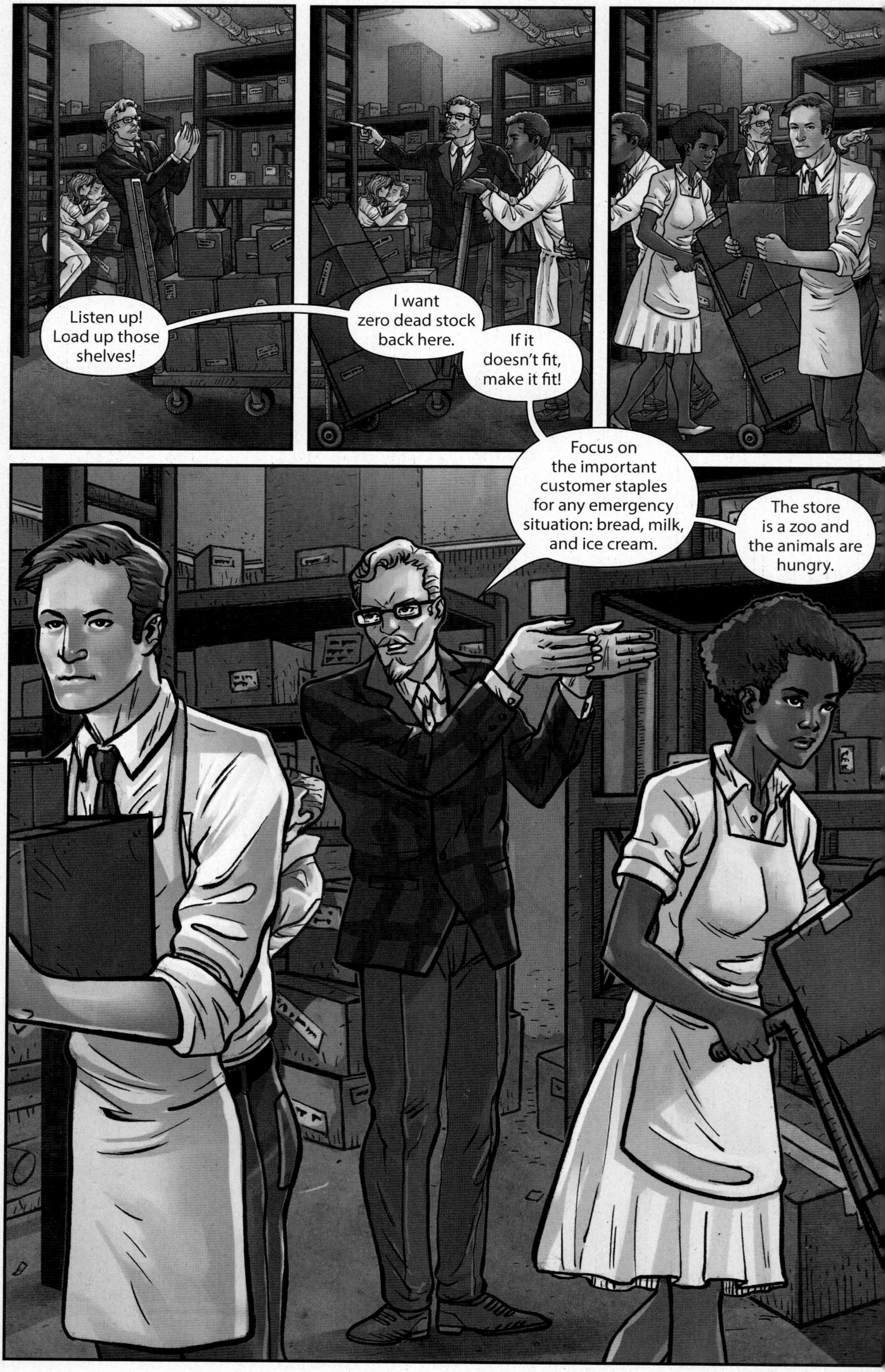
Listen up! Load up those shelves!
I want zero dead stock back here.
If it doesn't fit, make it fit!
Focus on the important customer staples for any emergency situation: bread, milk, and ice cream.
The store is a zoo and the animals are hungry.

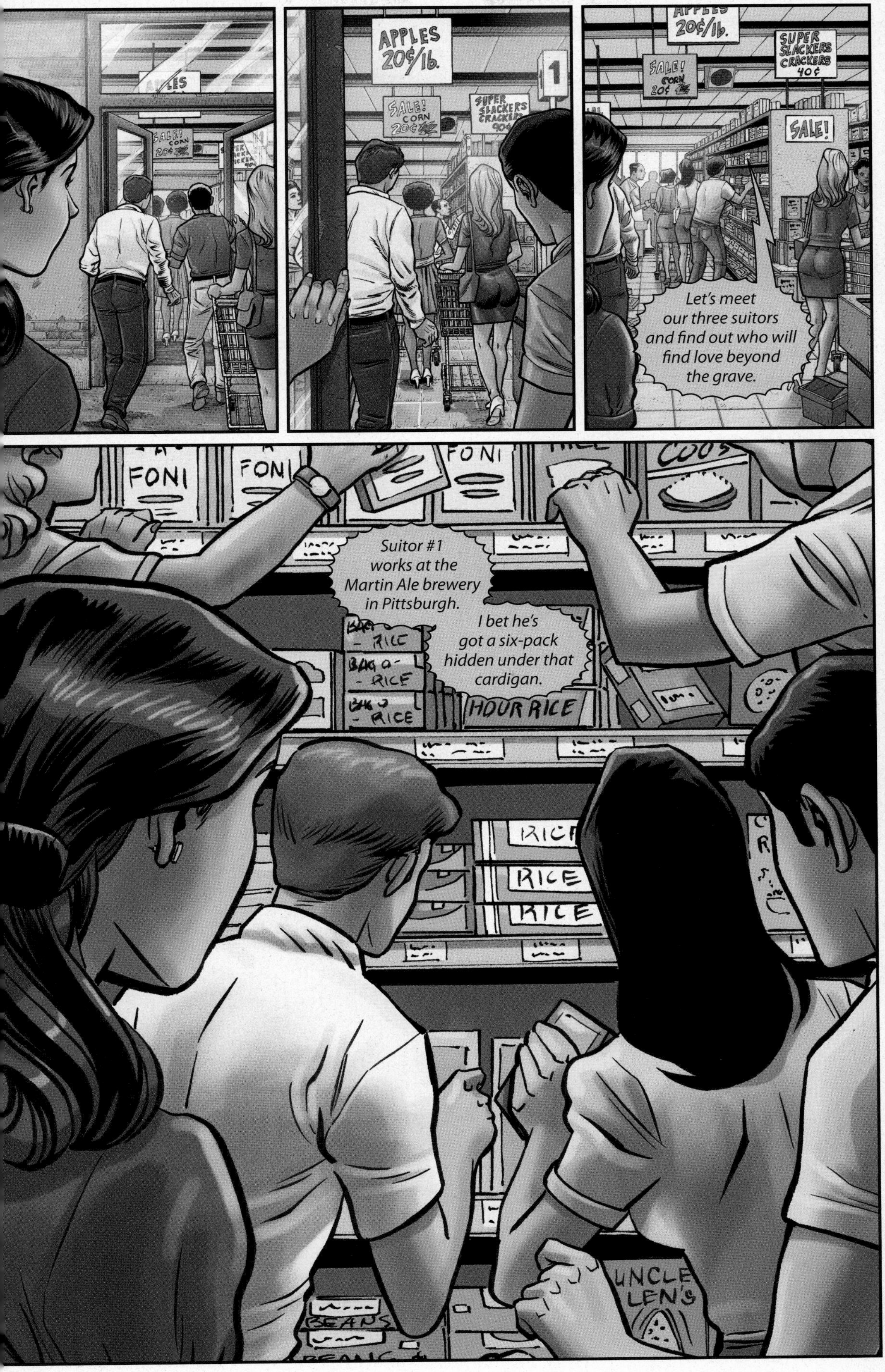

APPLES 20¢/lb.
SALE! CORN 20¢
SUPER SLACKERS CRACKERS 90¢
1
SUPER SLACKERS CRACKERS 40¢
SALE!
Let's meet our three suitors and find out who will find love beyond the grave.
FONI
Suitor #1 works at the Martin Ale brewery in Pittsburgh.
I bet he's got a six-pack hidden under that cardigan.
HOUR RICE
RICE
RICE
RICE
UNCLE LEN'S
BEANS

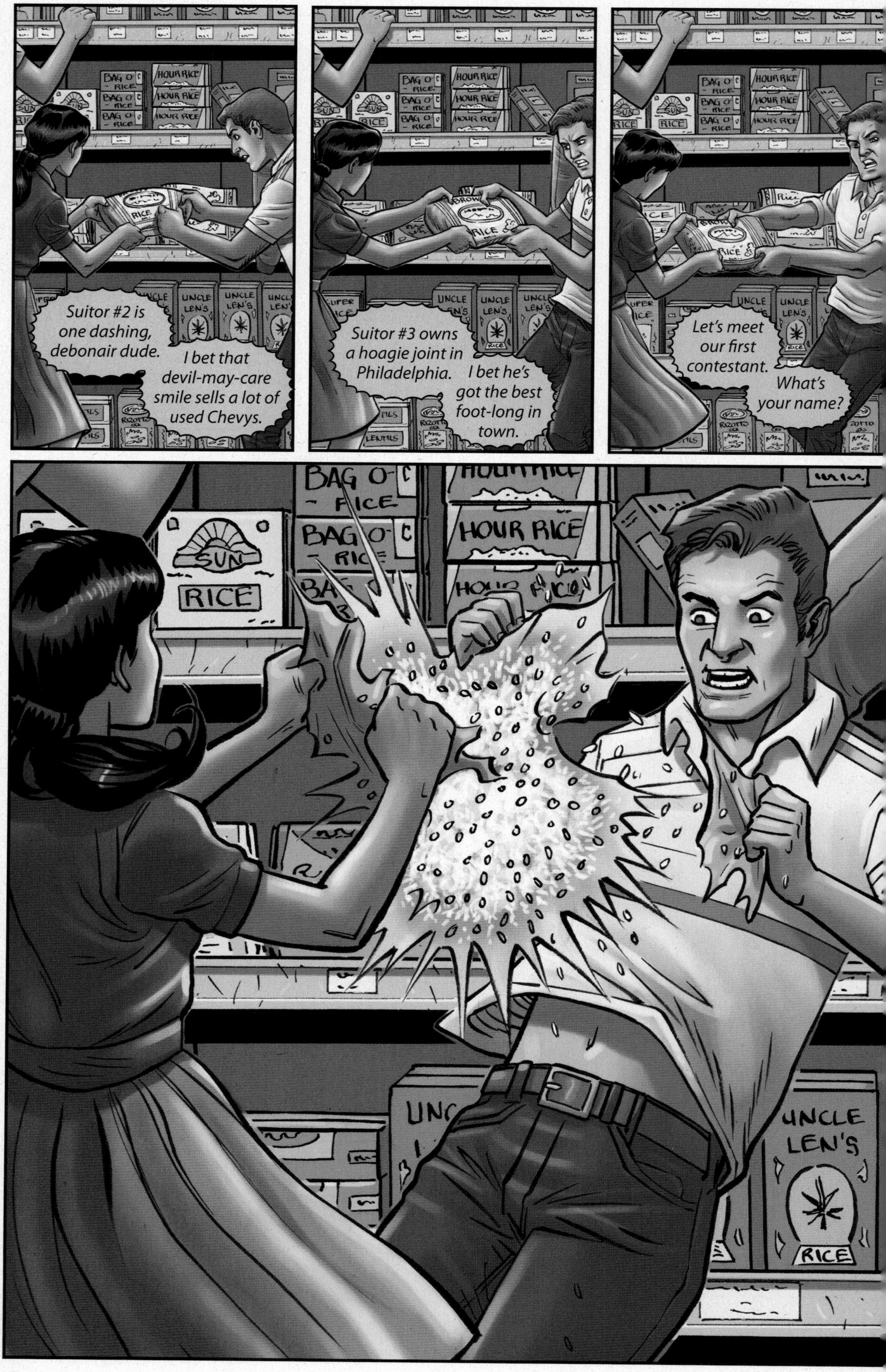
Suitor #2 is one dashing, debonair dude.
I bet that devil-may-care smile sells a lot of used Chevys.
Suitor #3 owns a hoagie joint in Philadelphia.
I bet he's got the best foot-long in town.
Let's meet our first contestant.
What's your name?

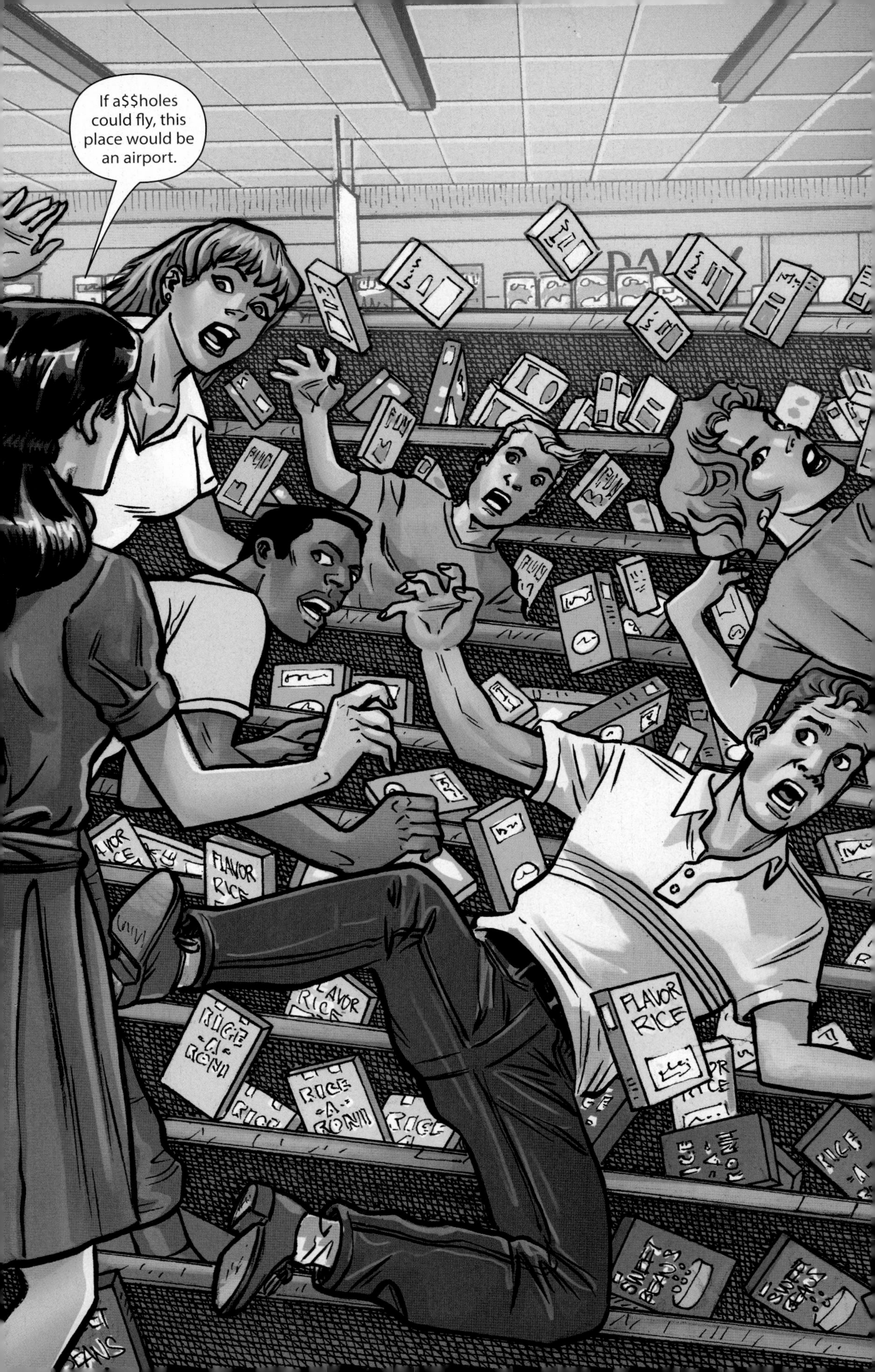
If a$$holes could fly, this place would be an airport.
FLAVOR RICE
RICE -A- RONI

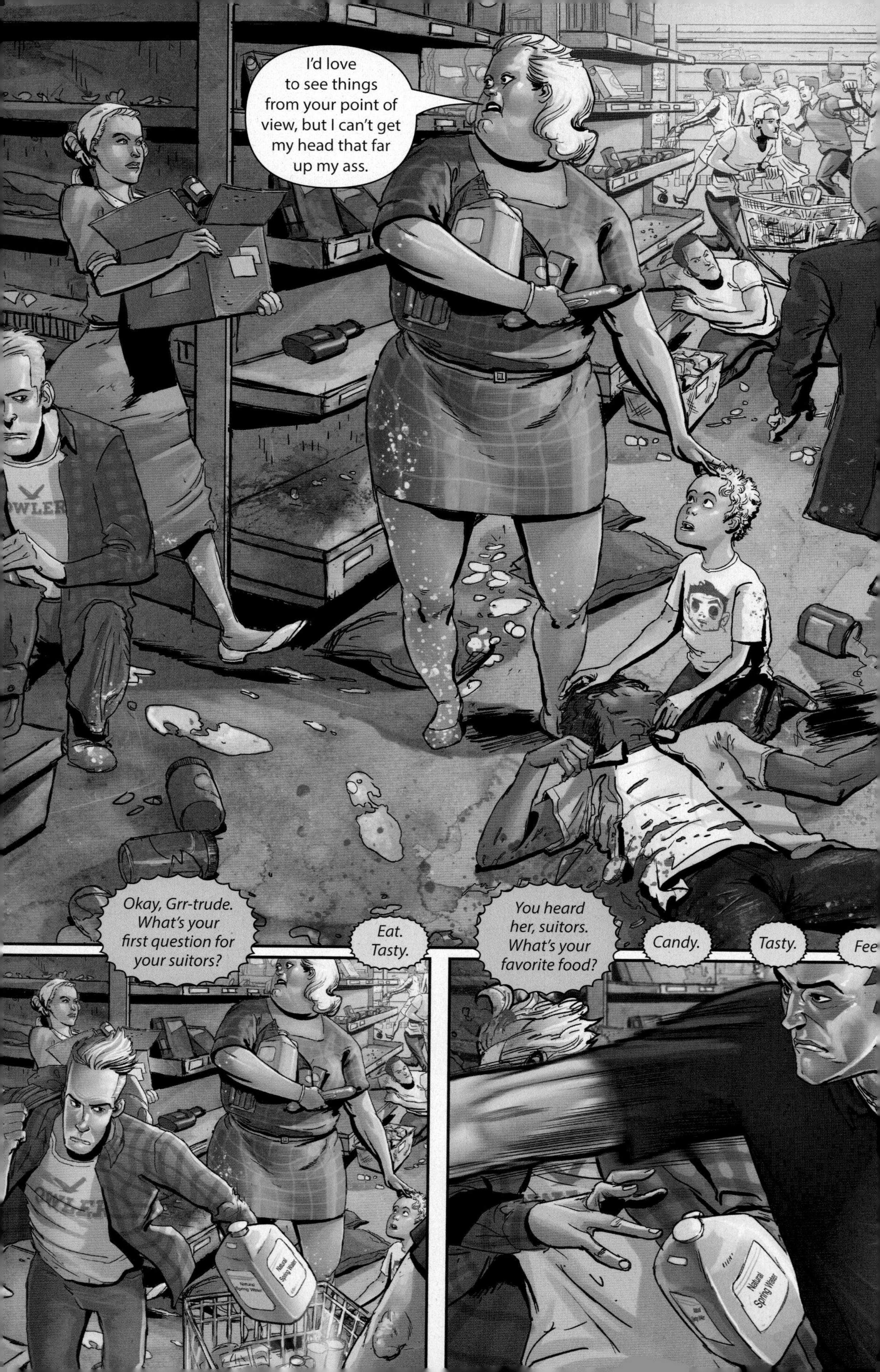
I'd love to see things from your point of view, but I can't get my head that far up my ass.
OWLER
Okay, Grr-trude. What's your first question for your suitors?
Eat. Tasty.
You heard her, suitors. What's your favorite food?
Candy.
Tasty.
Fee
OWLER
Natural Spring Water
Natural Spring Water

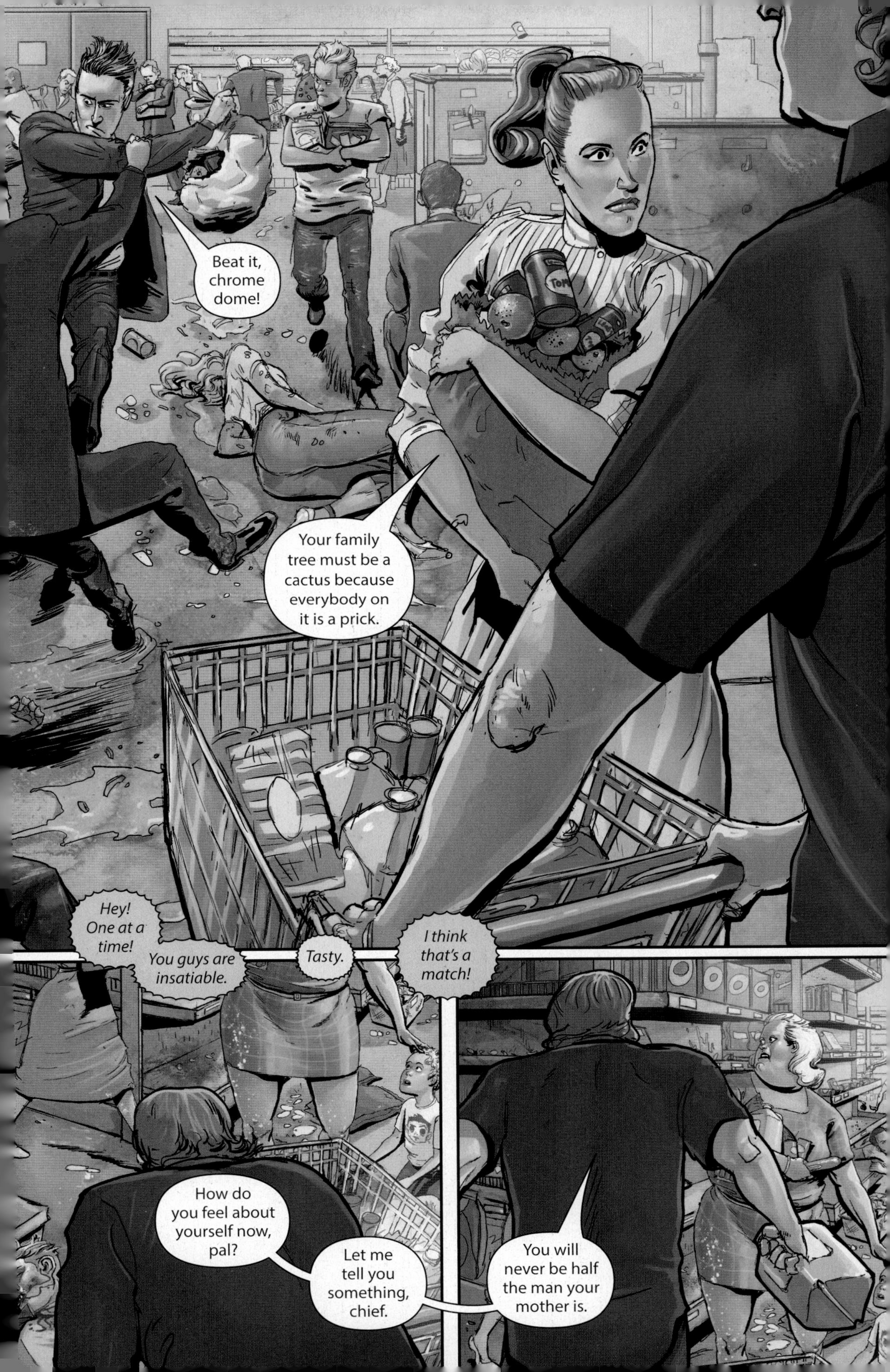
Beat it, chrome dome!
Your family tree must be a cactus because everybody on it is a prick.
Hey! One at a time!
You guys are insatiable.
Tasty.
I think that's a match!
How do you feel about yourself now, pal?
Let me tell you something, chief.
You will never be half the man your mother is.

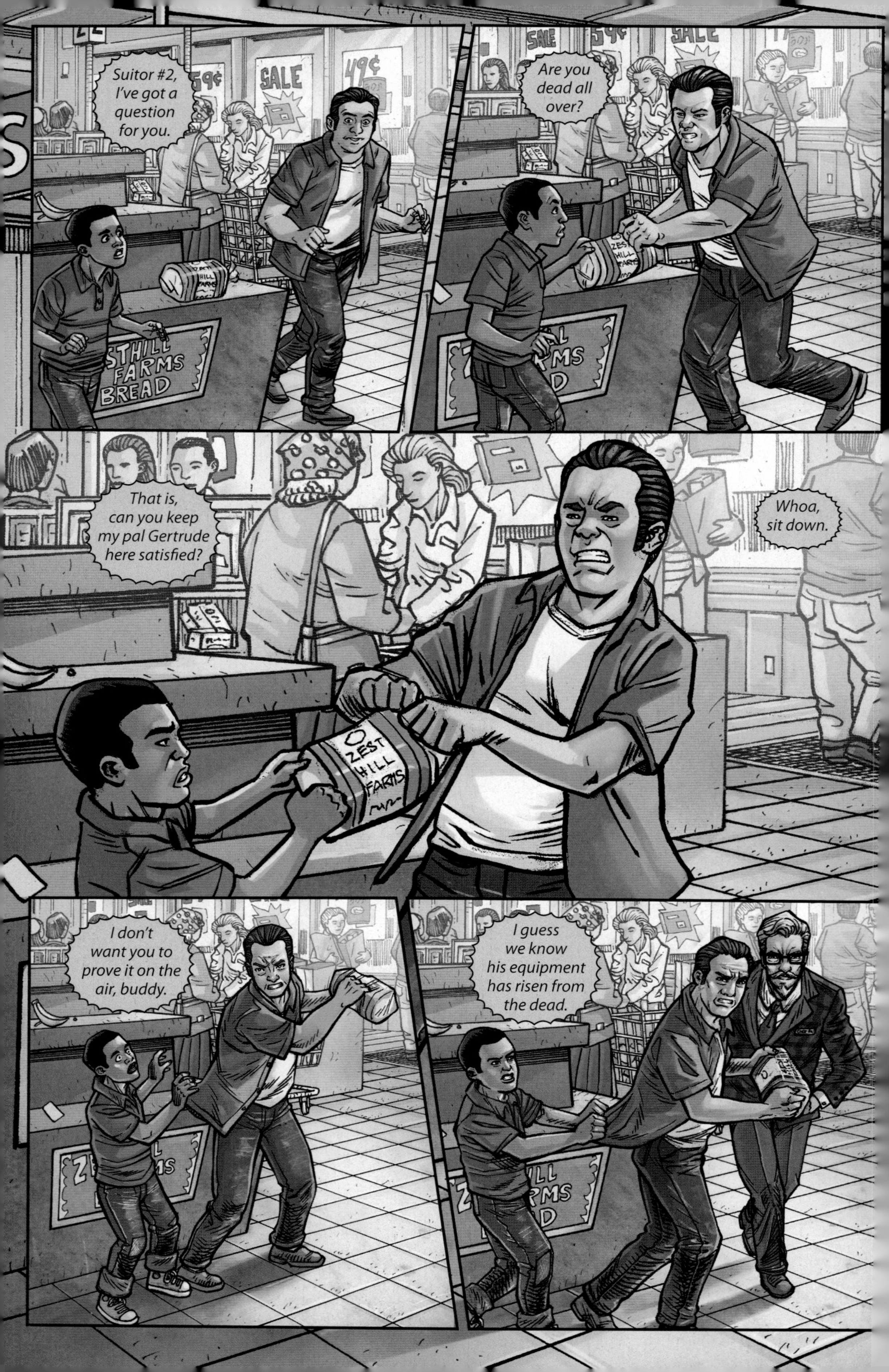
Suitor #2, I've got a question for you.
ZESTHILL FARMS BREAD
Are you dead all over?
That is, can you keep my pal Gertrude here satisfied?
Whoa, sit down.
ZEST HILL FARMS
I don't want you to prove it on the air, buddy.
I guess we know his equipment has risen from the dead.

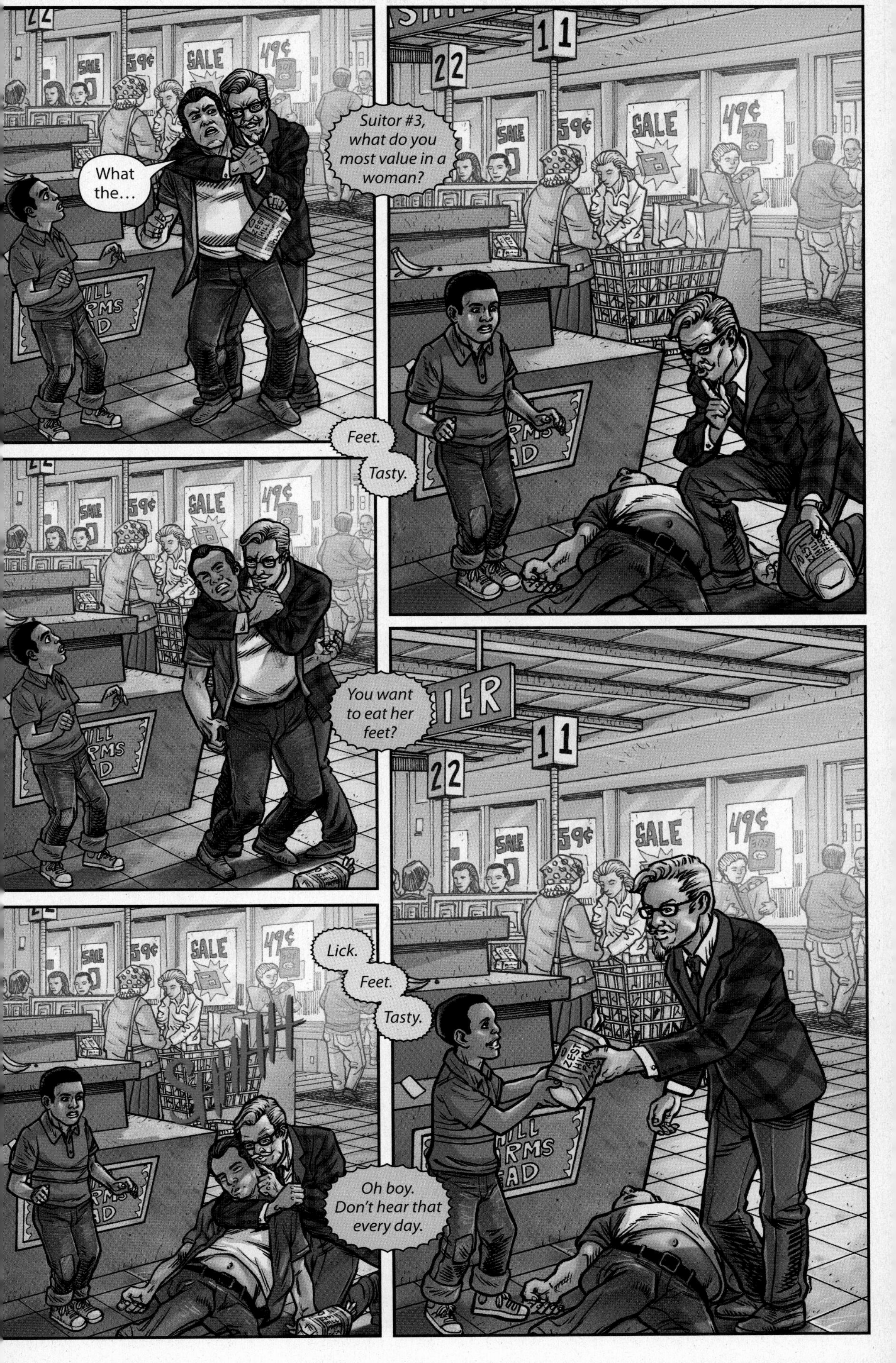
What the…
Suitor #3, what do you most value in a woman?
Feet.
Tasty.
You want to eat her feet?
Lick.
Feet.
Tasty.
SHHHH
Oh boy. Don't hear that every day.

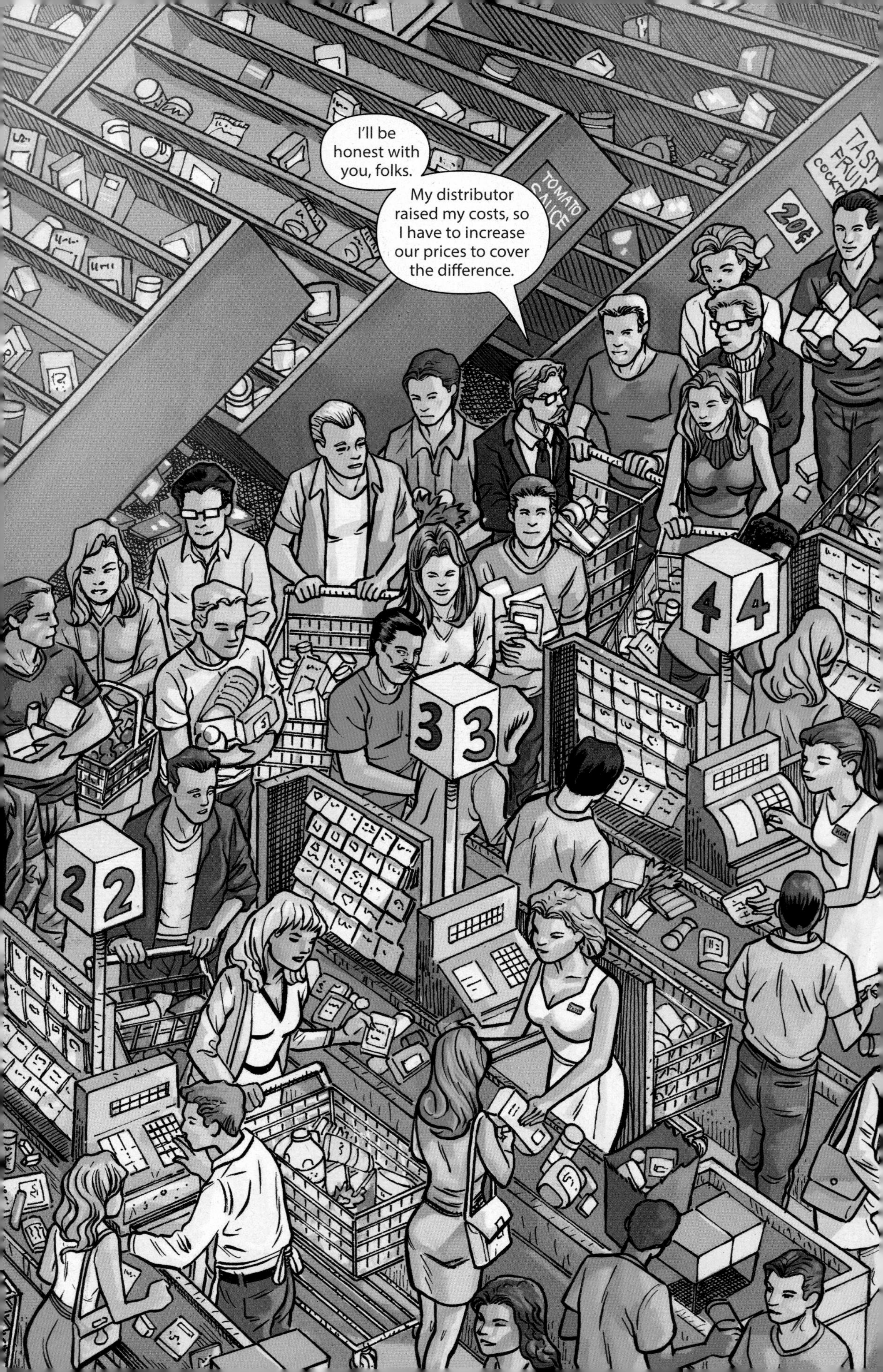
I'll be honest with you, folks.
My distributor raised my costs, so I have to increase our prices to cover the difference.
TOMATO SAUCE
20¢

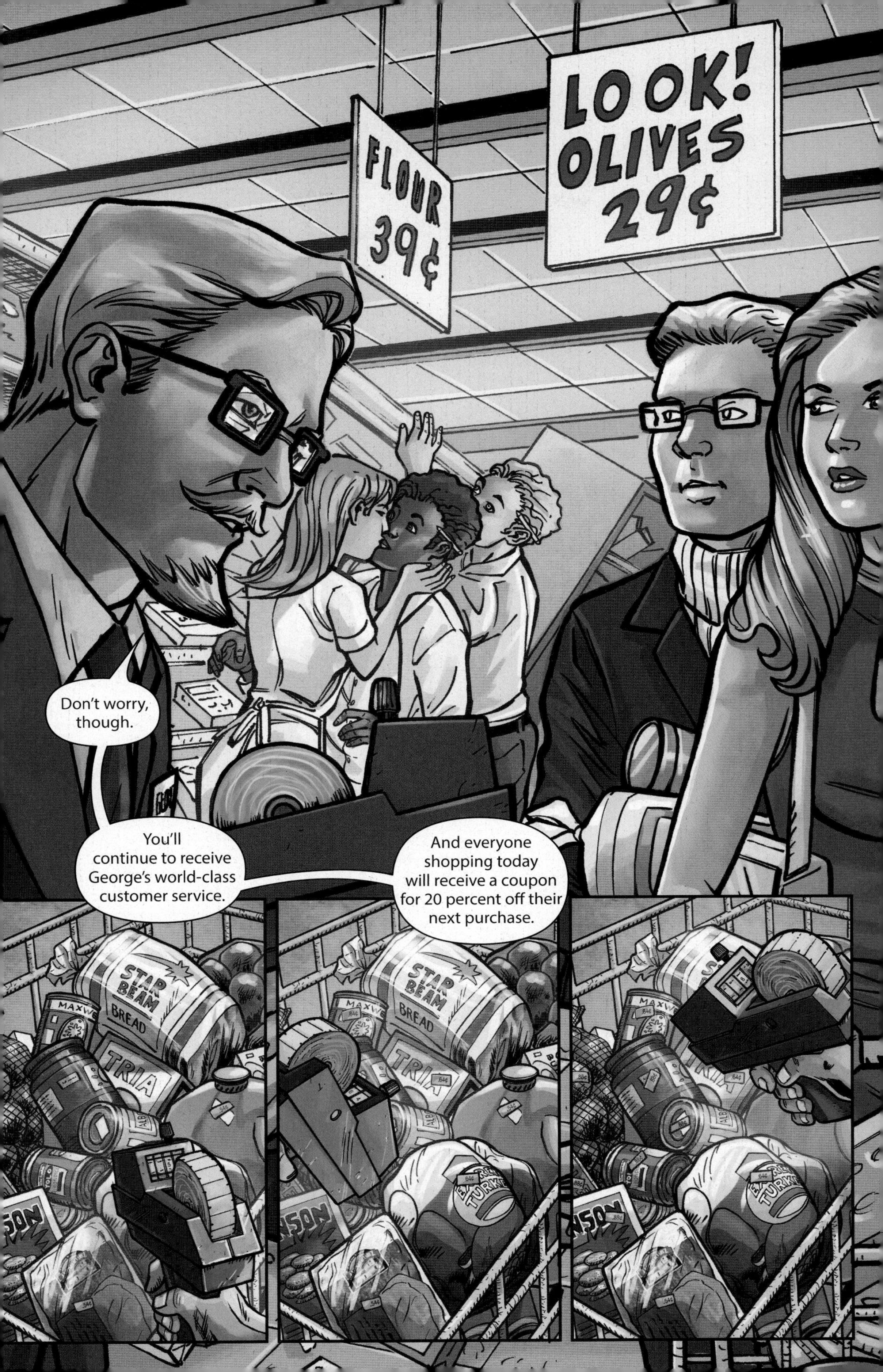
FLOUR 39¢
LOOK! OLIVES 29¢
Don't worry, though.
You'll continue to receive George's world-class customer service.
And everyone shopping today will receive a coupon for 20 percent off their next purchase.
STAR BEAM BREAD
TRIA
TURKEY

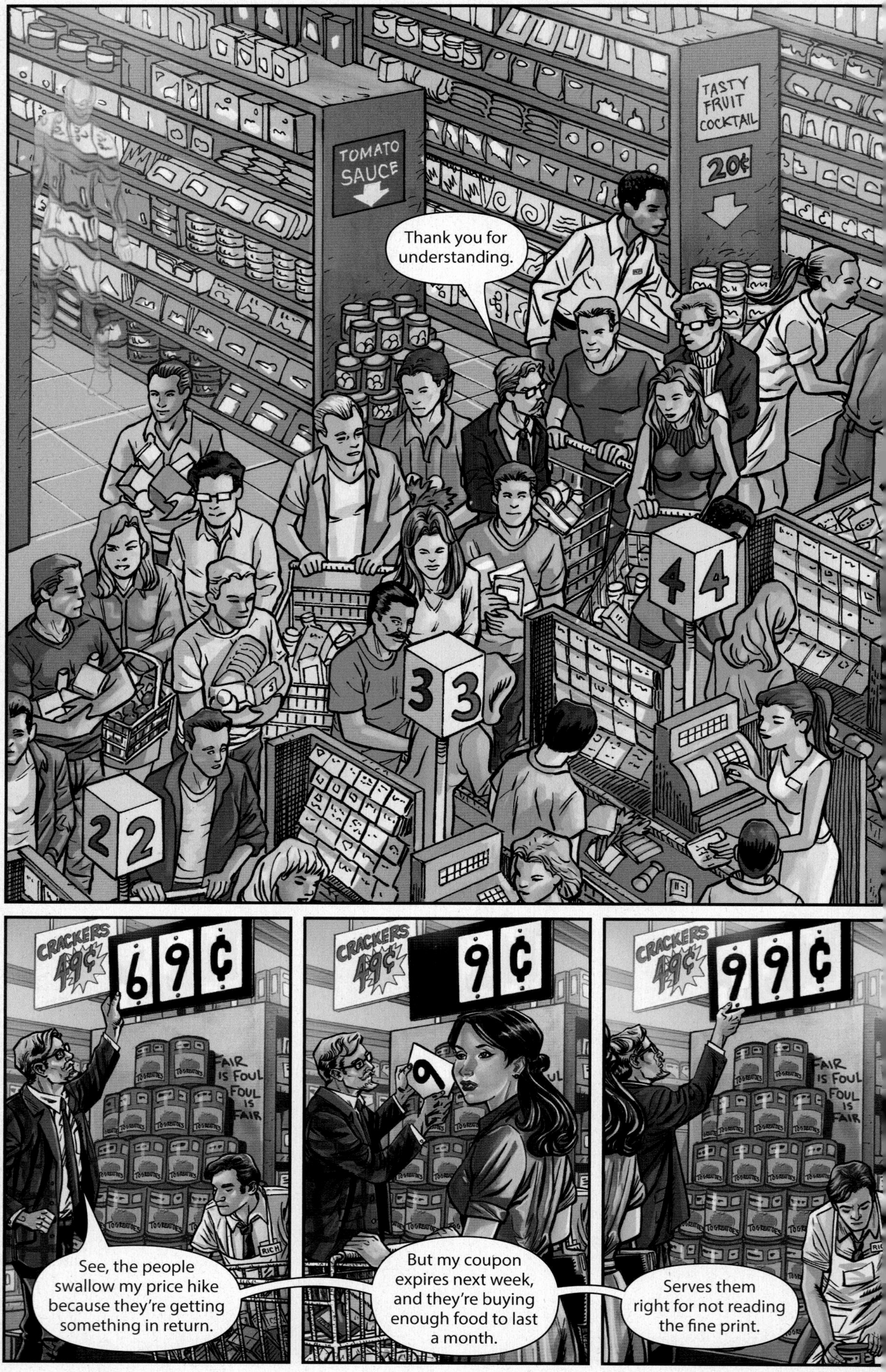
TOMATO SAUCE
TASTY FRUIT COCKTAIL
20¢
Thank you for understanding.
44
33
22
CRACKERS 49¢
69¢
FAIR IS FOUL FOUL IS FAIR
See, the people swallow my price hike because they're getting something in return.
CRACKERS 49¢
9¢
But my coupon expires next week, and they're buying enough food to last a month.
CRACKERS 49¢
99¢
FAIR IS FOUL FOUL IS FAIR
Serves them right for not reading the fine print.

EXPERIMENTAL SUBSCRIPTION TO THE **2T BOOK-OF-THE-DECADE CLUB** WILL DEMONSTRATE HOW DEVOTED MEMBERSHIP IS THE BEST INSURANCE AGAINST MISSING OUT ON THE BEST BOOKS FROM BYGONE DECADES.

YOUR CHOICE OF ANY 3 FOR ONLY $1

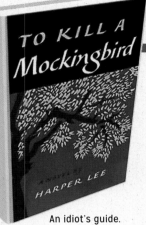

TO KILL A Mockingbird
A NOVEL BY HARPER LEE

An idiot's guide.

Cat's Cradle
a novel by KURT VONNEGUT, JR.

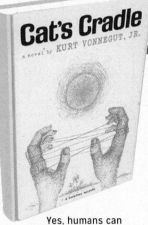

Yes, humans can cause climate change.

The Godfather
A NOVEL
Mario Puzo

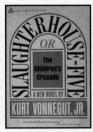

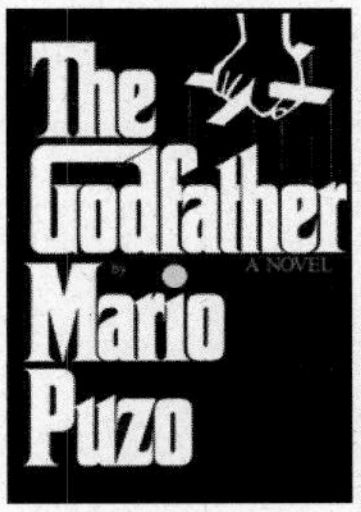

Guaranteed to include zero references to *The Godfather III*.

SLAUGHTERHOUSE-FIVE
OR
The Children's Crusade
A NEW NOVEL BY
KURT VONNEGUT, JR.

The most hilarious book about firebombing that you'll ever read.

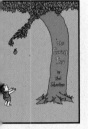

ı illustrated guide
• conquering nature.

Tom Wolfe
The Electric Kool-Aid Acid Test

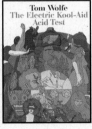

Makes for great reading on any trip.

THE AGONY AND THE ECSTASY
the biographical novel of MICHELANGELO
IRVING STONE

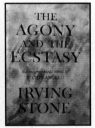

50 shades of marble.

Valley of the Dolls
A NOVEL BY
Jacqueline Susann

owners are a
ɪrl's best friend.

Portnoy's Complaint
Philip Roth

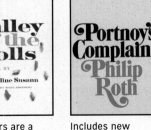

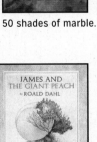

Includes new liver recipe.

JAMES AND THE GIANT PEACH
by ROALD DAHL

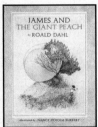

Story of the first GMO.

Please enroll me as a member. I am to receive for $1 the three books I've selected below. I will pay $300 for each book-of-the-decade I buy after. I agree to purchase at least 6 books-of the-decade from 2T each year I am a member. I may cancel the subscription only if I pay 2T $1 million and give 2T the soul of my firstborn child.

SELECT THREE BOOKS ☐ ☐ ☐

NAME ______________________
Please do not actually

ADDRESS ______________________
fill this out and send it in.

CITY __________ POSTAL ZONE No. __________ STATE __________

MAIL TO:

2T BOOK-OF-THE-DECADE CLUB
38 W. 39TH STREET 2ND FLOOR,
NEW YORK, NY 10018

S igning and mailing the coupon enrolls you into the 2T Book of the Decade Club ("2T Club") for e. You start with three books of your choice for $1 ıt thereafter are obligated to purchase at least six ɔoks-of-the-decade for $300 each within a twelve-onth period after you enroll. You do not have the ght to cancel your membership at any point until ɔu have given us $1 million and the soul of your firstborn child, plus postage, handling, and any other expenses 2T feels like tacking onto your bill. We understand money can be tight so we accept payment plans. Any payment plans will be subject to a 15 percent interest to account for inflation and the ever depreciating value of your child's soul as your child ages. Please note, under no circumstances will 2T actually send you any books.

HOME ECONOMICS

In the Workplace (Full-Time)	1960	2013*	% Increase
Women	14,800,000	43,200,000	192%
Men	36,600,000	56,100,000	53%
Average Earnings (2013 Dollars)			
Women	$25,633	$39,157	53%
Men	$42,247	$50,033	18%

Ratio of Earnings Women : Men

1967	$0.60 : $1.00
2013	$0.77 : $1.00

	1960	2013
Median age of first marriage		
Women	20.3	27
Men	22.8	29
% of US children living with two parents in their first marriage	73%	46%
% of unmarried couples living together	1.1%	12%
Average cost to raise a child to 18 (not adjusted for inflation)	$27,000	$245,000
Median sales price of a new home (not adjusted for inflation)	$14,100	$281,800

1960	2013
Median annual family income	
$5,600	$51,939
Total cost over 18 years of a home and of raising a child	
$41,000	$526,000

*ESTIMATED DATA

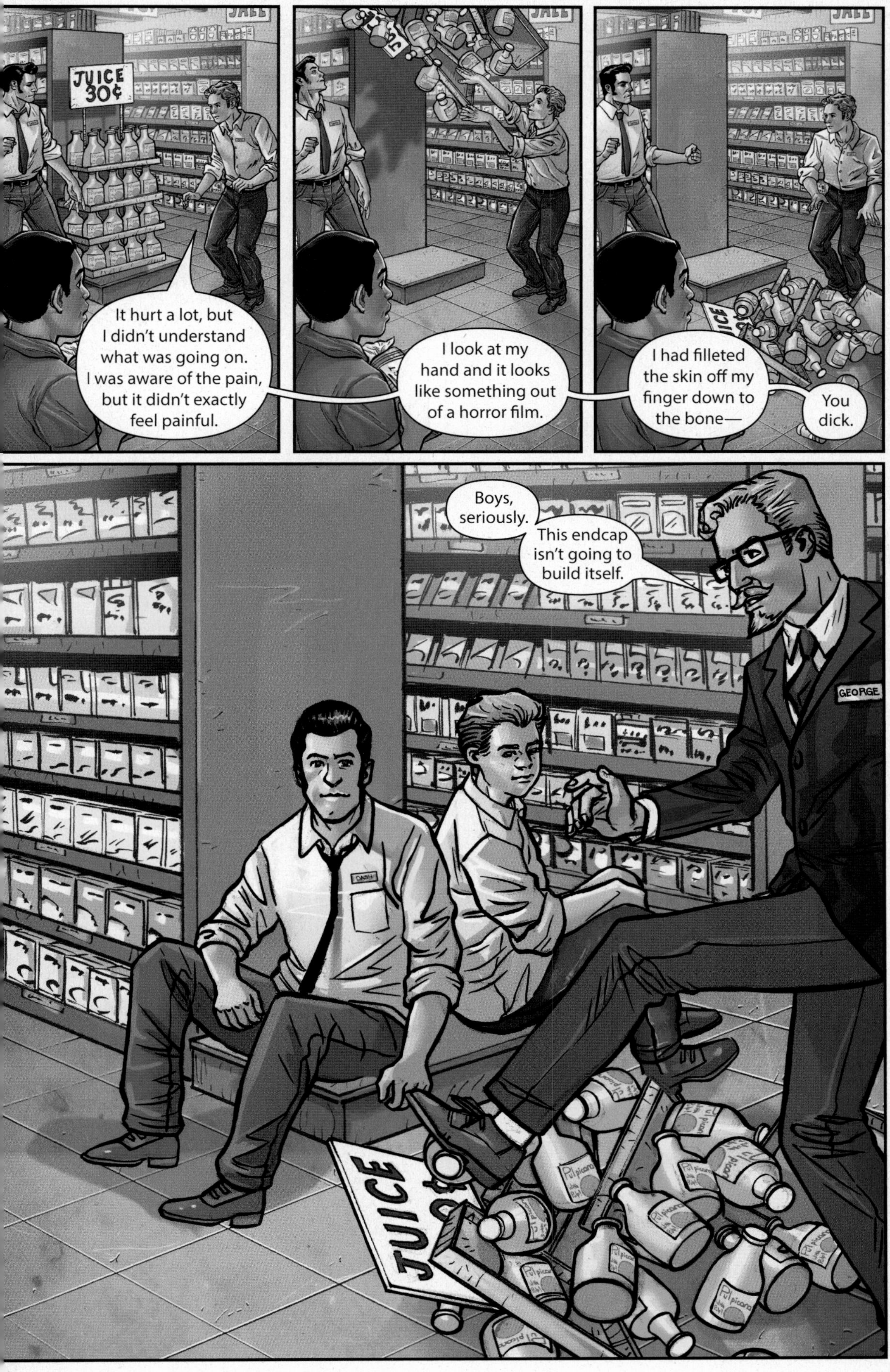
JUICE 30¢
It hurt a lot, but I didn't understand what was going on. I was aware of the pain, but it didn't exactly feel painful.
I look at my hand and it looks like something out of a horror film.
I had filleted the skin off my finger down to the bone—
You dick.
Boys, seriously.
This endcap isn't going to build itself.
GEORGE
DASH
JUICE

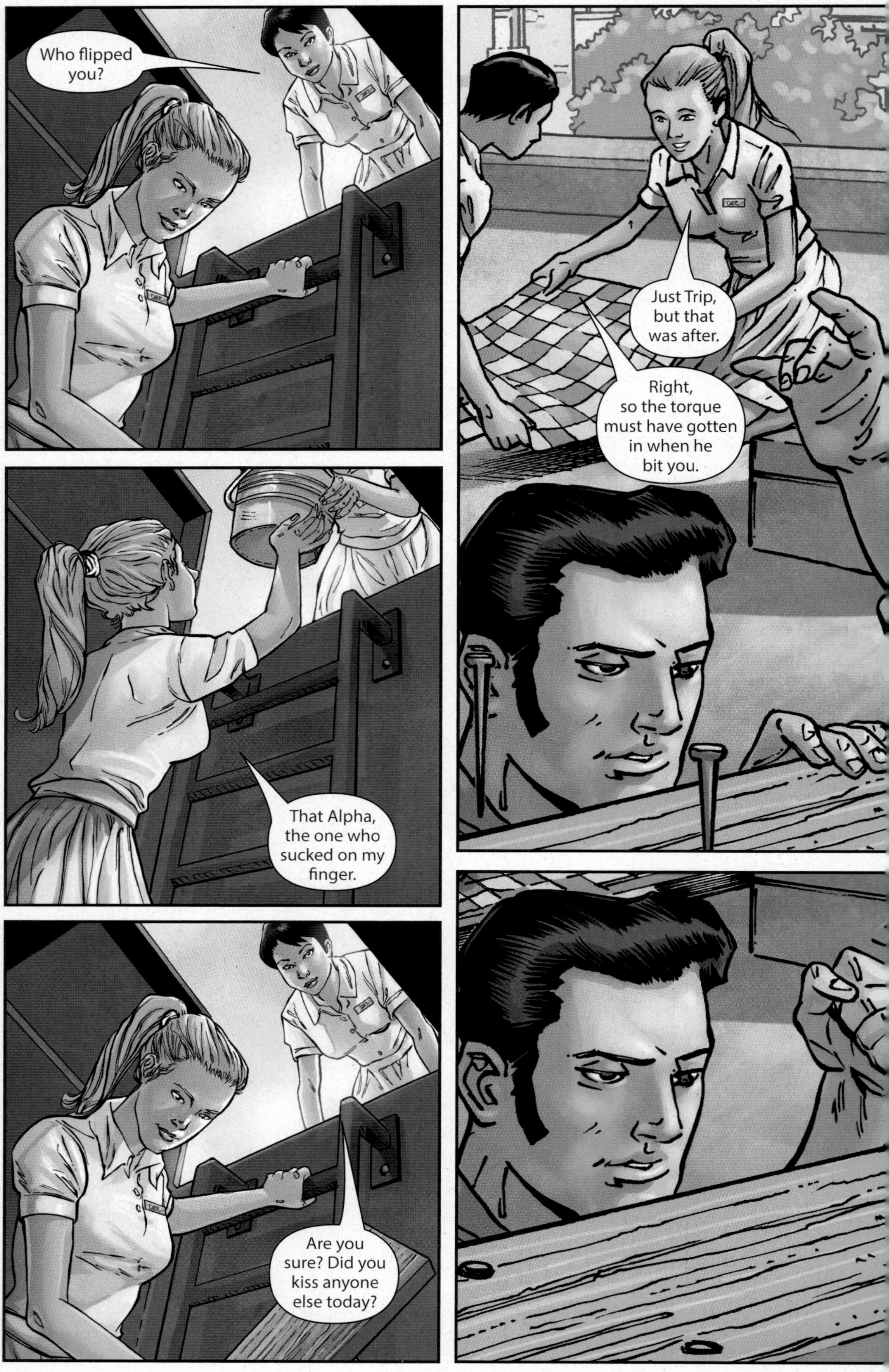
Who flipped you?
That Alpha, the one who sucked on my finger.
Are you sure? Did you kiss anyone else today?
Just Trip, but that was after.
Right, so the torque must have gotten in when he bit you.

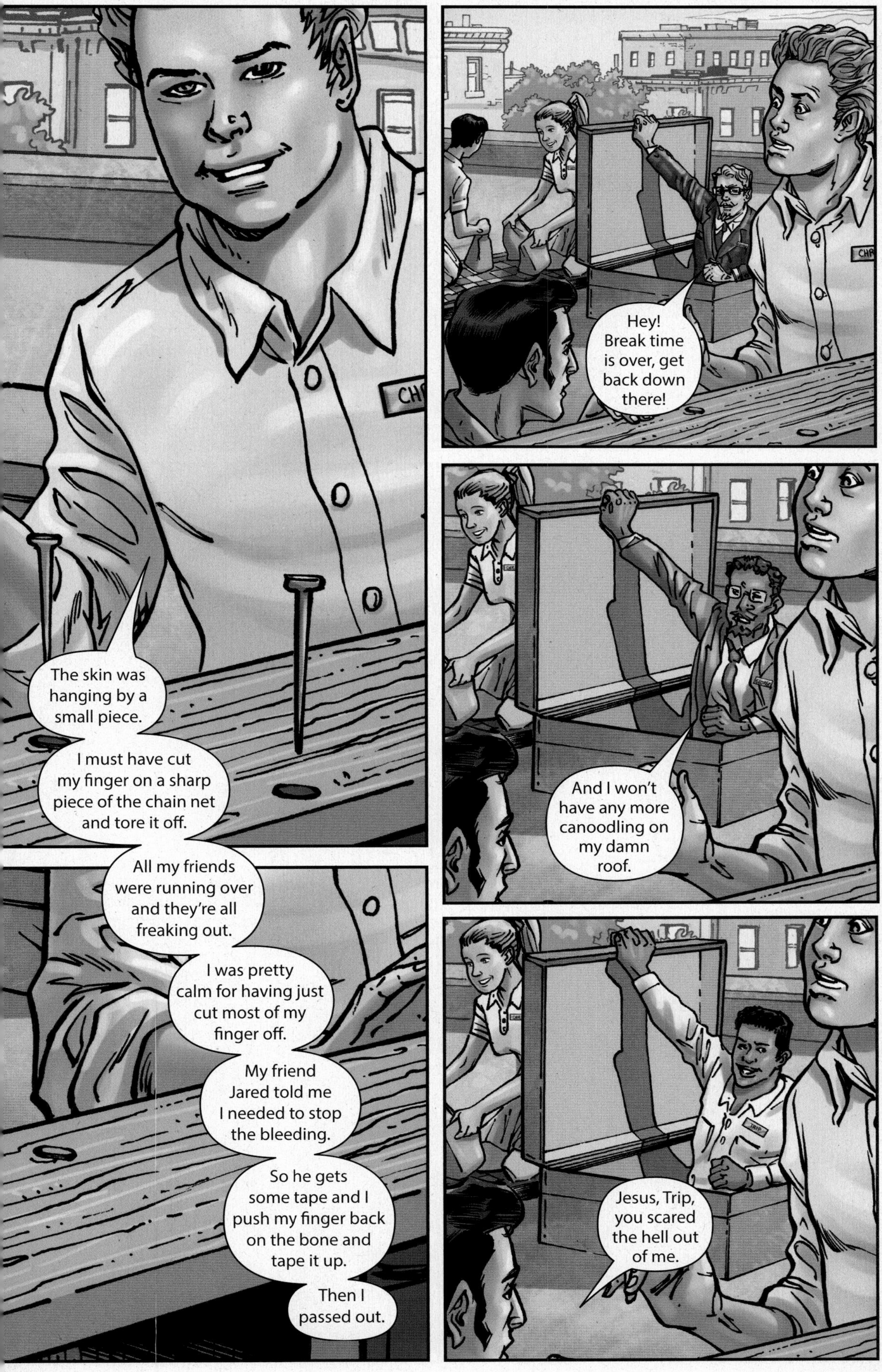
The skin was hanging by a small piece.
I must have cut my finger on a sharp piece of the chain net and tore it off.
All my friends were running over and they're all freaking out.
I was pretty calm for having just cut most of my finger off.
My friend Jared told me I needed to stop the bleeding.
So he gets some tape and I push my finger back on the bone and tape it up.
Then I passed out.
Hey! Break time is over, get back down there!
And I won't have any more canoodling on my damn roof.
Jesus, Trip, you scared the hell out of me.

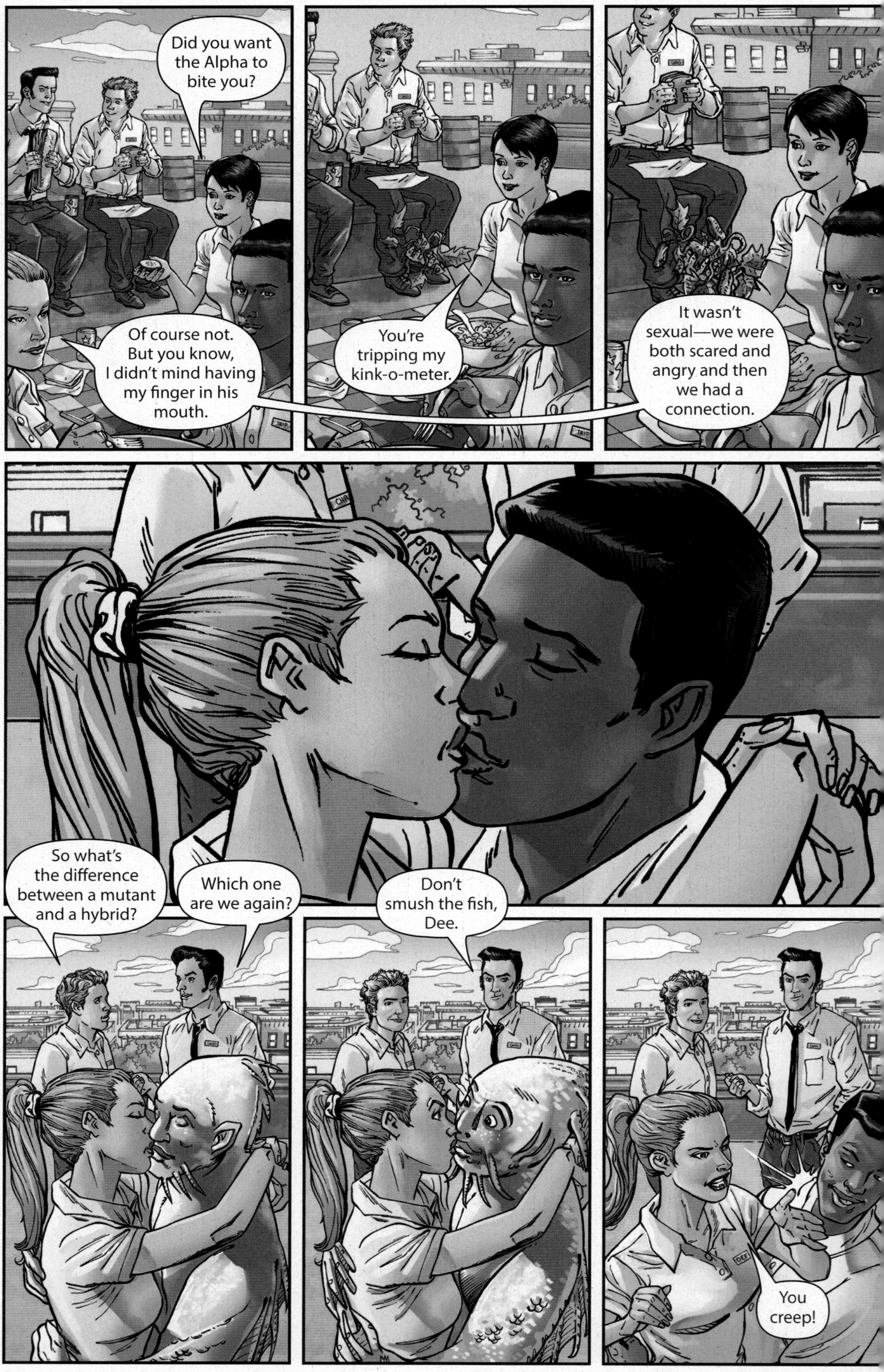
Did you want the Alpha to bite you?
Of course not. But you know, I didn't mind having my finger in his mouth.
You're tripping my kink-o-meter.
It wasn't sexual—we were both scared and angry and then we had a connection.
So what's the difference between a mutant and a hybrid?
Which one are we again?
Don't smush the fish, Dee.
You creep!

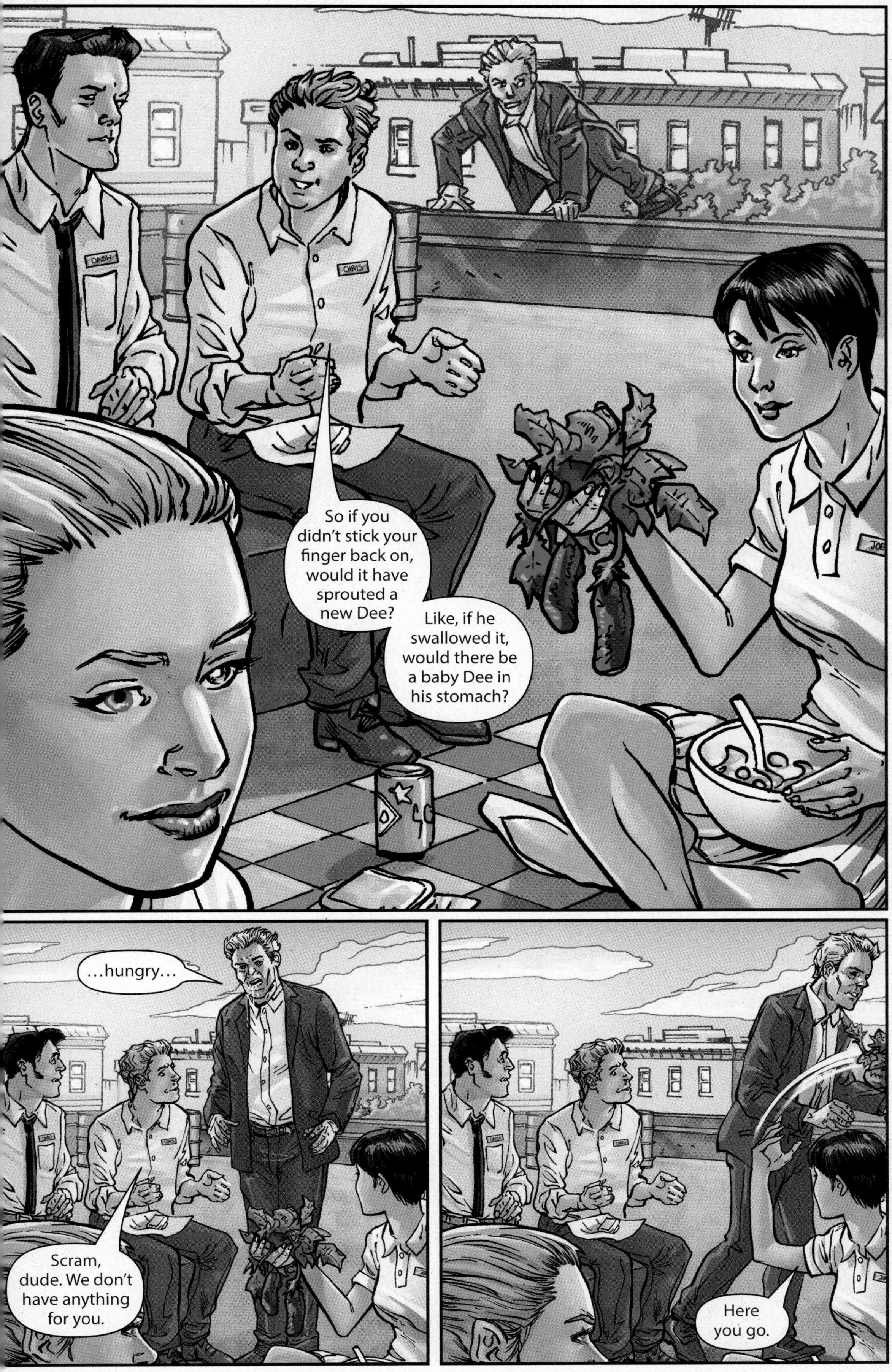
DASH
CHRIS
JOE
So if you didn't stick your finger back on, would it have sprouted a new Dee?
Like, if he swallowed it, would there be a baby Dee in his stomach?
…hungry…
Scram, dude. We don't have anything for you.
Here you go.

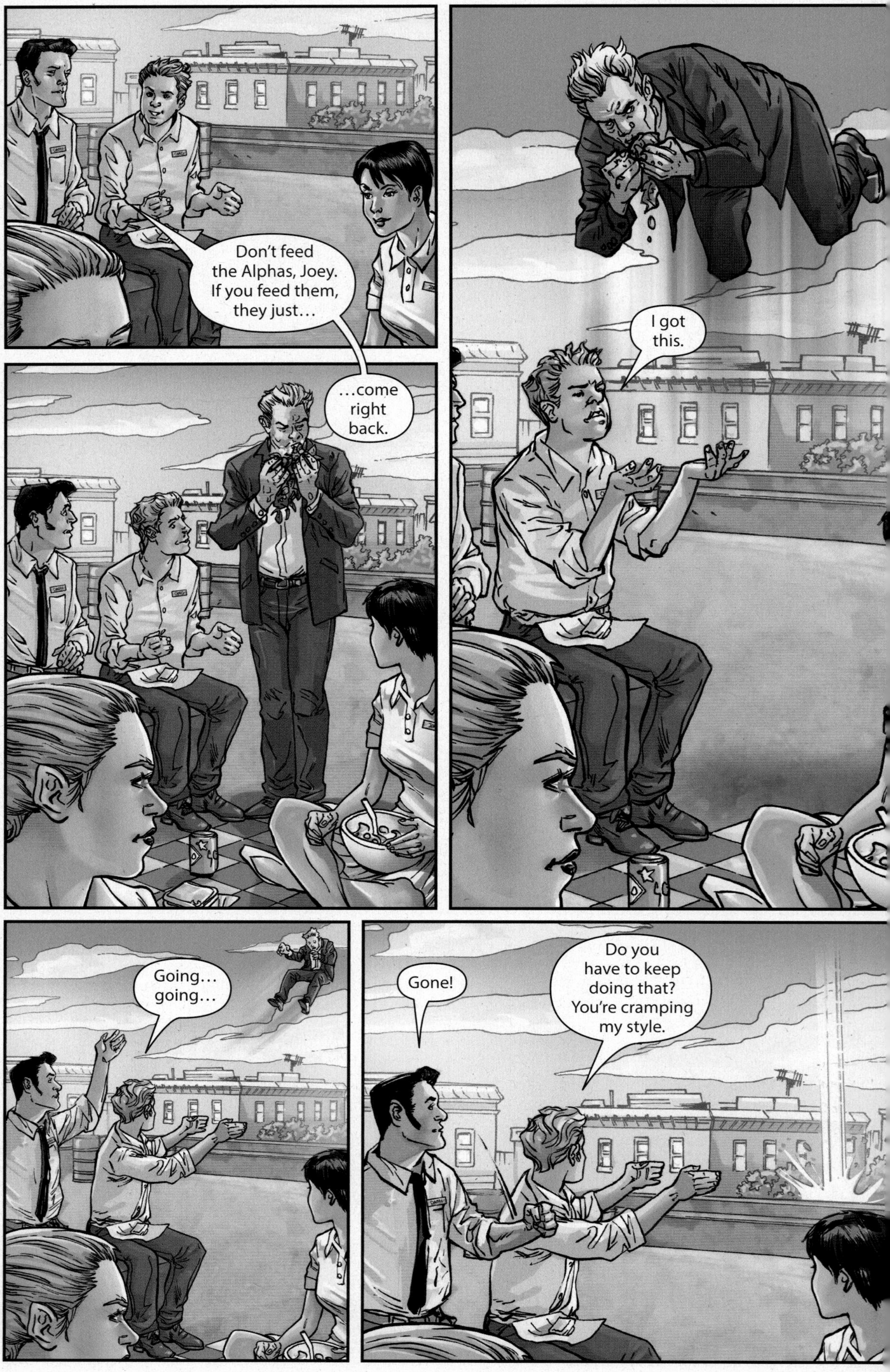
Don't feed the Alphas, Joey. If you feed them, they just…
…come right back.
I got this.
Going… going…
Gone!
Do you have to keep doing that? You're cramping my style.

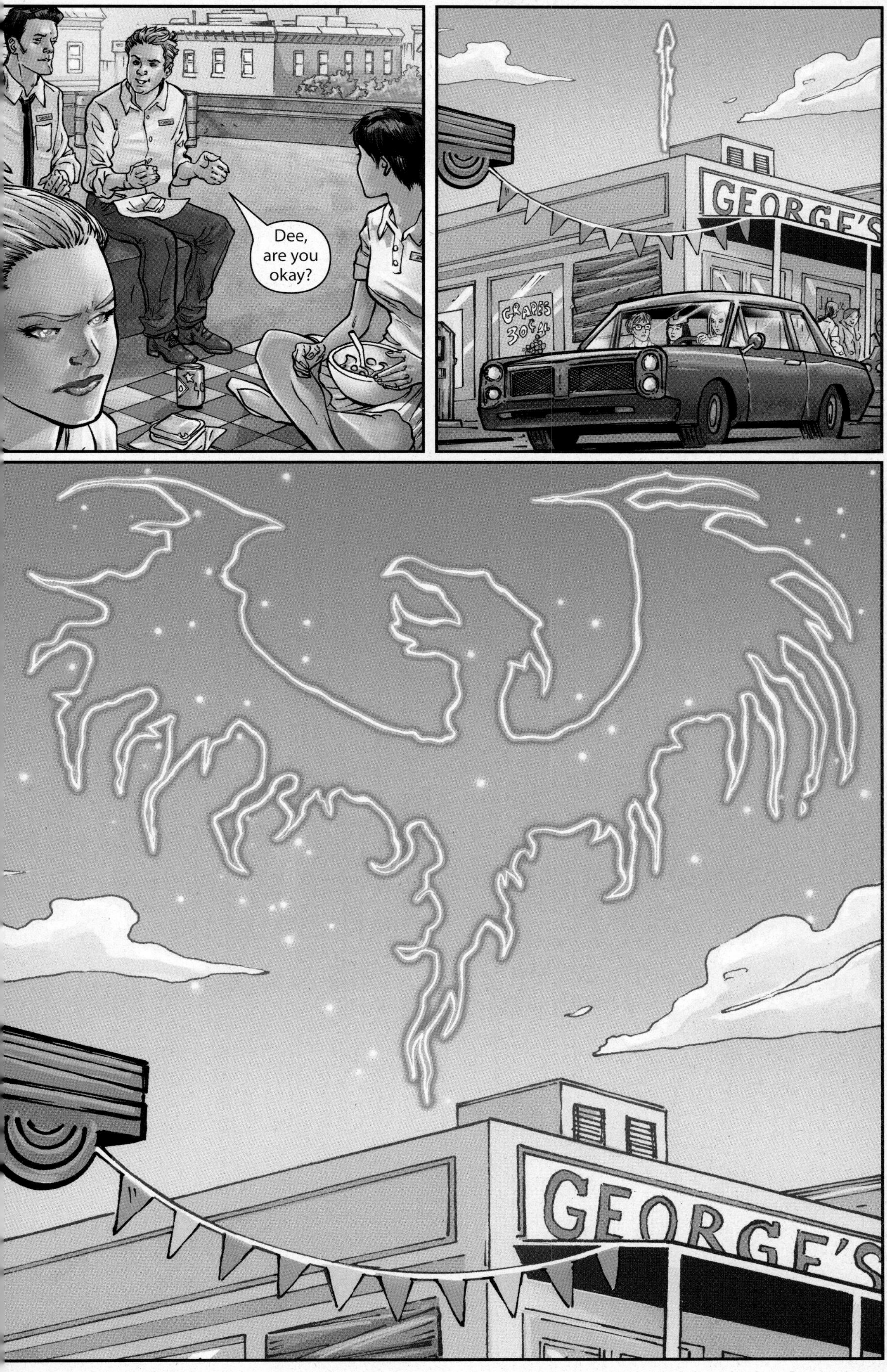
Dee, are you okay?
GRAPES 30¢ lb.
GEORGE'S
GEORGE'S

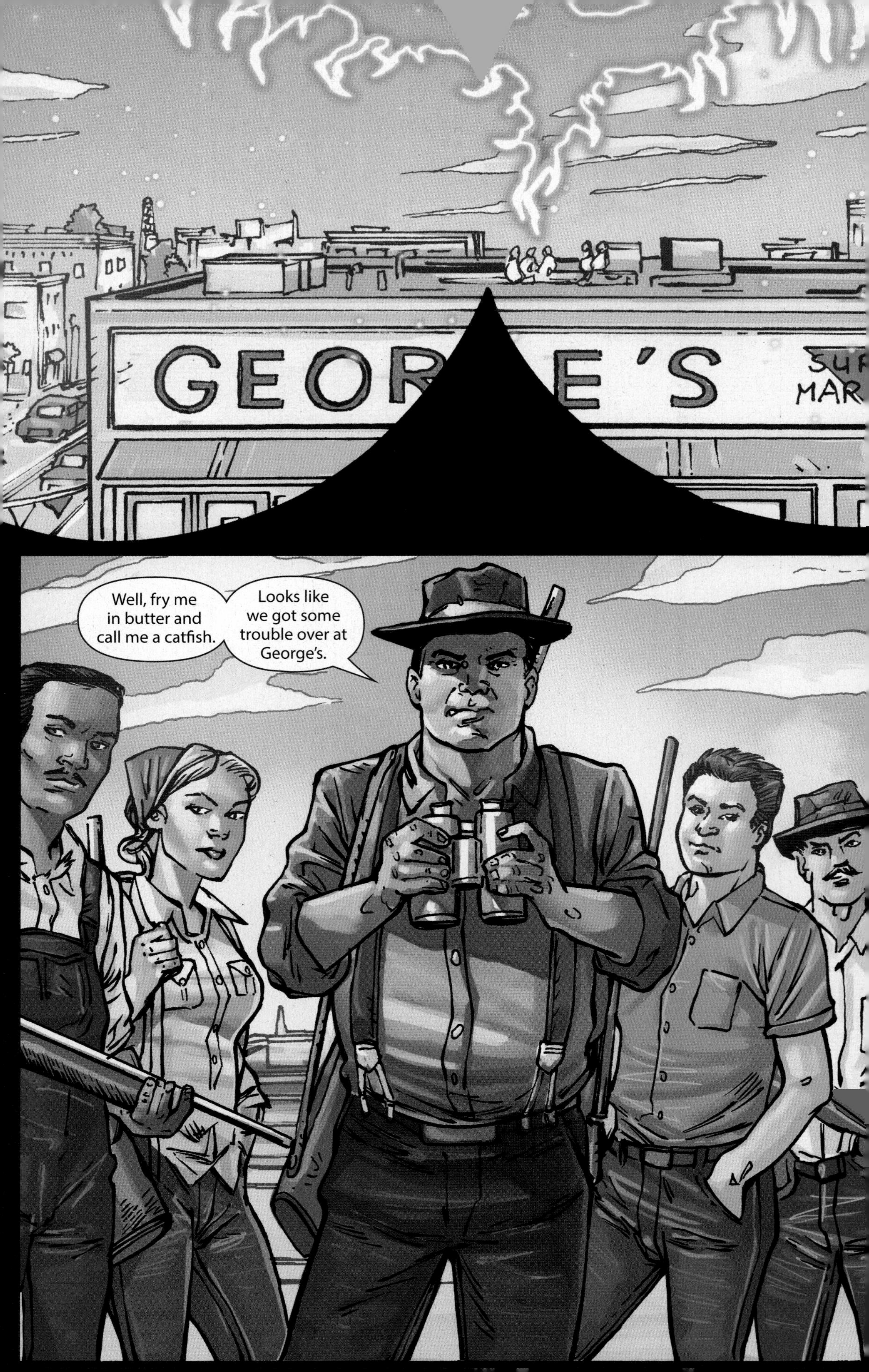
Well, fry me in butter and call me a catfish.
Looks like we got some trouble over at George's.

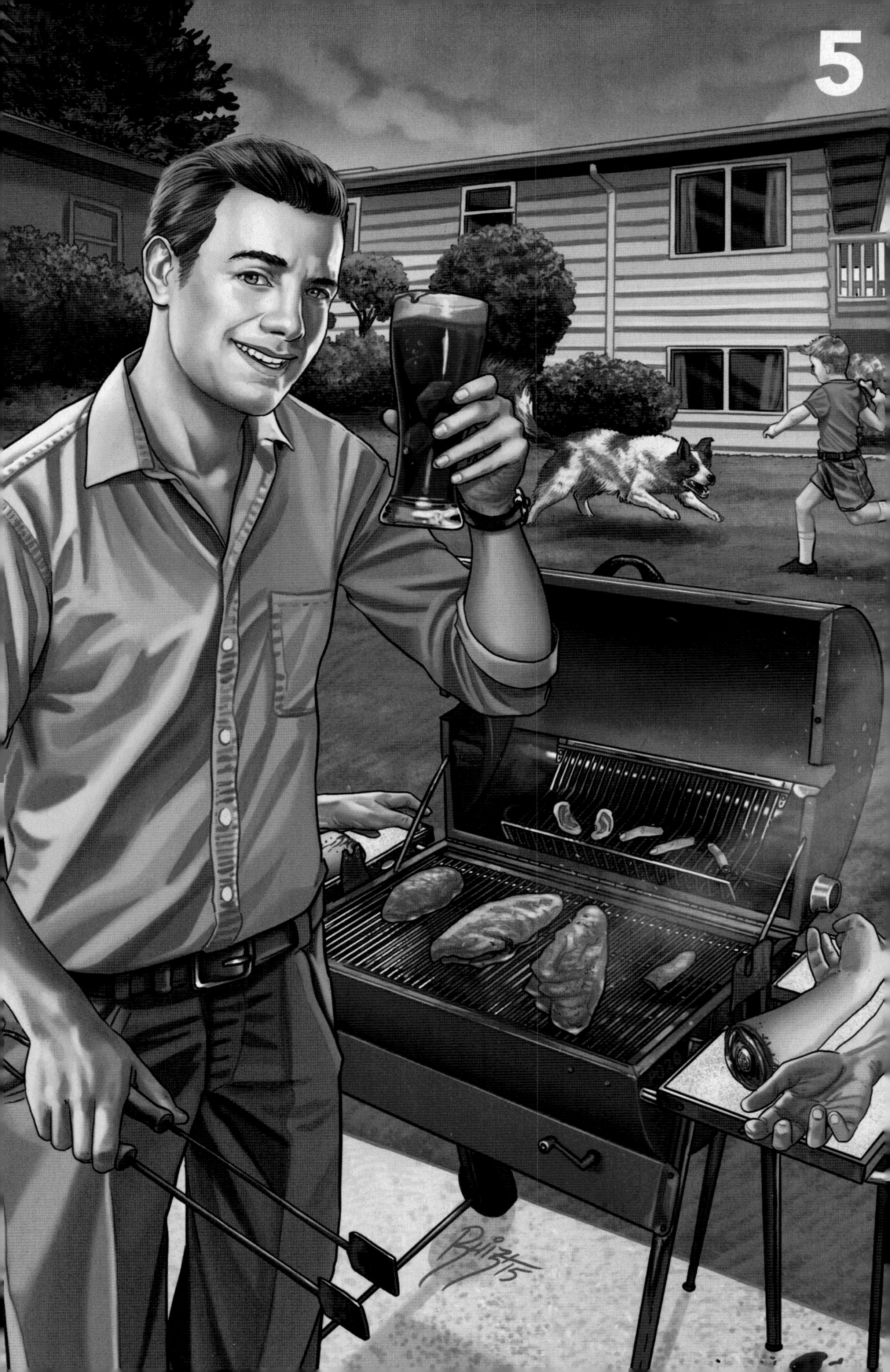
5

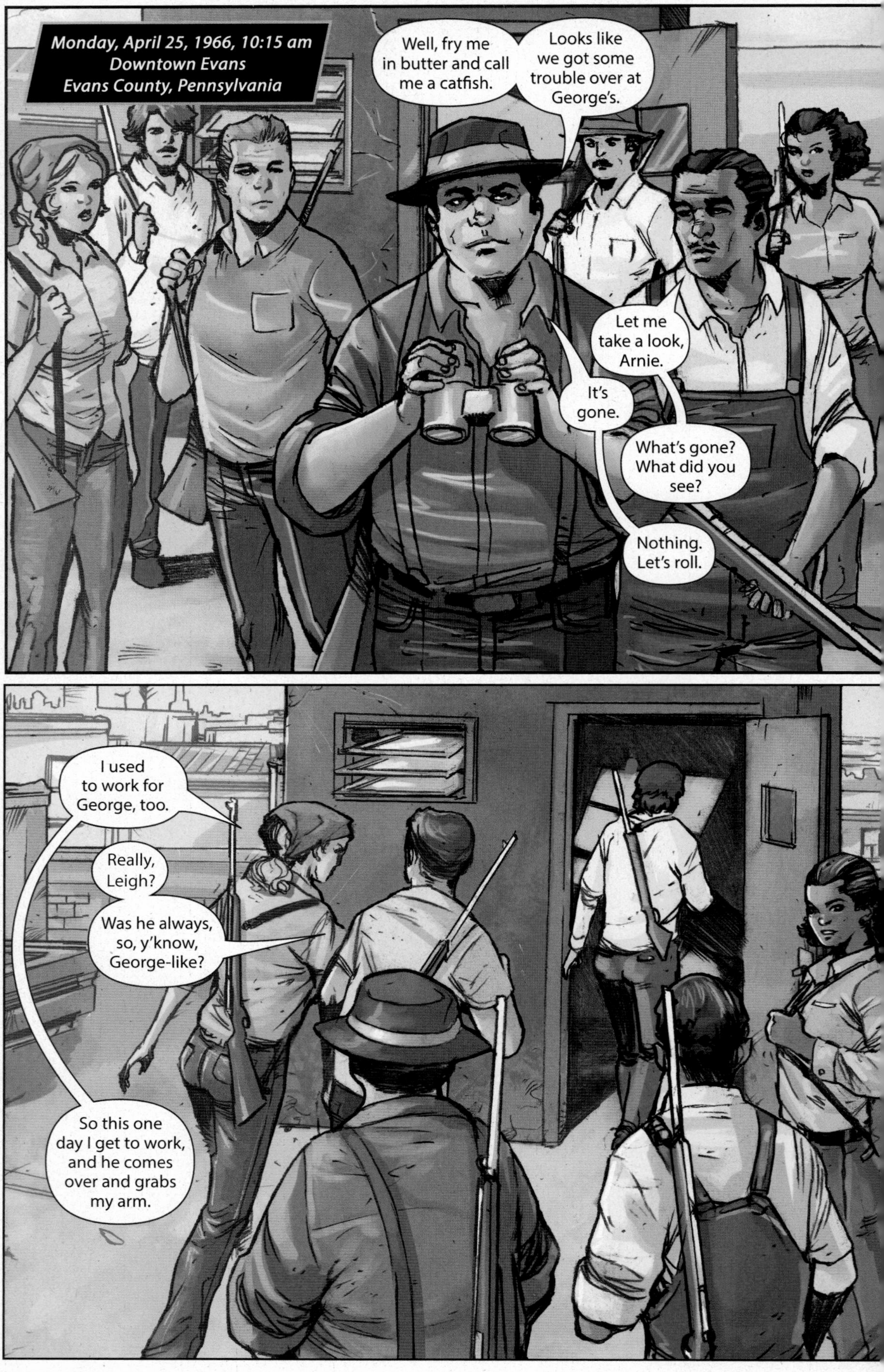
Monday, April 25, 1966, 10:15 am
Downtown Evans
Evans County, Pennsylvania
Well, fry me in butter and call me a catfish.
Looks like we got some trouble over at George's.
Let me take a look, Arnie.
It's gone.
What's gone? What did you see?
Nothing. Let's roll.
I used to work for George, too.
Really, Leigh?
Was he always, so, y'know, George-like?
So this one day I get to work, and he comes over and grabs my arm.

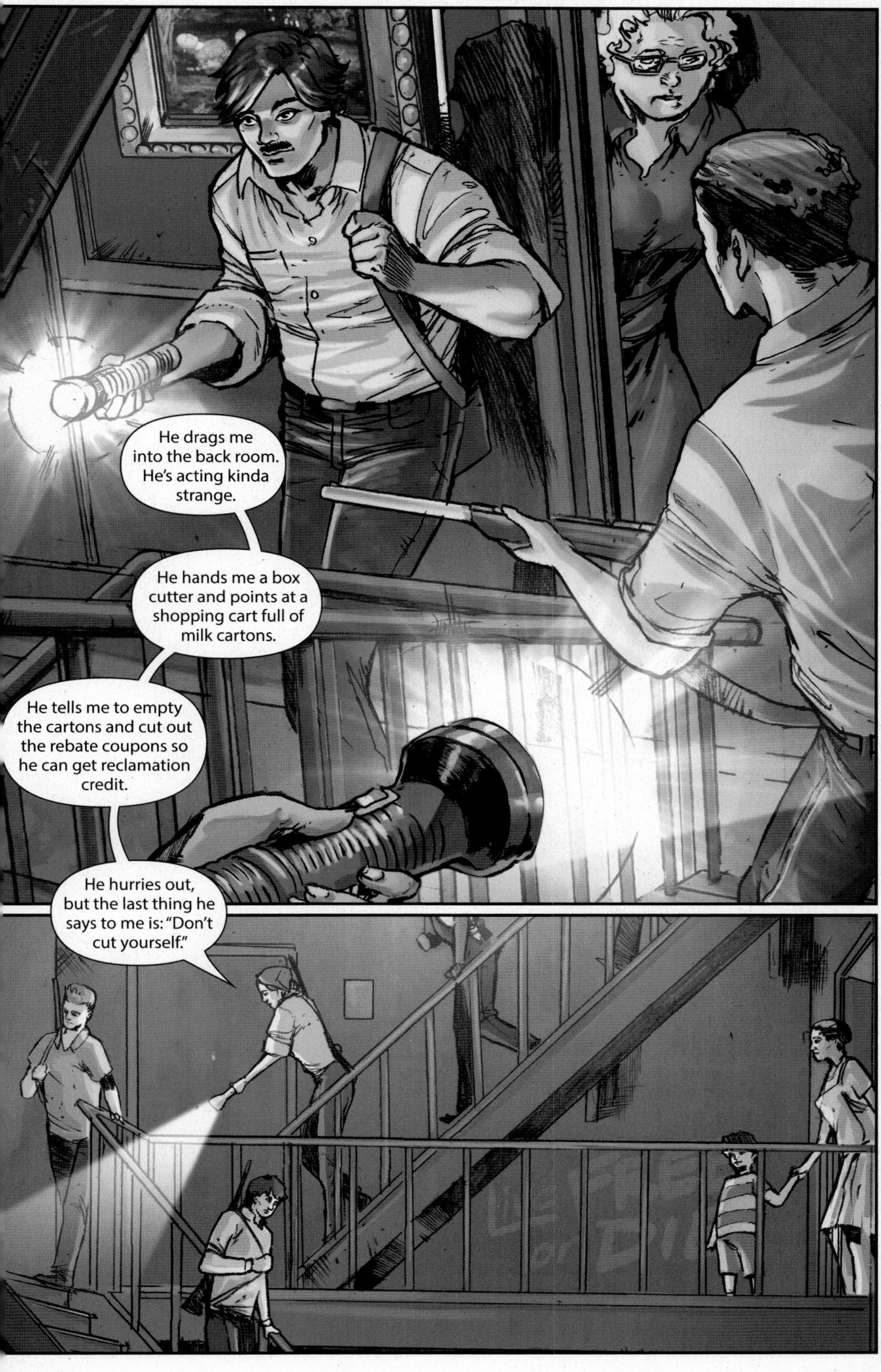
He drags me into the back room. He's acting kinda strange.
He hands me a box cutter and points at a shopping cart full of milk cartons.
He tells me to empty the cartons and cut out the rebate coupons so he can get reclamation credit.
He hurries out, but the last thing he says to me is: "Don't cut yourself."

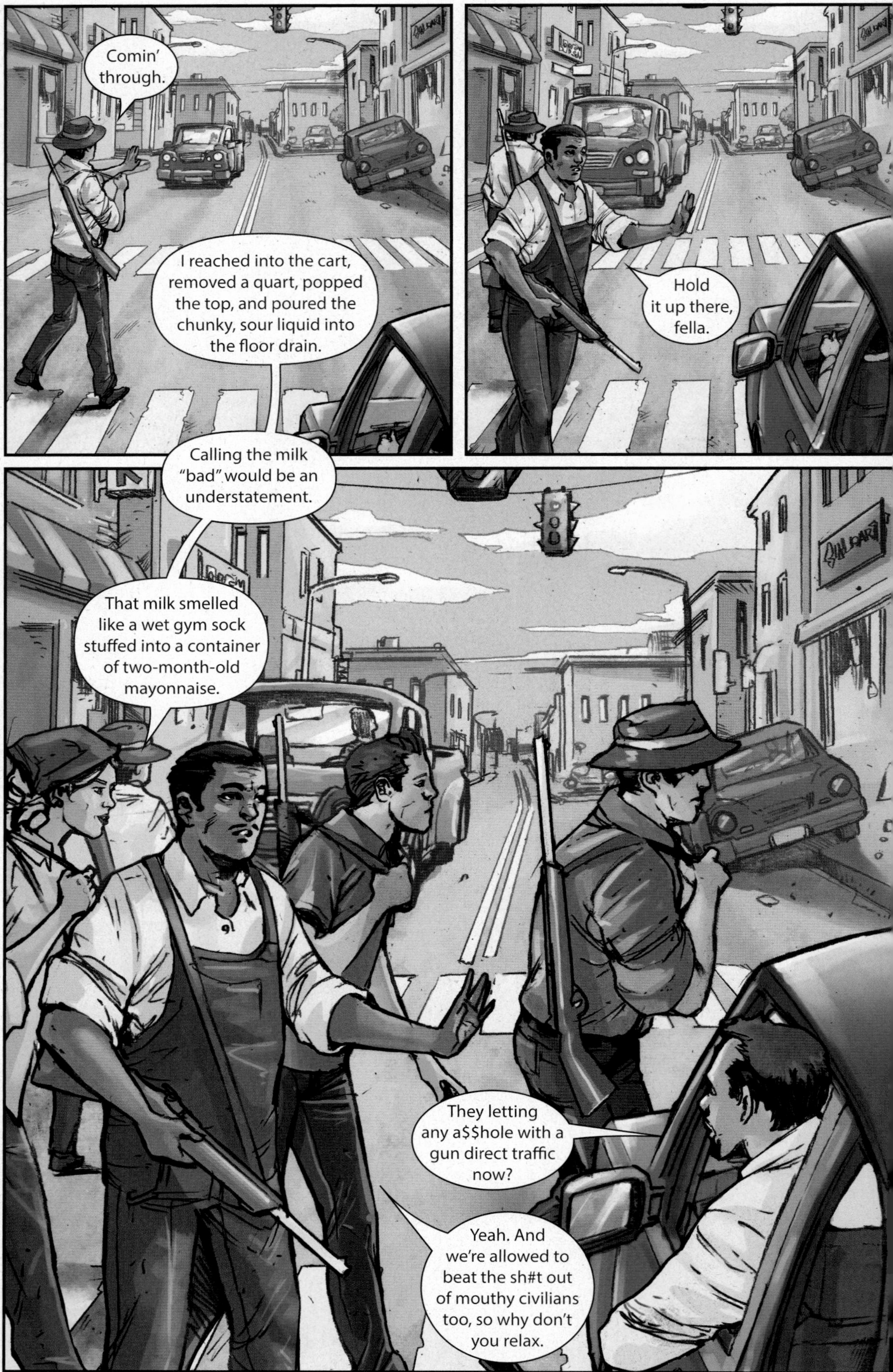
Comin' through.
I reached into the cart, removed a quart, popped the top, and poured the chunky, sour liquid into the floor drain.
Hold it up there, fella.
Calling the milk "bad" would be an understatement.
That milk smelled like a wet gym sock stuffed into a container of two-month-old mayonnaise.
They letting any a$$hole with a gun direct traffic now?
Yeah. And we're allowed to beat the sh#t out of mouthy civilians too, so why don't you relax.

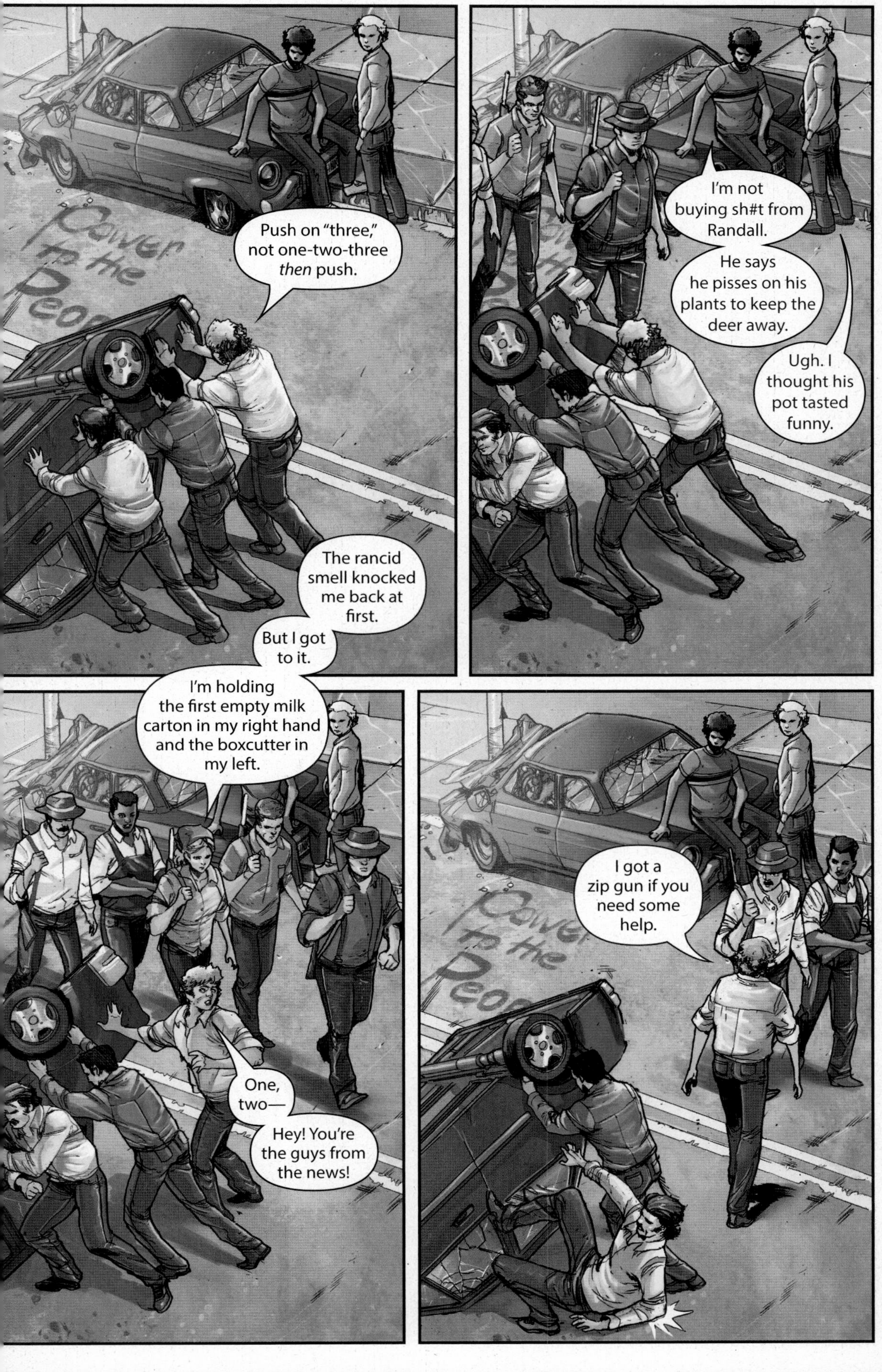

Push on "three," not one-two-three *then* push.
The rancid smell knocked me back at first.
But I got to it.
I'm not buying sh#t from Randall.
He says he pisses on his plants to keep the deer away.
Ugh. I thought his pot tasted funny.
I'm holding the first empty milk carton in my right hand and the boxcutter in my left.
One, two—
Hey! You're the guys from the news!
I got a zip gun if you need some help.

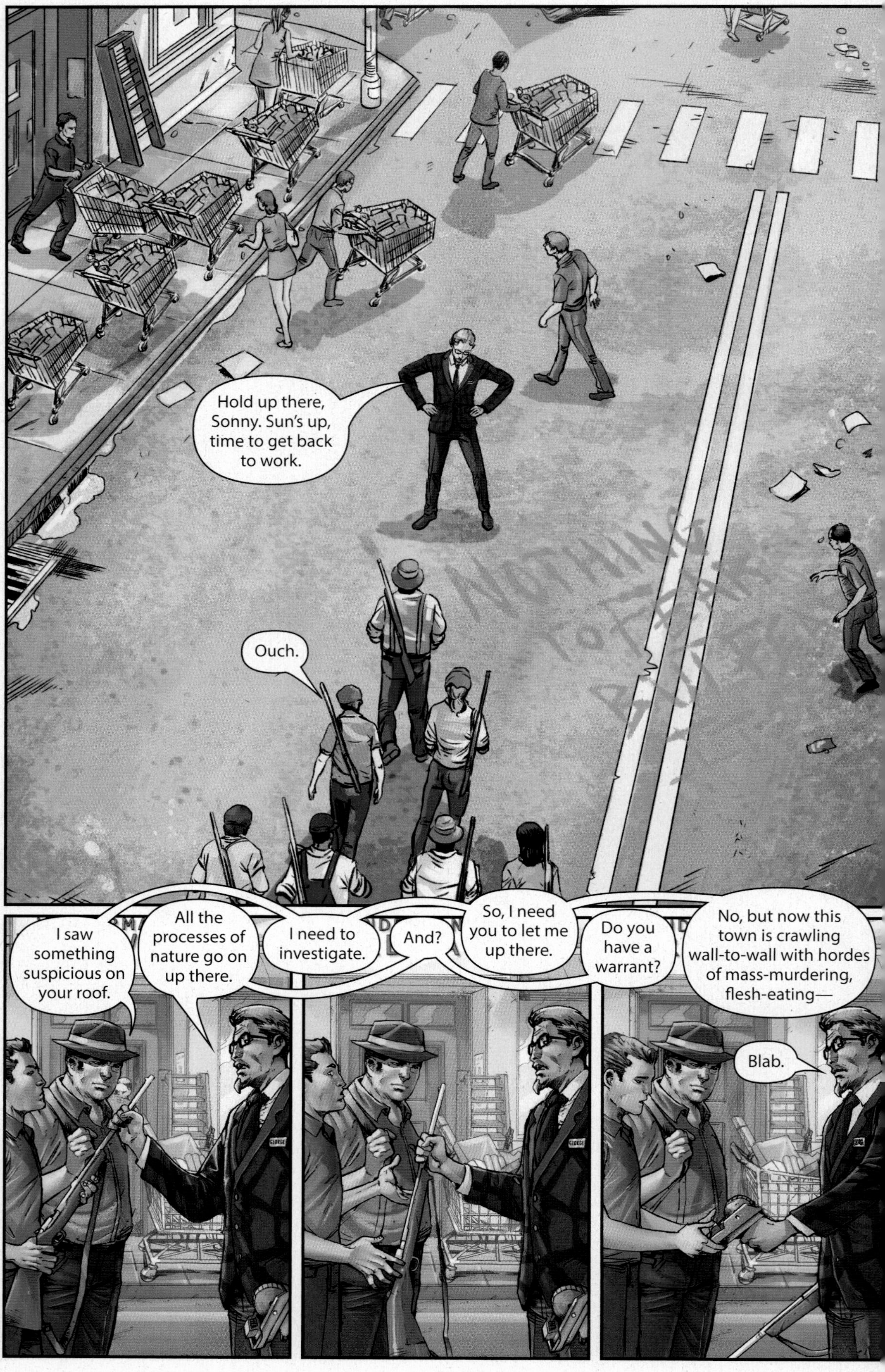
Hold up there, Sonny. Sun's up, time to get back to work.
Ouch.
I saw something suspicious on your roof.
All the processes of nature go on up there.
I need to investigate.
And?
So, I need you to let me up there.
Do you have a warrant?
No, but now this town is crawling wall-to-wall with hordes of mass-murdering, flesh-eating—
Blab.

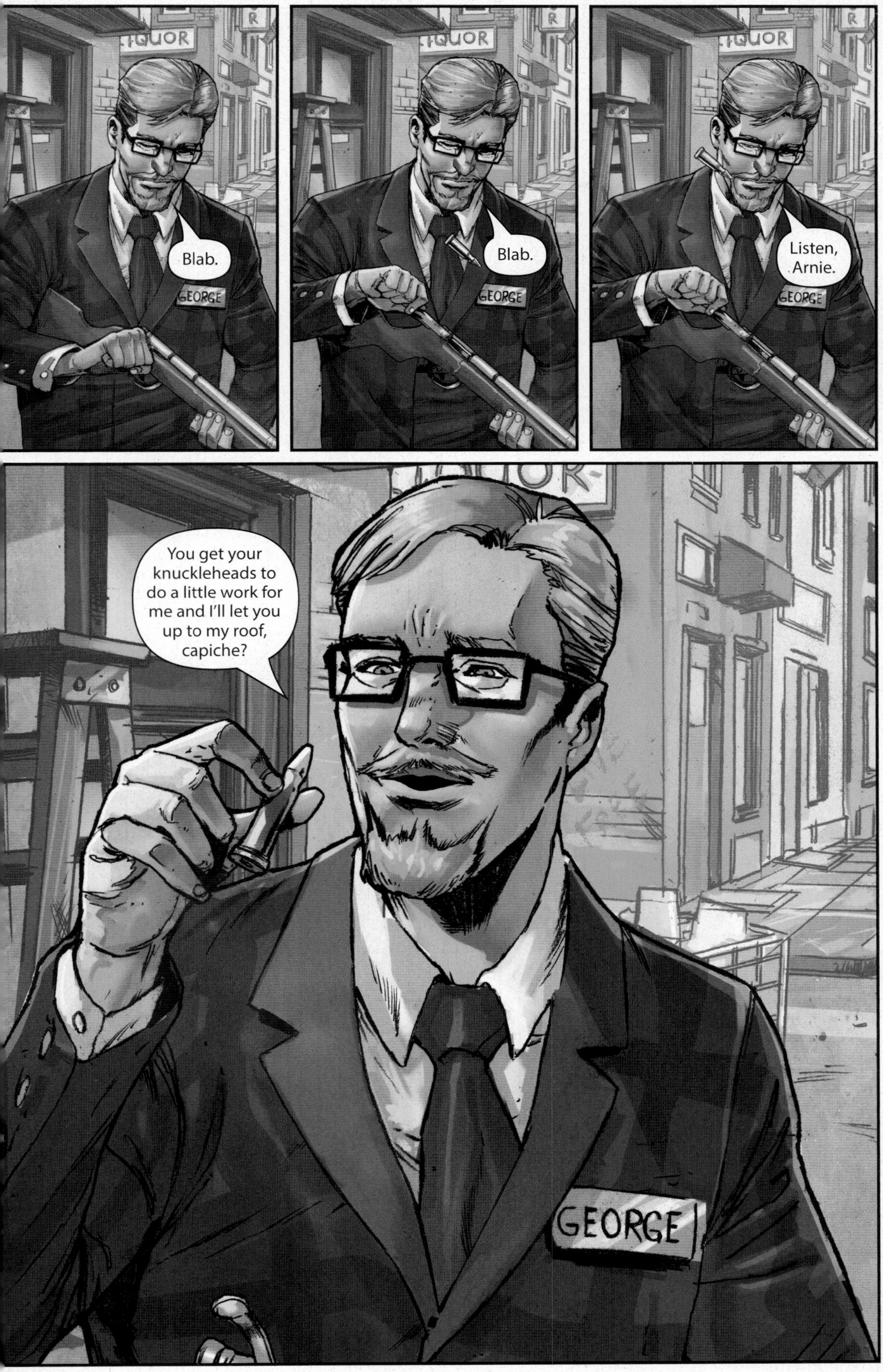

IQUOR
GEORGE
Blab.
Blab.
Listen, Arnie.
You get your knuckleheads to do a little work for me and I'll let you up to my roof, capiche?
GEORGE

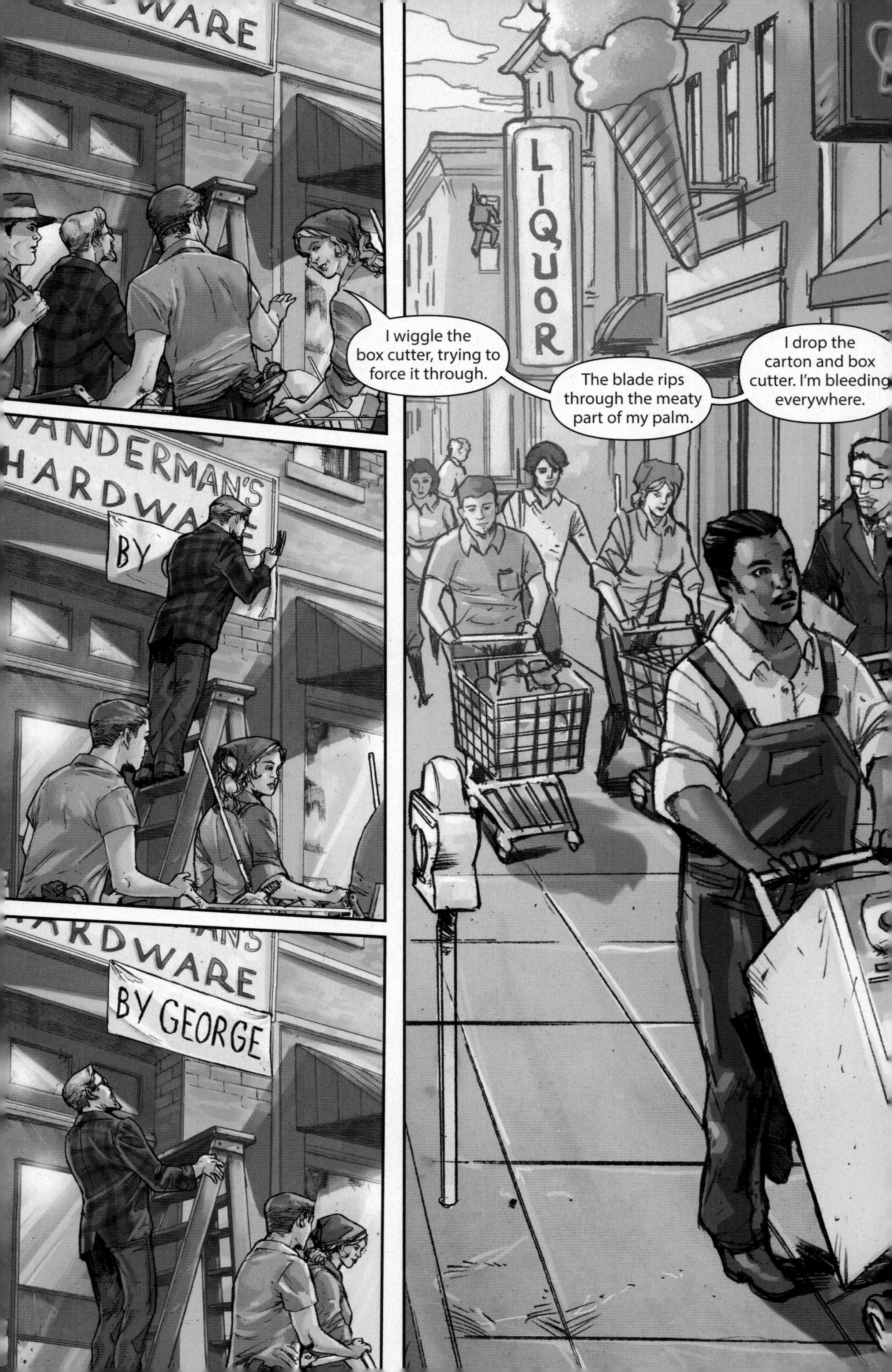
WARE
VANDERMAN'S
HARDWARE
BY G
ARDWARE
BY GEORGE
LIQUOR
I wiggle the box cutter, trying to force it through.
The blade rips through the meaty part of my palm.
I drop the carton and box cutter. I'm bleeding everywhere.

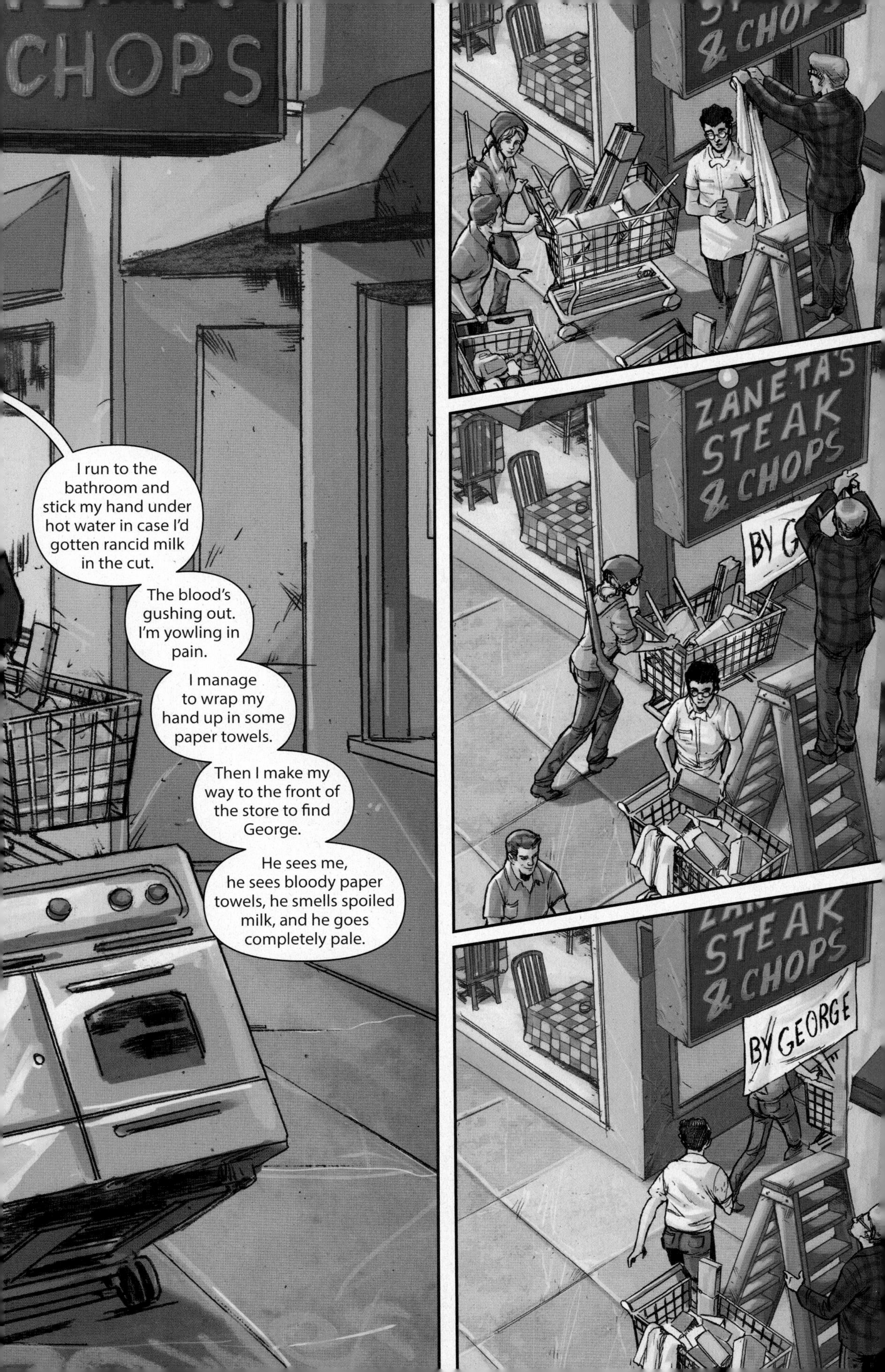
CHOPS
I run to the bathroom and stick my hand under hot water in case I'd gotten rancid milk in the cut.
The blood's gushing out. I'm yowling in pain.
I manage to wrap my hand up in some paper towels.
Then I make my way to the front of the store to find George.
He sees me, he sees bloody paper towels, he smells spoiled milk, and he goes completely pale.
& CHOPS
ZANETA'S STEAK & CHOPS
BY G
STEAK & CHOPS
BY GEORGE

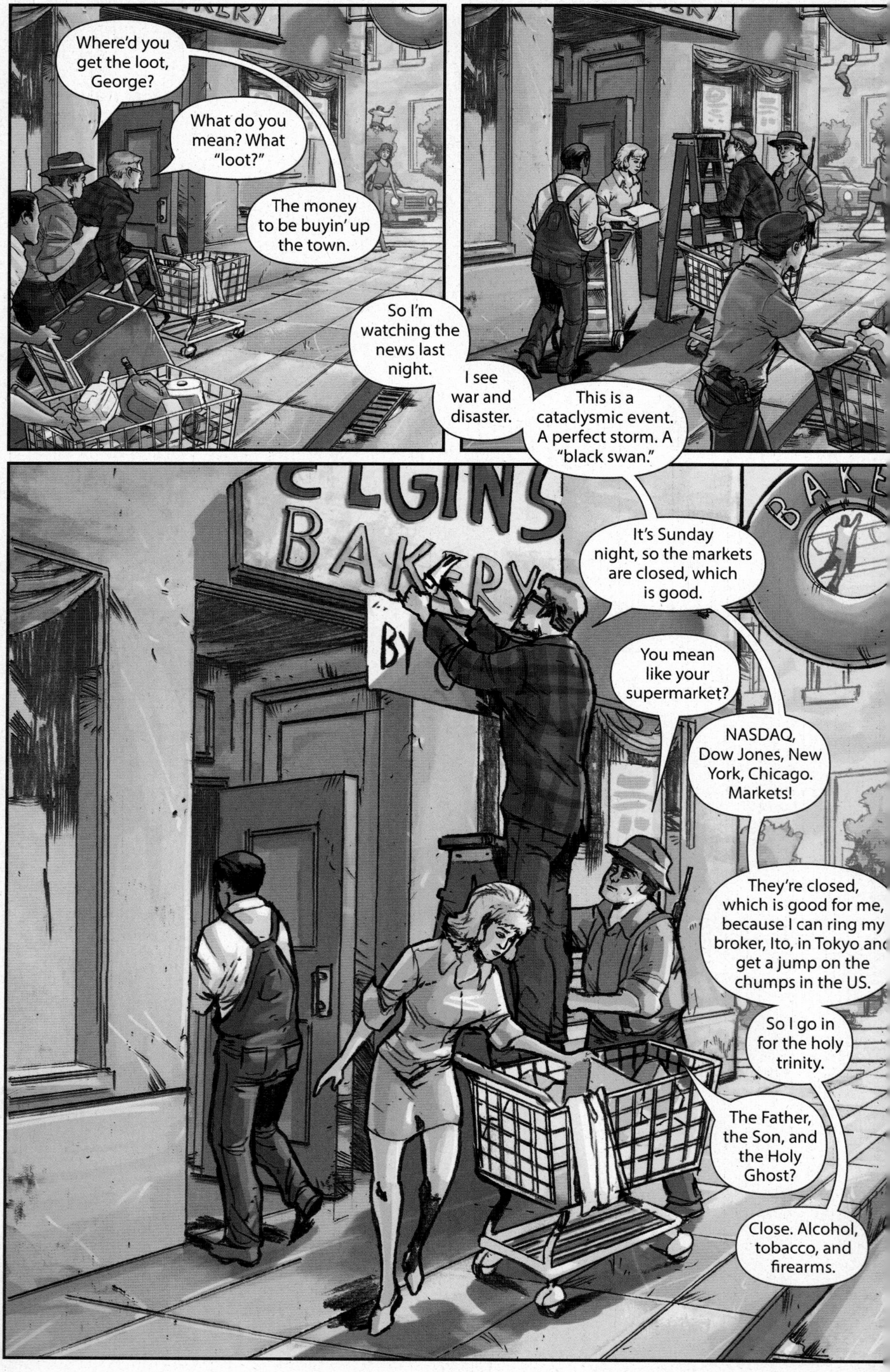

Where'd you get the loot, George?
What do you mean? What "loot?"
The money to be buyin' up the town.
So I'm watching the news last night.
I see war and disaster.
This is a cataclysmic event. A perfect storm. A "black swan."
ELGINS BAKERY
BAKE
BY
It's Sunday night, so the markets are closed, which is good.
You mean like your supermarket?
NASDAQ, Dow Jones, New York, Chicago. Markets!
They're closed, which is good for me, because I can ring my broker, Ito, in Tokyo and get a jump on the chumps in the US.
So I go in for the holy trinity.
The Father, the Son, and the Holy Ghost?
Close. Alcohol, tobacco, and firearms.

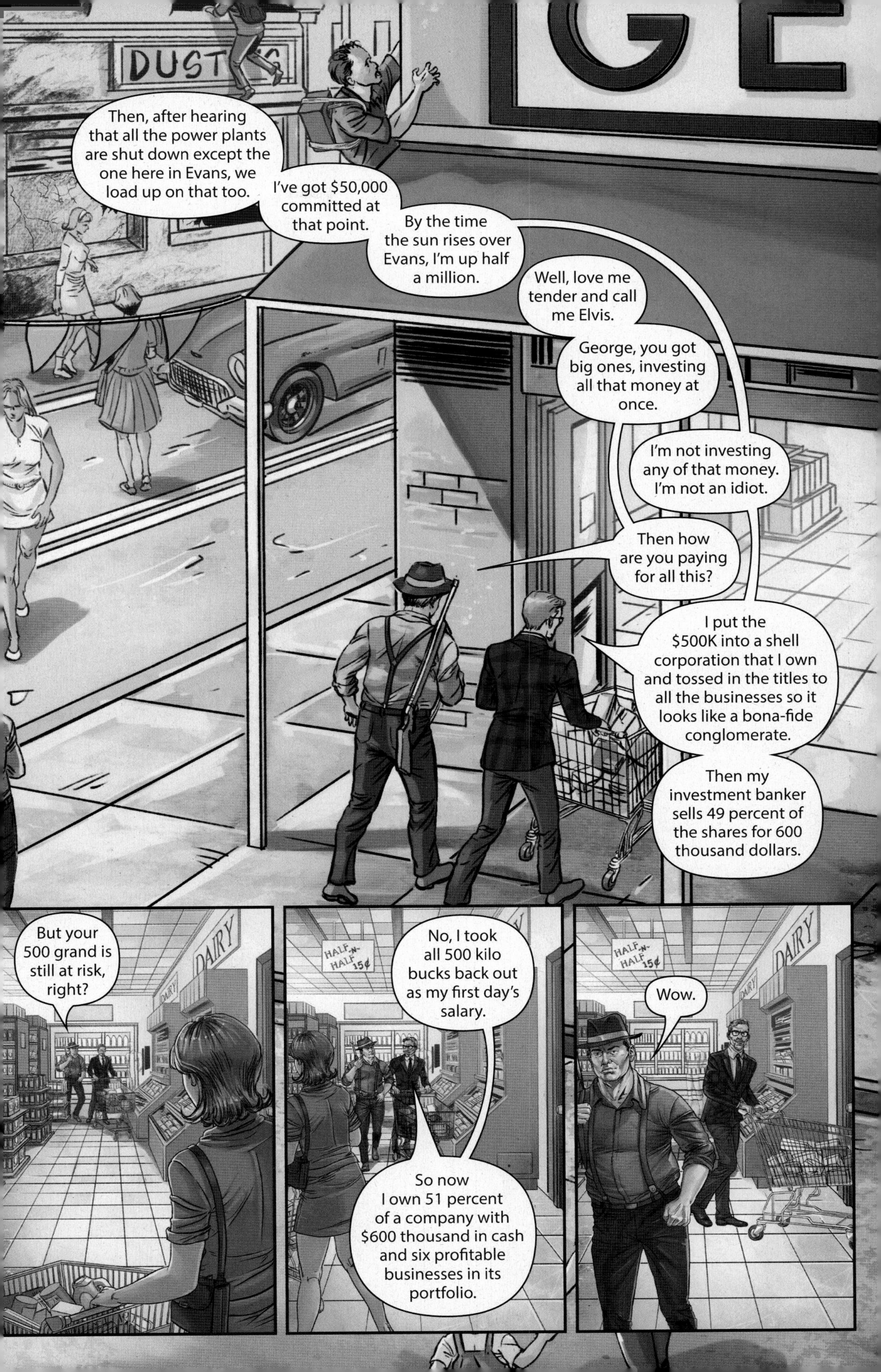
DUST
Then, after hearing that all the power plants are shut down except the one here in Evans, we load up on that too.
I've got $50,000 committed at that point.
By the time the sun rises over Evans, I'm up half a million.
Well, love me tender and call me Elvis.
George, you got big ones, investing all that money at once.
I'm not investing any of that money. I'm not an idiot.
Then how are you paying for all this?
I put the $500K into a shell corporation that I own and tossed in the titles to all the businesses so it looks like a bona-fide conglomerate.
Then my investment banker sells 49 percent of the shares for 600 thousand dollars.
But your 500 grand is still at risk, right?
DAIRY
HALF-N-HALF 15¢
No, I took all 500 kilo bucks back out as my first day's salary.
So now I own 51 percent of a company with $600 thousand in cash and six profitable businesses in its portfolio.
Wow.

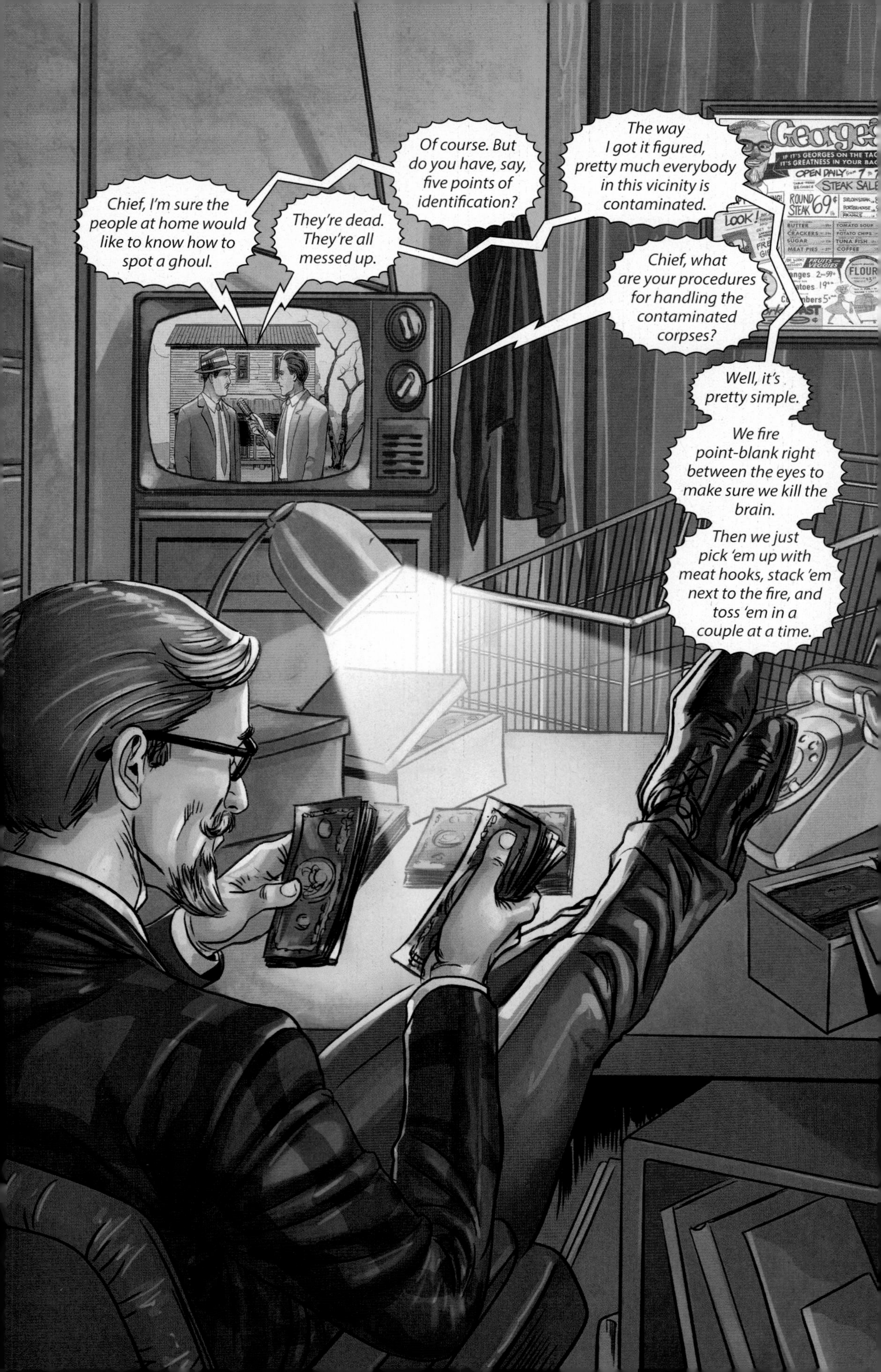
Chief, I'm sure the people at home would like to know how to spot a ghoul.
They're dead. They're all messed up.
Of course. But do you have, say, five points of identification?
The way I got it figured, pretty much everybody in this vicinity is contaminated.
Chief, what are your procedures for handling the contaminated corpses?
Well, it's pretty simple.
We fire point-blank right between the eyes to make sure we kill the brain.
Then we just pick 'em up with meat hooks, stack 'em next to the fire, and toss 'em in a couple at a time.
Georges
IF IT'S GEORGES ON THE TAG IT'S GREATNESS IN YOUR BAG
OPEN DAILY
STEAK SALE
ROUND STEAK 69¢
LOOK!
BUTTER
CRACKERS
SUGAR
MEAT PIES
TOMATO SOUP
POTATO CHIPS
TUNA FISH
COFFEE
FRUITS VEGGIES
FLOUR

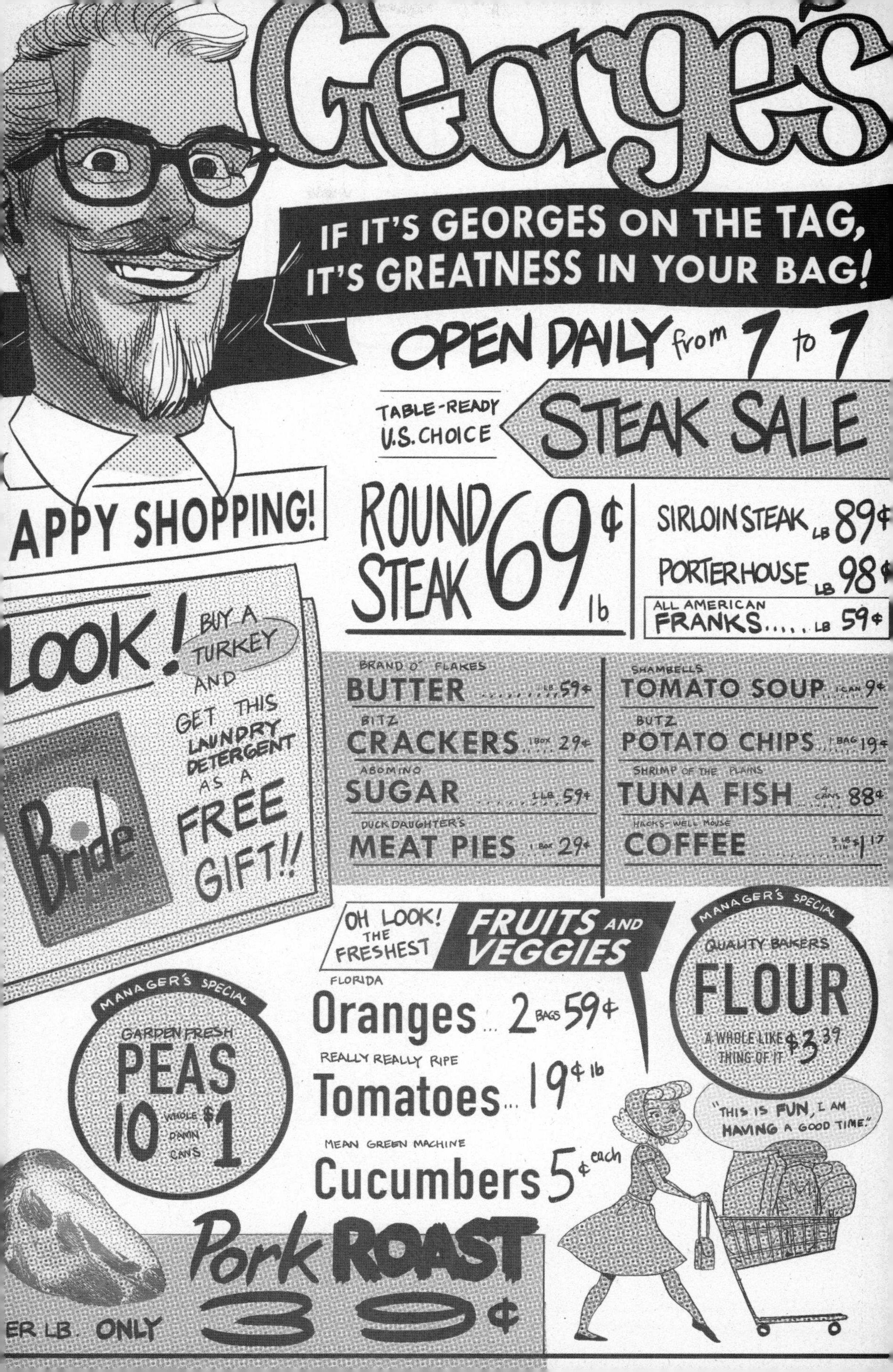

George's
IF IT'S GEORGES ON THE TAG, IT'S GREATNESS IN YOUR BAG!
OPEN DAILY from 7 to 7
TABLE-READY U.S. CHOICE
STEAK SALE
APPY SHOPPING!
ROUND STEAK 69¢ lb
SIRLOIN STEAK LB 89¢
PORTERHOUSE LB 98¢
ALL AMERICAN FRANKS..... LB 59¢
LOOK! BUY A TURKEY AND GET THIS LAUNDRY DETERGENT AS A FREE GIFT!!
Bride
BRAND O' FLAKES BUTTER LB 59¢
BITZ CRACKERS 1 BOX 29¢
ABOMINO SUGAR 1 LB 59¢
DUCK DAUGHTER'S MEAT PIES 1 BOX 29¢
SHAMBELLS TOMATO SOUP 1 CAN 9¢
BUTZ POTATO CHIPS 1 BAG 19¢
SHRIMP OF THE PLAINS TUNA FISH 4 CANS 88¢
HACKS-WELL MOUSE COFFEE 3 LB TIN $1.17
OH LOOK! THE FRESHEST
FRUITS AND VEGGIES
FLORIDA Oranges... 2 BAGS 59¢
REALLY REALLY RIPE Tomatoes... 19¢ lb
MEAN GREEN MACHINE Cucumbers 5¢ each
MANAGER'S SPECIAL
QUALITY BAKERS FLOUR
A WHOLE LIKE THING OF IT $3.39
"THIS IS FUN, I AM HAVING A GOOD TIME."
MANAGER'S SPECIAL
GARDEN FRESH PEAS
10 WHOLE DAMN CANS $1
Pork ROAST 39¢
ER LB. ONLY

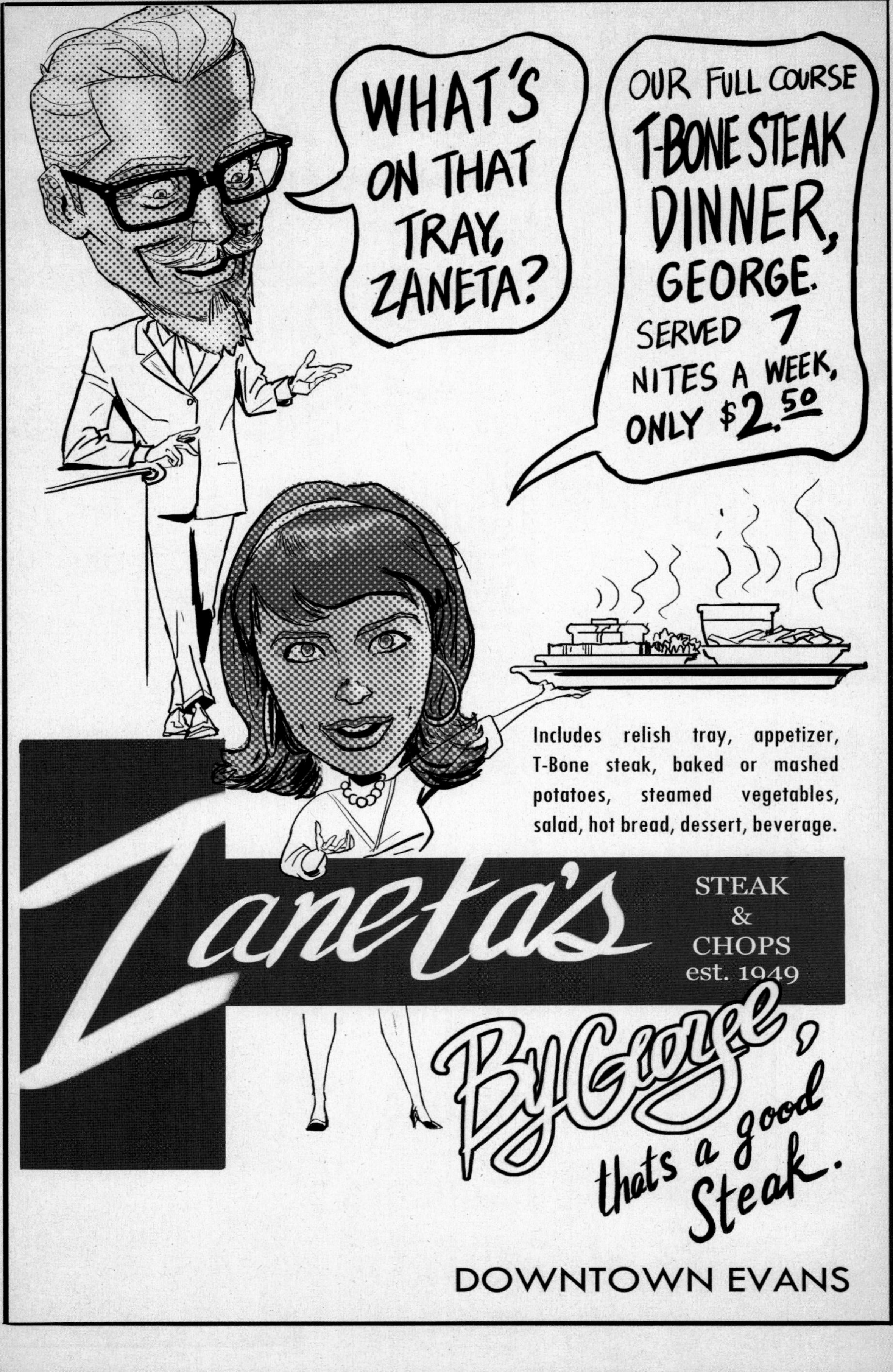

WHAT'S ON THAT TRAY, ZANETA?
OUR FULL COURSE T-BONE STEAK DINNER, GEORGE. SERVED 7 NITES A WEEK, ONLY $2.50
Includes relish tray, appetizer, T-Bone steak, baked or mashed potatoes, steamed vegetables, salad, hot bread, dessert, beverage.
Zaneta's
STEAK & CHOPS est. 1949
By George, thats a good Steak.
DOWNTOWN EVANS

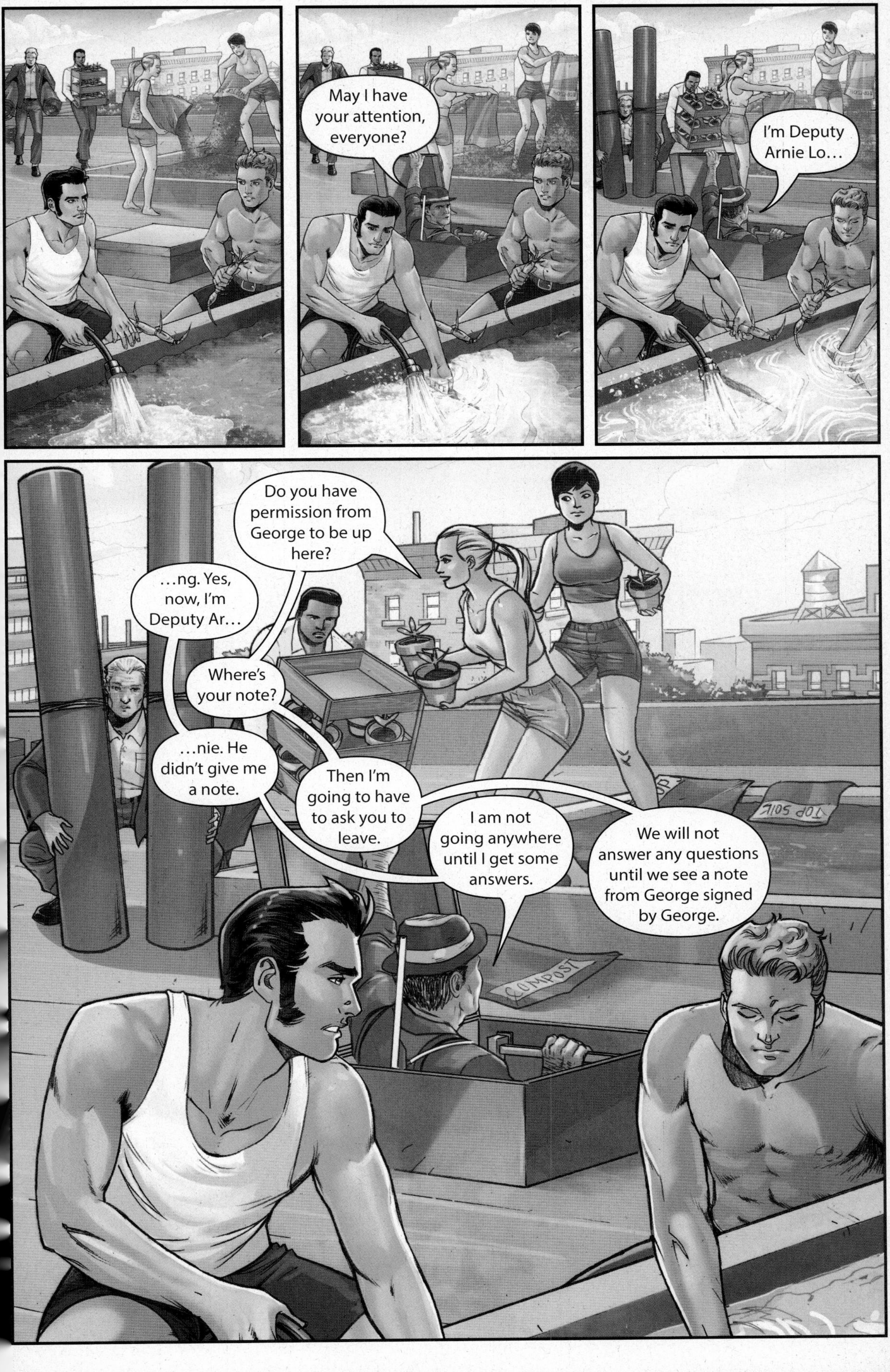
May I have your attention, everyone?
I'm Deputy Arnie Lo…
Do you have permission from George to be up here?
…ng. Yes, now, I'm Deputy Ar…
Where's your note?
…nie. He didn't give me a note.
Then I'm going to have to ask you to leave.
I am not going anywhere until I get some answers.
We will not answer any questions until we see a note from George signed by George.
COMPOST

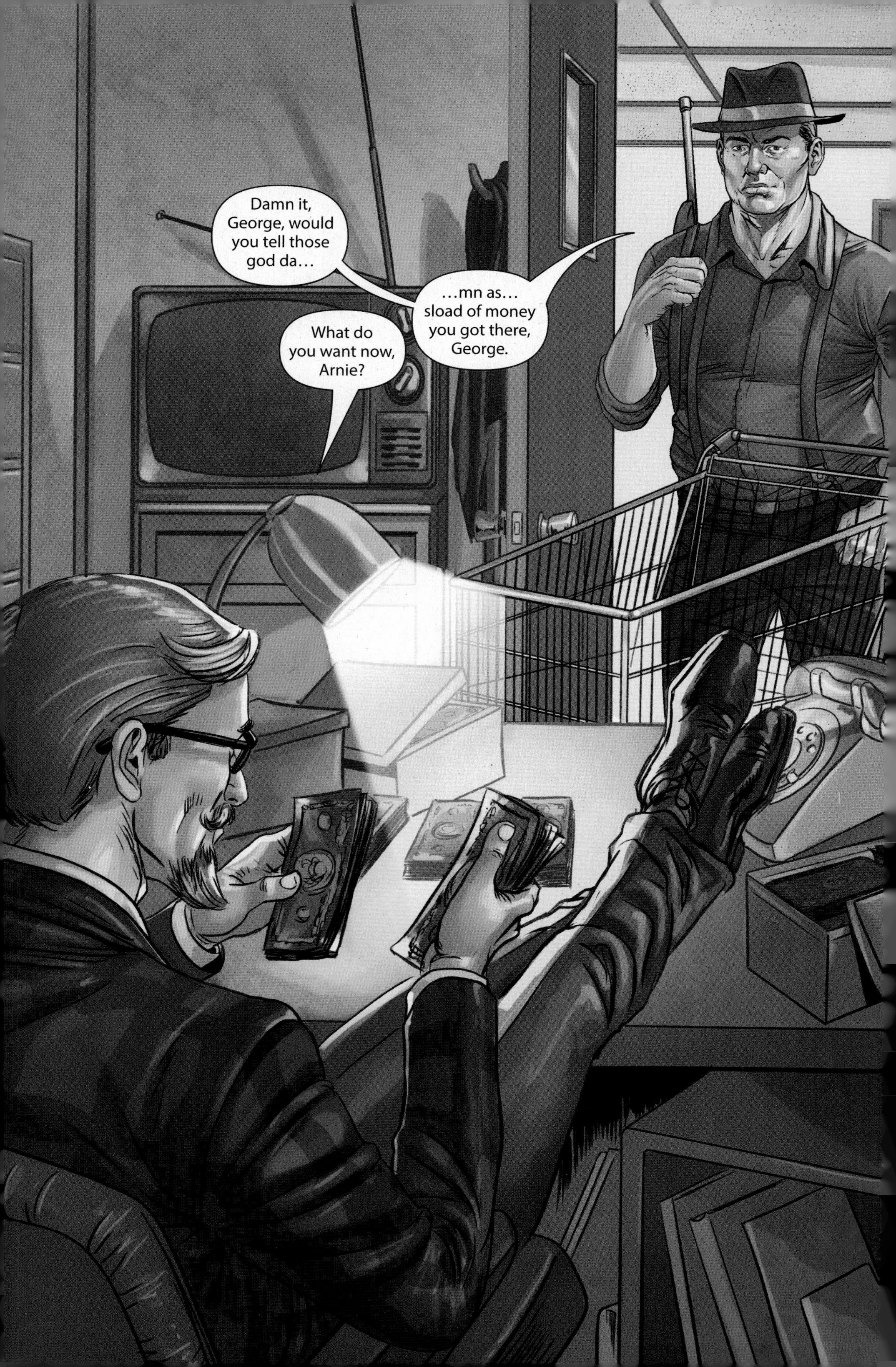

What do you want now, Arnie?
Damn it, George, would you tell those god da…
…mn as… sload of money you got there, George.

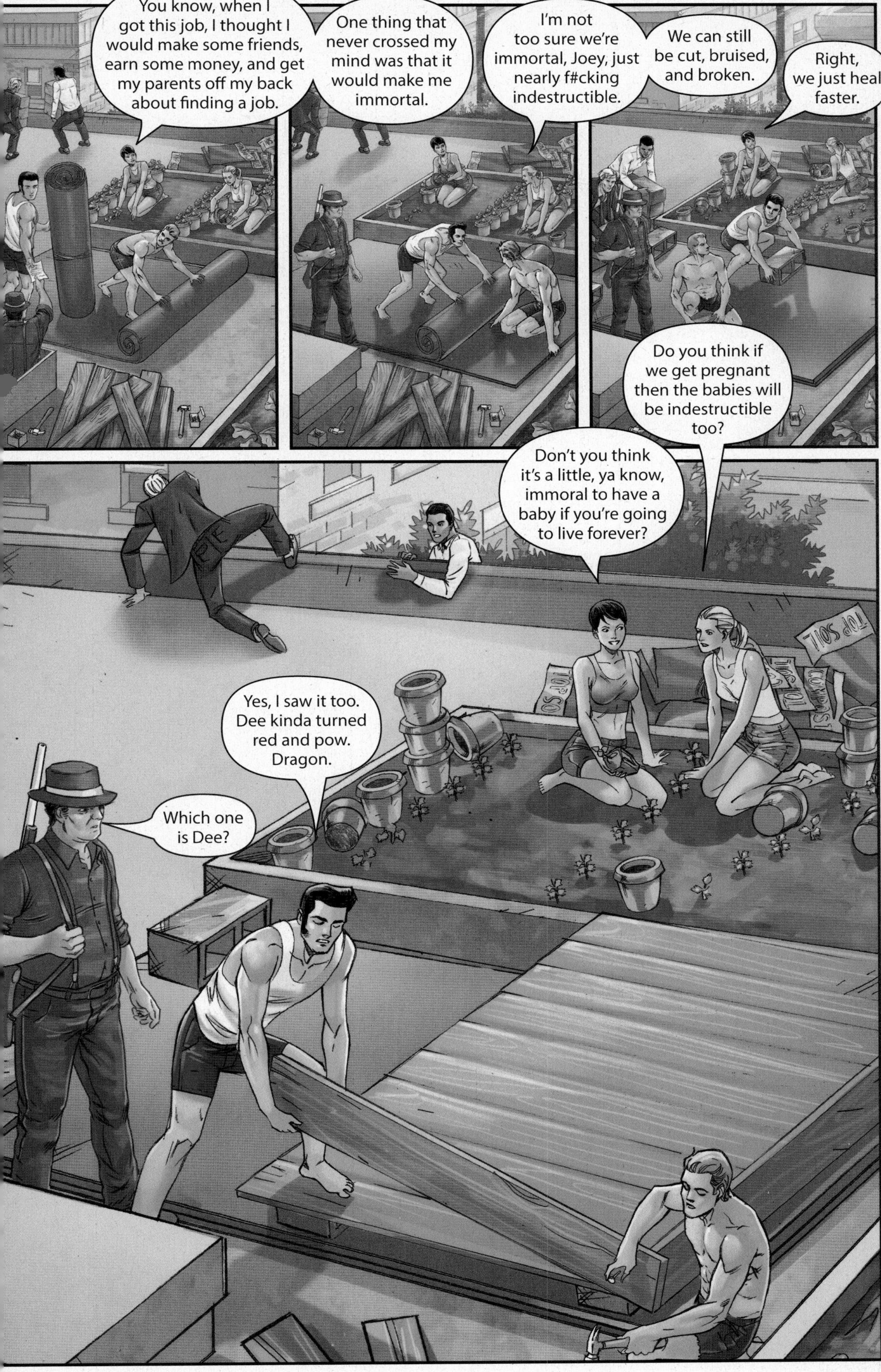
You know, when I got this job, I thought I would make some friends, earn some money, and get my parents off my back about finding a job.
One thing that never crossed my mind was that it would make me immortal.
I'm not too sure we're immortal, Joey, just nearly f#cking indestructible.
We can still be cut, bruised, and broken.
Right, we just heal faster.
Do you think if we get pregnant then the babies will be indestructible too?
Don't you think it's a little, ya know, immoral to have a baby if you're going to live forever?
TOP SOIL
Yes, I saw it too. Dee kinda turned red and pow. Dragon.
Which one is Dee?

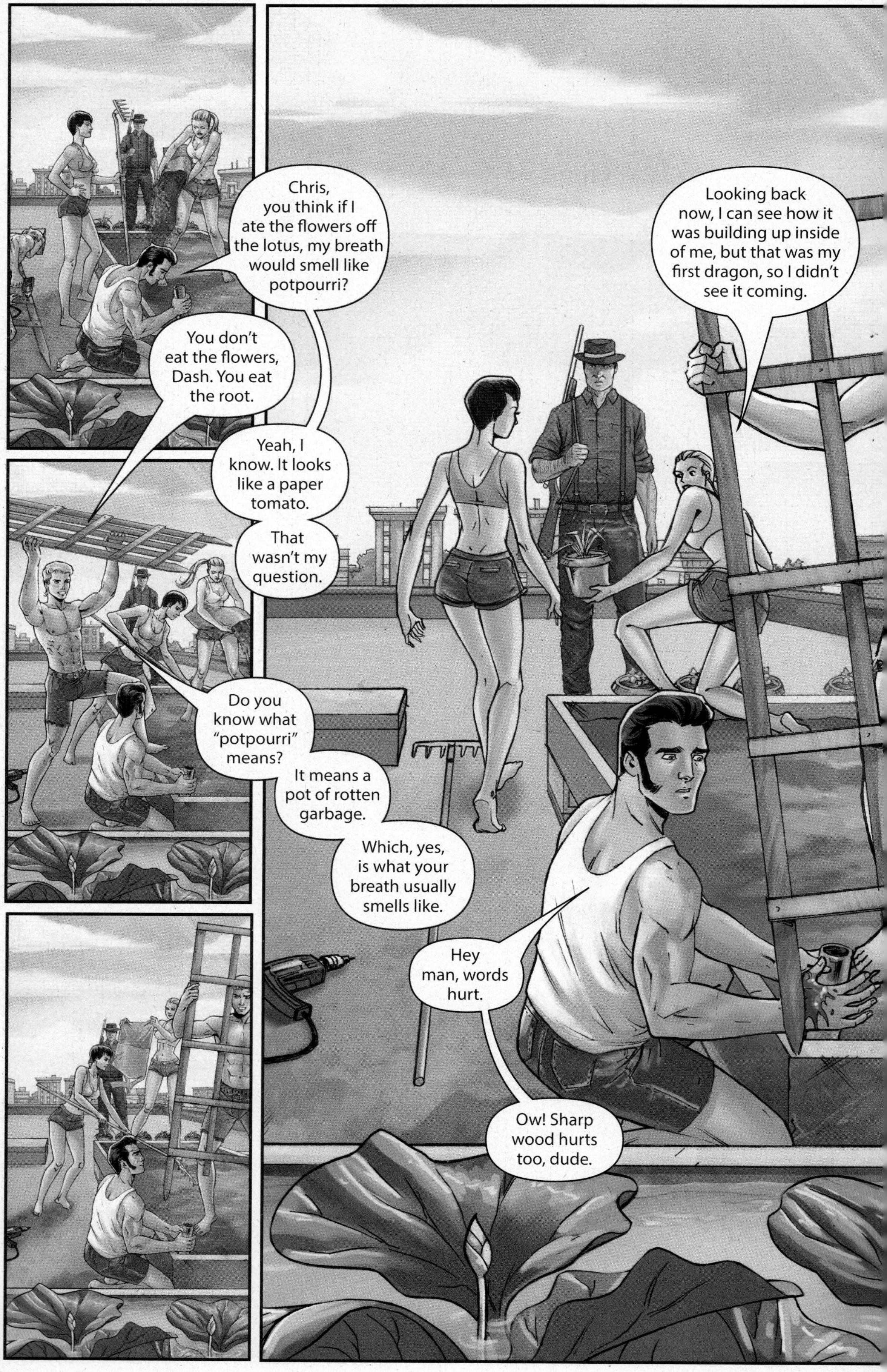
Chris, you think if I ate the flowers off the lotus, my breath would smell like potpourri?
You don't eat the flowers, Dash. You eat the root.
Yeah, I know. It looks like a paper tomato.
That wasn't my question.
Do you know what "potpourri" means?
It means a pot of rotten garbage.
Which, yes, is what your breath usually smells like.
Looking back now, I can see how it was building up inside of me, but that was my first dragon, so I didn't see it coming.
Hey man, words hurt.
Ow! Sharp wood hurts too, dude.

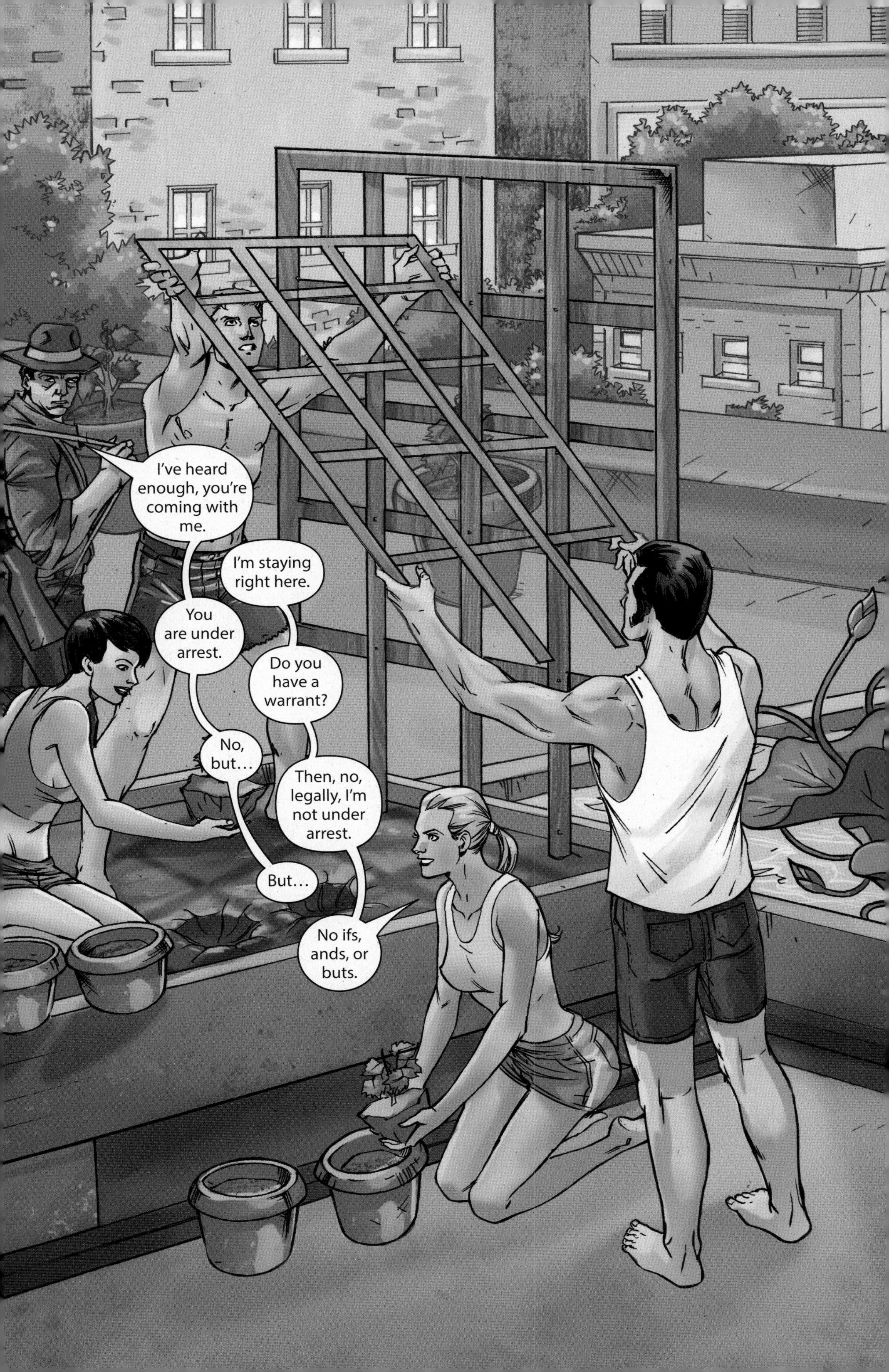
I've heard enough, you're coming with me.
I'm staying right here.
You are under arrest.
Do you have a warrant?
No, but…
Then, no, legally, I'm not under arrest.
But…
No ifs, ands, or buts.

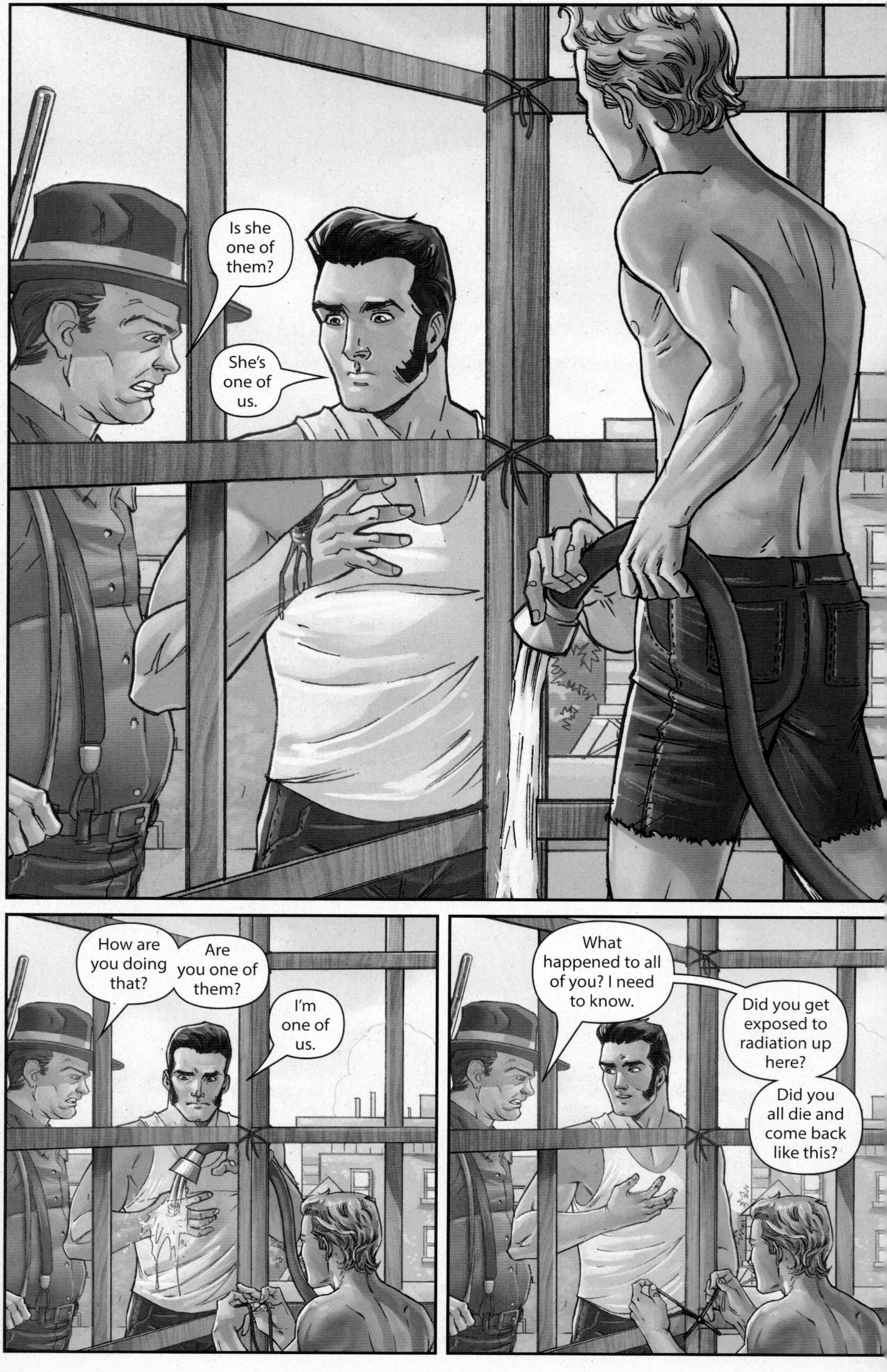
Is she one of them?
She's one of us.
How are you doing that?
Are you one of them?
I'm one of us.
What happened to all of you? I need to know.
Did you get exposed to radiation up here?
Did you all die and come back like this?

BY GEORGE, that's good cake.

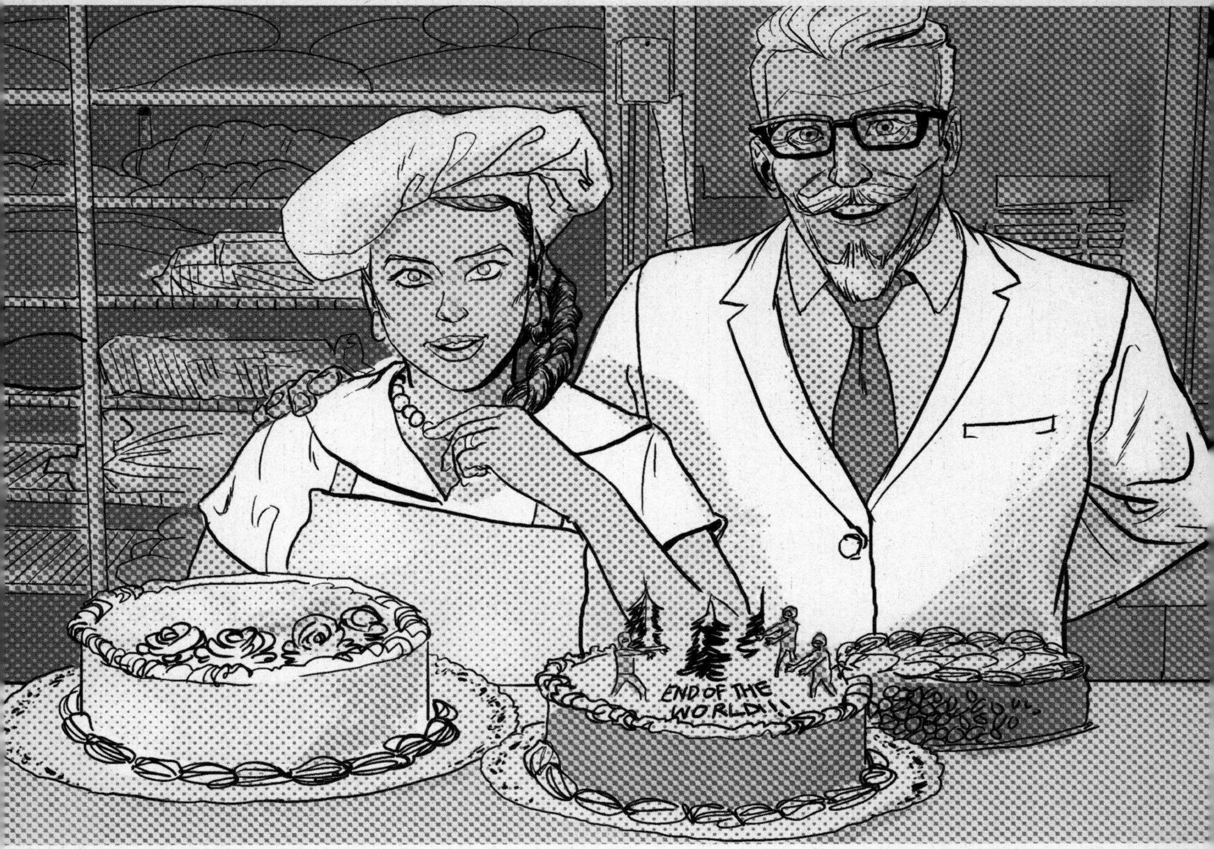
END OF THE WORLD!!!

At ELGIN'S BAKERY,

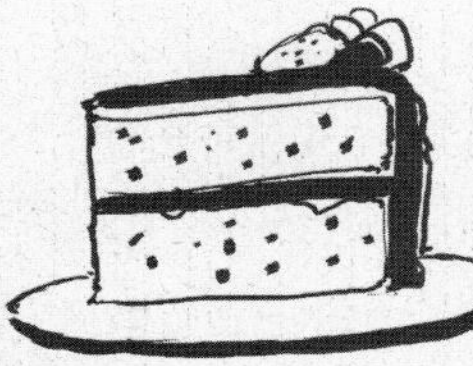 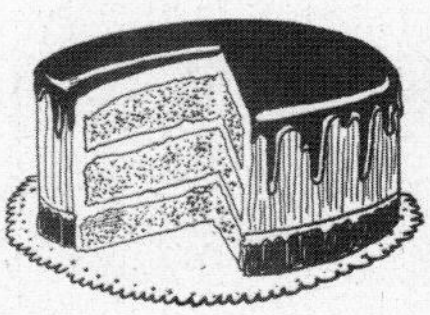 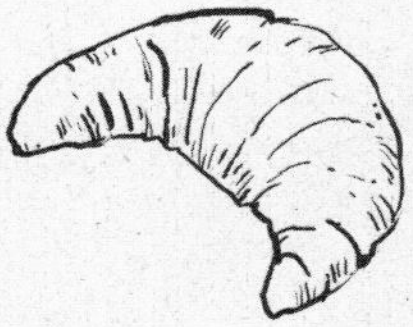

We are more than ready for all occasions. Whether it be a BIRTHDAY or WEDDING cake, we deliver! Not only are we fast - we use our famous Elgin's recipes. A loving mix of quality and tradition, delivered right to your doorstep.

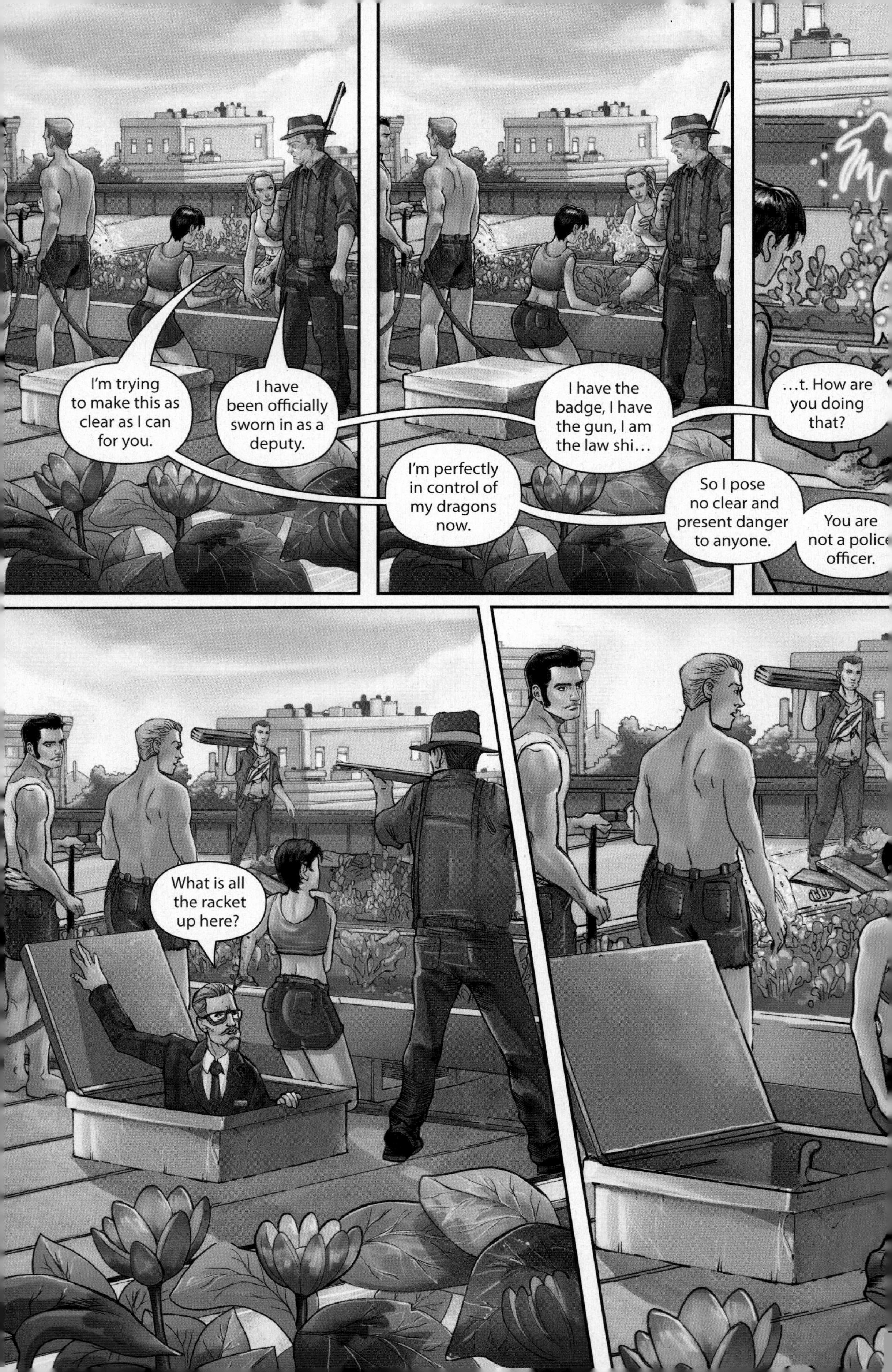
I'm trying to make this as clear as I can for you.
I have been officially sworn in as a deputy.
I'm perfectly in control of my dragons now.
I have the badge, I have the gun, I am the law shi…
So I pose no clear and present danger to anyone.
…t. How are you doing that?
You are not a police officer.
What is all the racket up here?

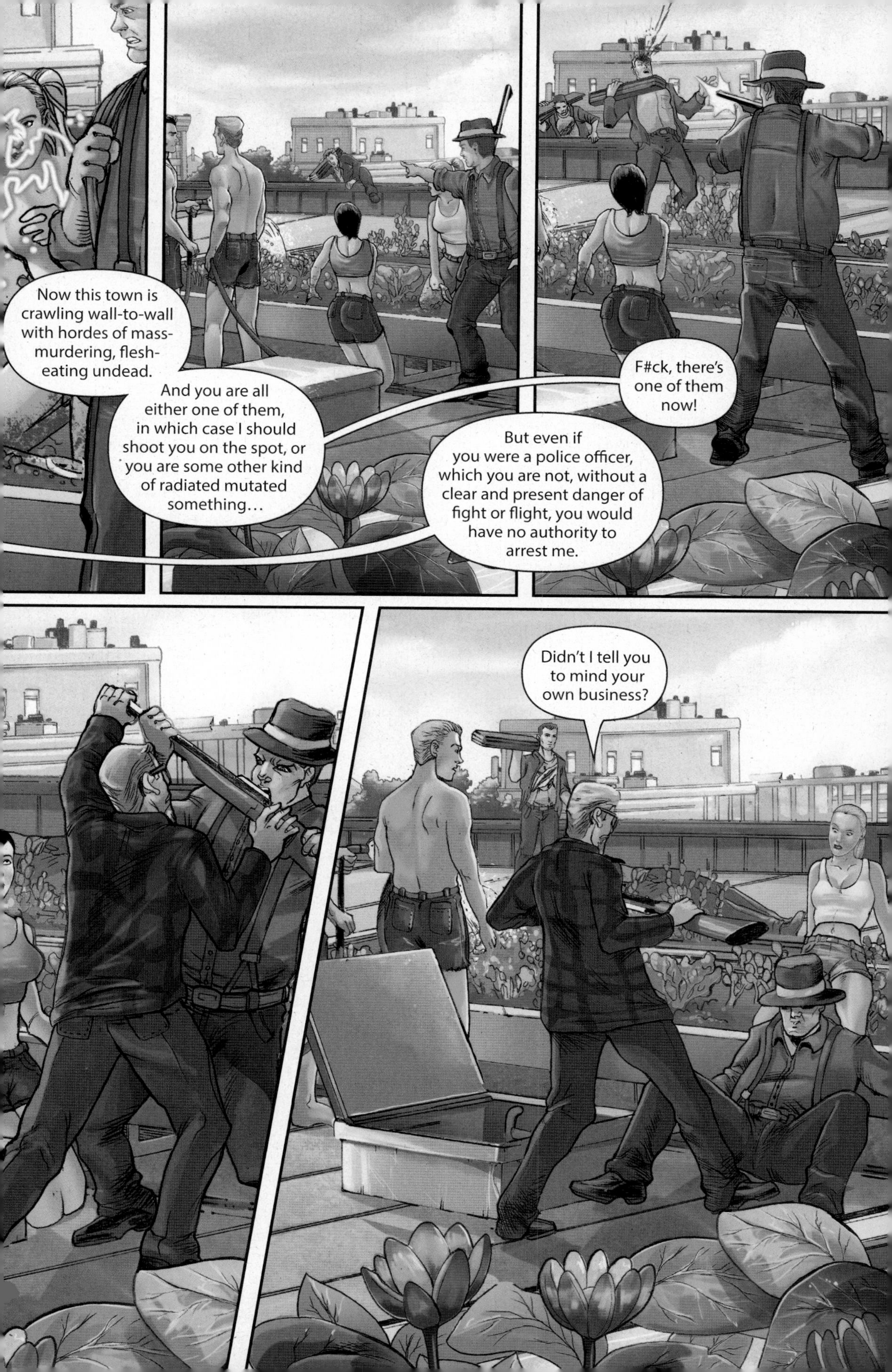
Now this town is crawling wall-to-wall with hordes of mass-murdering, flesh-eating undead.
And you are all either one of them, in which case I should shoot you on the spot, or you are some other kind of radiated mutated something…
But even if you were a police officer, which you are not, without a clear and present danger of fight or flight, you would have no authority to arrest me.
F#ck, there's one of them now!
Didn't I tell you to mind your own business?

THANK YOU
FOR YOUR CONTRIBUTIONS, COLLABORATION, AND SUPPORT.

Strauss Zelnick
Hao Zheng
Dwight Zimmerman
Marianne Yang
Billy Yocum
Butch & Susan Yocum
Jerry Wang
Allen Watson
Erik Welch
Peter Welch
Heather Werber
Adam Wexler
Dan Wickline
Mitchell Wojcik
Michael Worosz
Bob Wulff
Teodora Varga
Jean Vargas
Jorge Vieira
John Taddeo
Kenji Takabayashi
The Tan Family
Jamie Tanner
Jude Terror
Peter Thomatos
Zac Thompson
Patrick J. Sabol
Ethan Sacks
Aaron Sagers
April Salazar
Darren Sanchez
Jessica Schaeffer
Cassandra Schaffa
Maggie Searcy
Theresa Seliga
Dmitry Semenov
Gareb Shamus
Klaus Shmidheiser
Cori Silberman
Jeffrey Simons
Karl Slatoff
Mat Smart
Catherine Smyka
The Song Family
Jay Spence
Hans Spitzer
Anthony Steiner
Sage Stossel

Shannon Sullivan
Meaghan Summo
Chelsey Swilik
Ethan Rasiel
John Roberts
John Robinson
Hans Rodionoff
Mike Rosenzweig
Sharon & Blake Rowe
Dino Pai
Jason Parent
Ron Perazza
Rock Persaud
Michael Pfeiffer
Dominique Picard
Fred Pierce
Julia Pressman
Emmanuel Ogwang
Qui Nguyen
Nicole Nicoletti
Jai Nitz
Phil Novoa
Ralph Macchio
David Macho
Max MacDonald
Quinlan Maggio
Adriana Mark
Brian David Marshall
Mike Martucci
Peter Milligan
Jane Milrod
Steven & Jennifer Mitrano
Debi Moore
Michaela Murphy
Joey Leanzo
Tony Lee
Ken Levine
Josh Leuze
Kyle Levenick
Alan Lewis
Ping Liang
Stephen Liang
Jo Licht
Gui Karyo
Jordan Katz
Robert Keeley
James Kiernan

Jen King
Jaffa & Rick Kintigh
Maria Jagodka
Rose & Bill Jemas
Orissa Jenkins
The Jeong Family
Rich Johnston
Dan Jolly
Socko Jones
Meghan E. Jones
Justin Jordan
Nick Joyce
Alex Hamby
Harry Haramis
Daniel Heacox
The Heller Family
Peter Herrmann
Joshua Hixon
Jaime Hoerbelt
Audrey Hollister
Kay Honda
Matt Hoverman
Sean Hughes
Shaun Hurley
Daniel Gallina
Court Gebeau
Hayley Geftman-Gold
Greg Gibson
Flinn Gillan
Karen & Michael Gilmore
David Macho Gómez
Sarah Gordon
Andrew Granik
The Graves Family
Kathryn Greenbaum
John Greenbaum
Lisandro Gutierrez
John Falco
Adam Fenton
The Fishberg Family
Christopher Fiumano
The Flanagan Family
Jacquelyn Florio
Teresa Focarille
Drew Ford
Atom Freeman
Chris Eaton

Otto Eckstein
Carter Edwards
Daniel Einzig
Howard Emanuel
Jessica Eth
Vonnetta Ewing
Brian Dages
Keith Dallas
Kathleen Davis
Sean Clark Delaney
Shawn DeLoache
Gavin Dillinger
Christian Cafiero
Peter Carbonaro
Chris Casazza
Skye Chalmers
Ben Chamberlain
Larry Charlip
Muhammad Chaudhry
The Chou Family
Gary Cioni
Laura Feery Cioni
Paul Clark
Brian Clevinger
The Coast Family
Jesse James Criscione
Travis Czap
Maria Barreras
Peter Begler
Christopher Benton
Ian Berry
Guillaume Blais
Christina Blanch
Ralph Blaser
Siobhan Boes
Antoine Boisvert
Tommy Bolduc
Scott Bowers
Phil Boyle
KB Breiseth
Russ Brown
Gahl Buslov
Tony Buttino
Sandra Alcaide
Derek Anderson
Chris Arrant
Dorothy Ashley-Jones
The Ayala Family

All of us here at Double Take admire and respect the creators, cast, and crew of the 1968 film *Night of the Living Dead*. While no one affiliated with the film has been involved in the creation of these stories, their wonderful work inspired us.

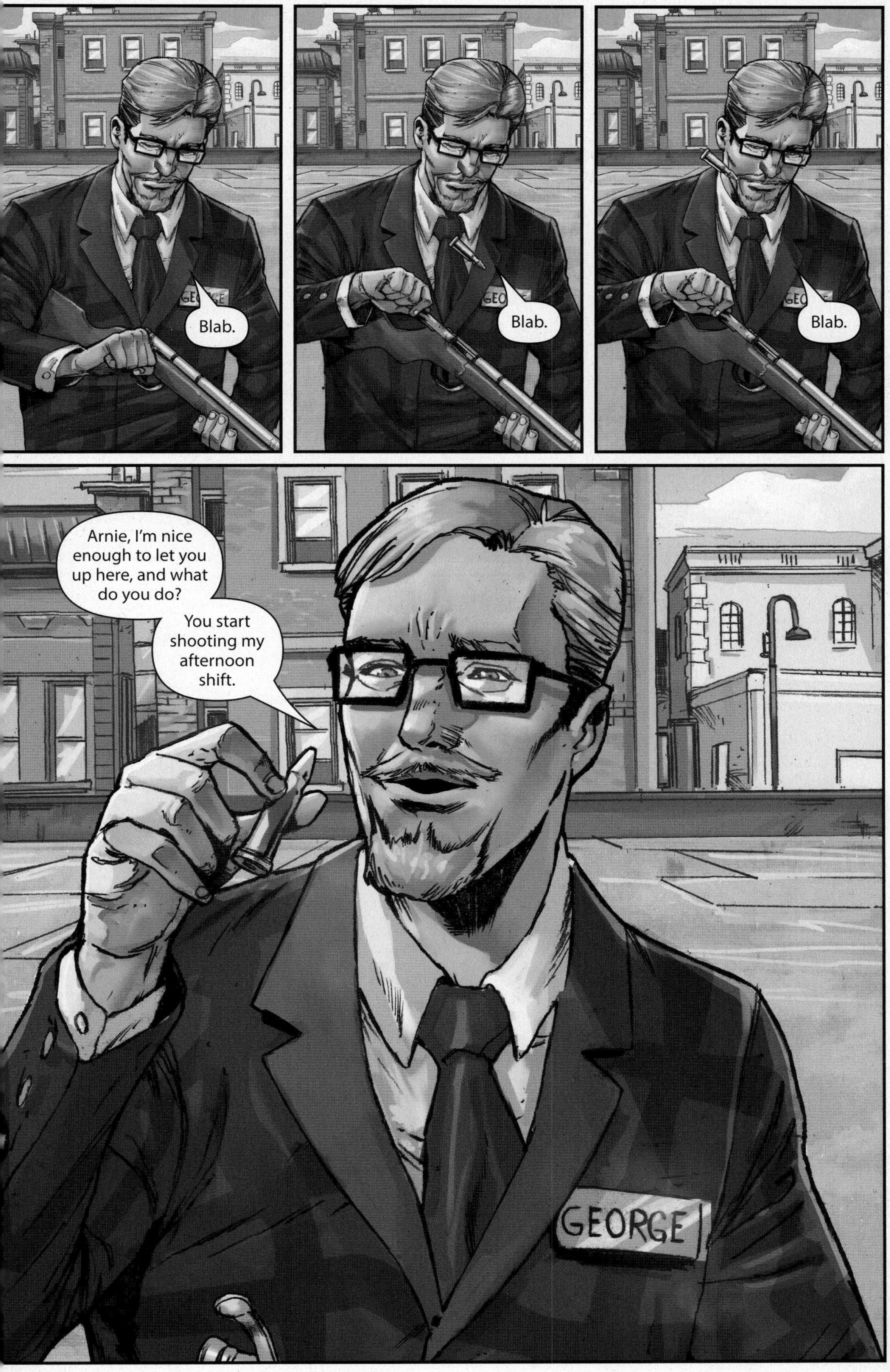
Blab.
Blab.
Blab.
Arnie, I'm nice enough to let you up here, and what do you do?
You start shooting my afternoon shift.
GEORGE

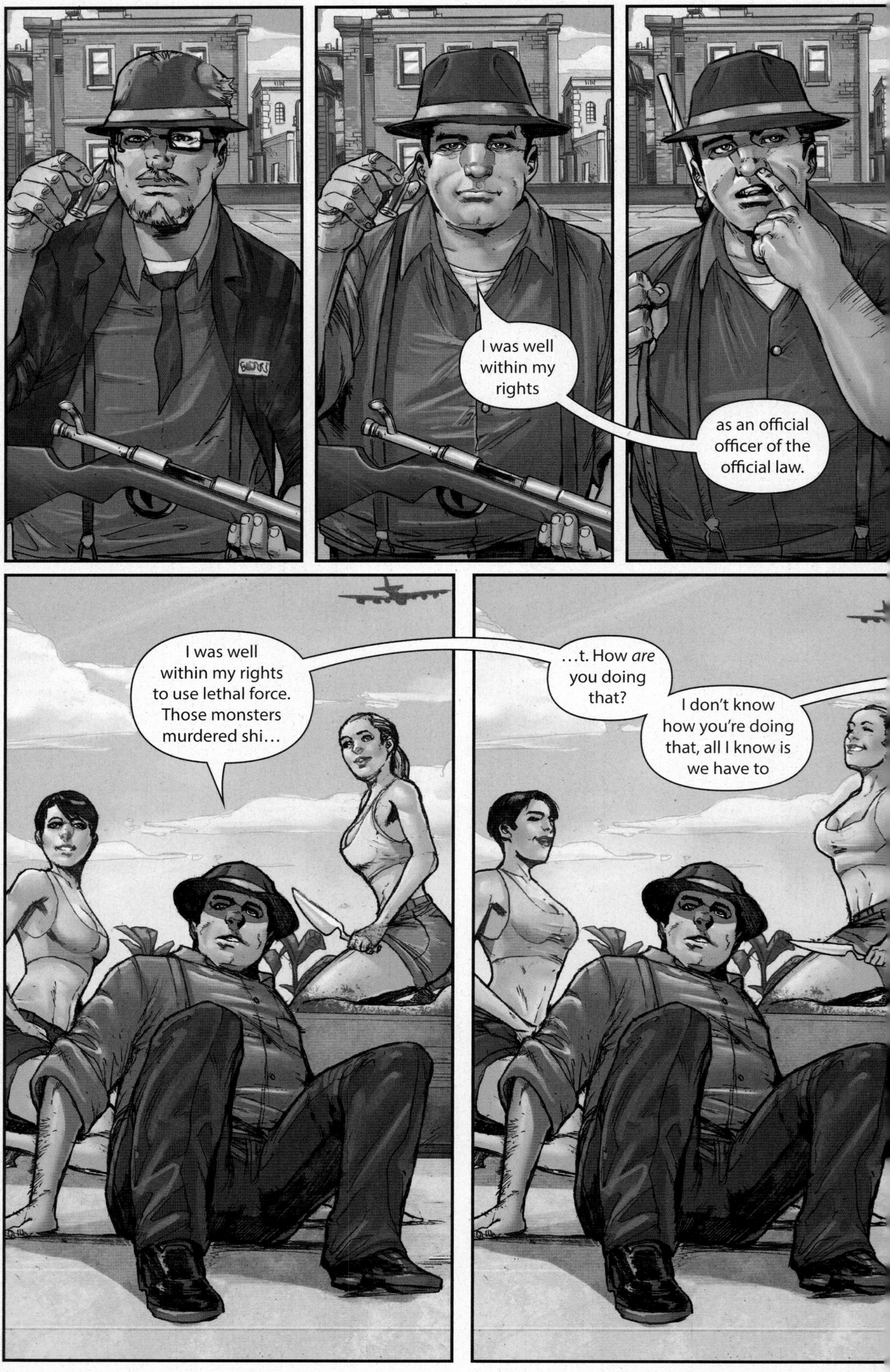

I was well within my rights
as an official officer of the official law.
I was well within my rights to use lethal force. Those monsters murdered shi…
…t. How *are* you doing that?
I don't know how you're doing that, all I know is we have to

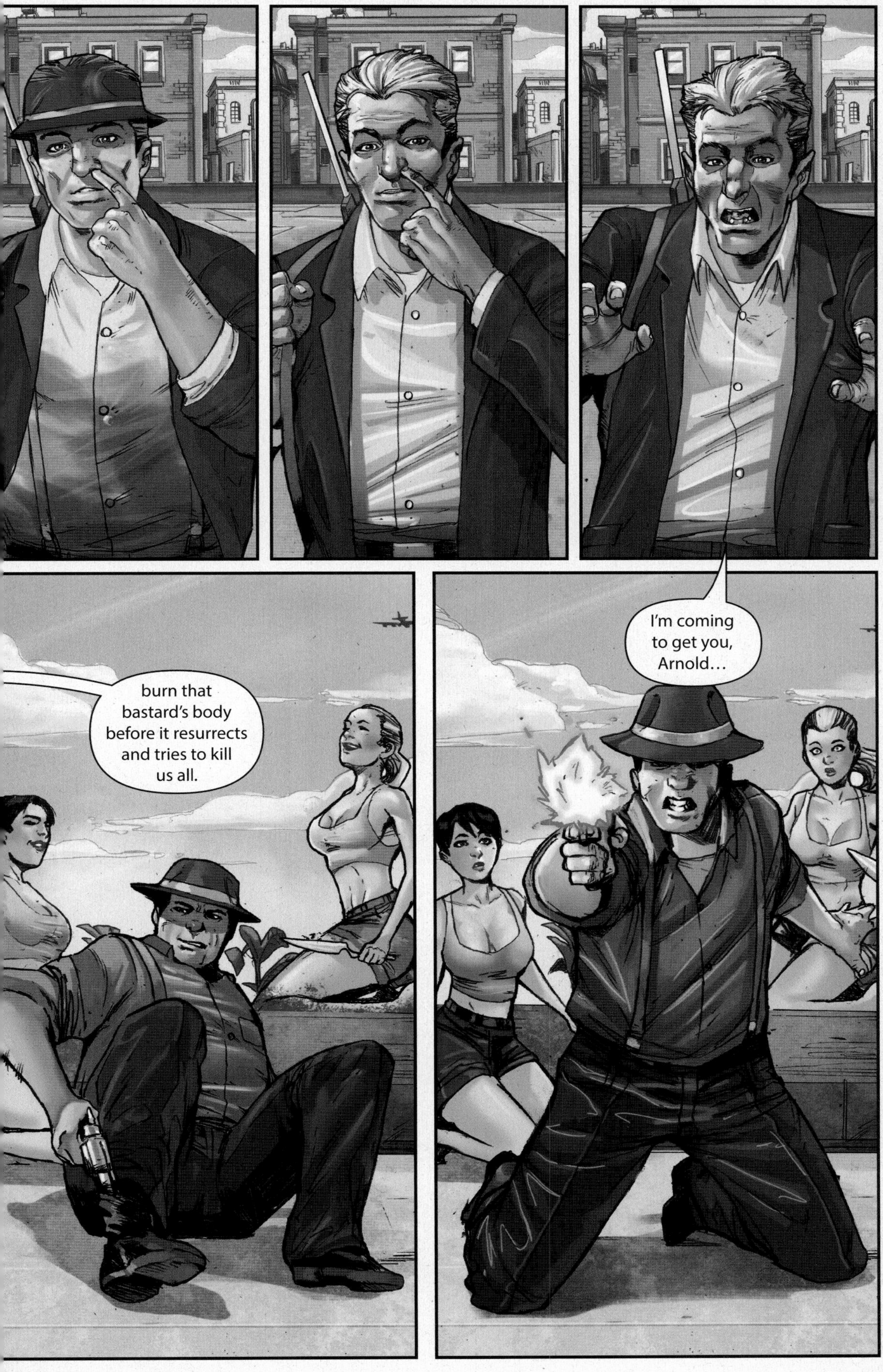
burn that bastard's body before it resurrects and tries to kill us all.
I'm coming to get you, Arnold…

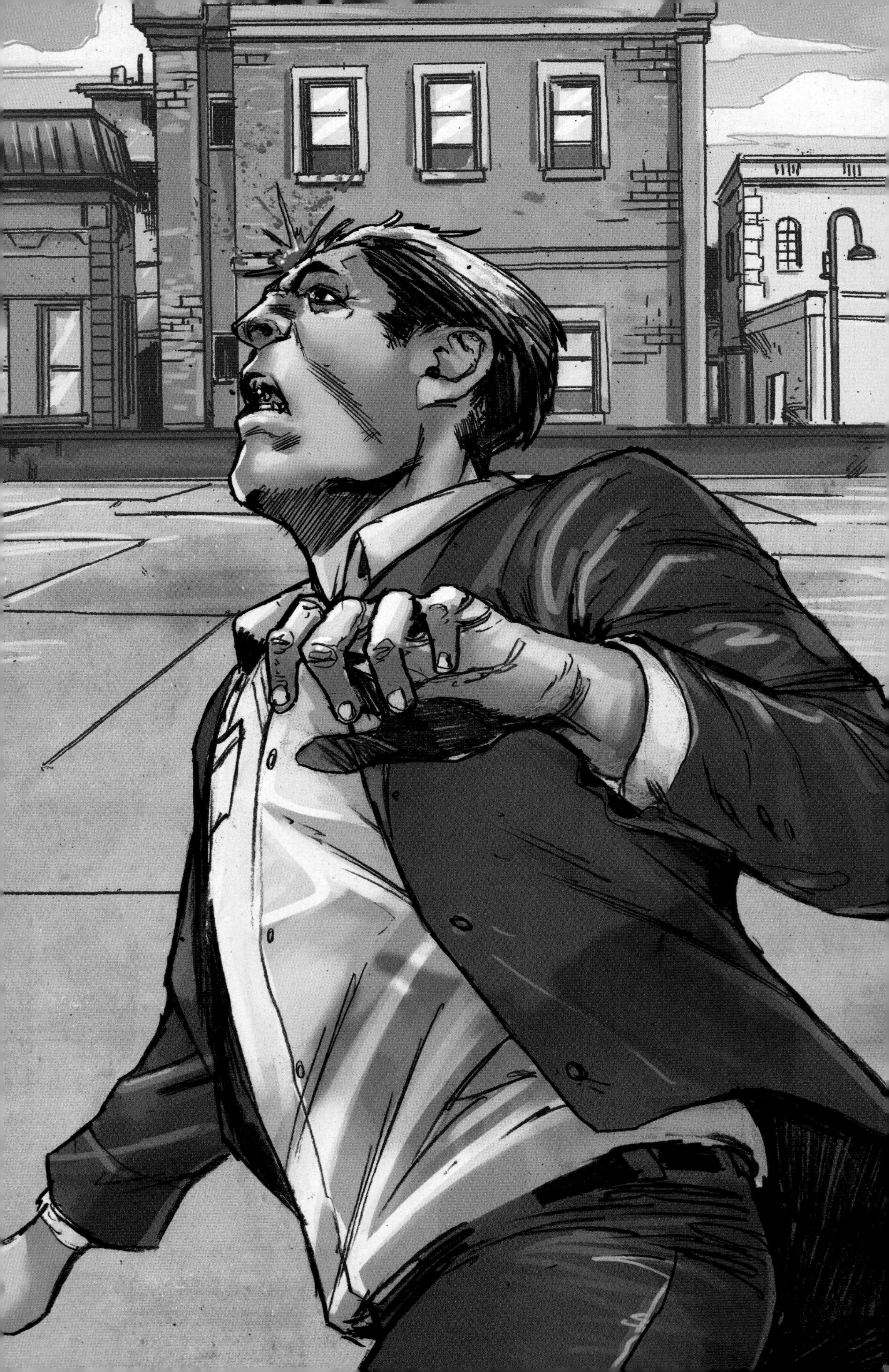

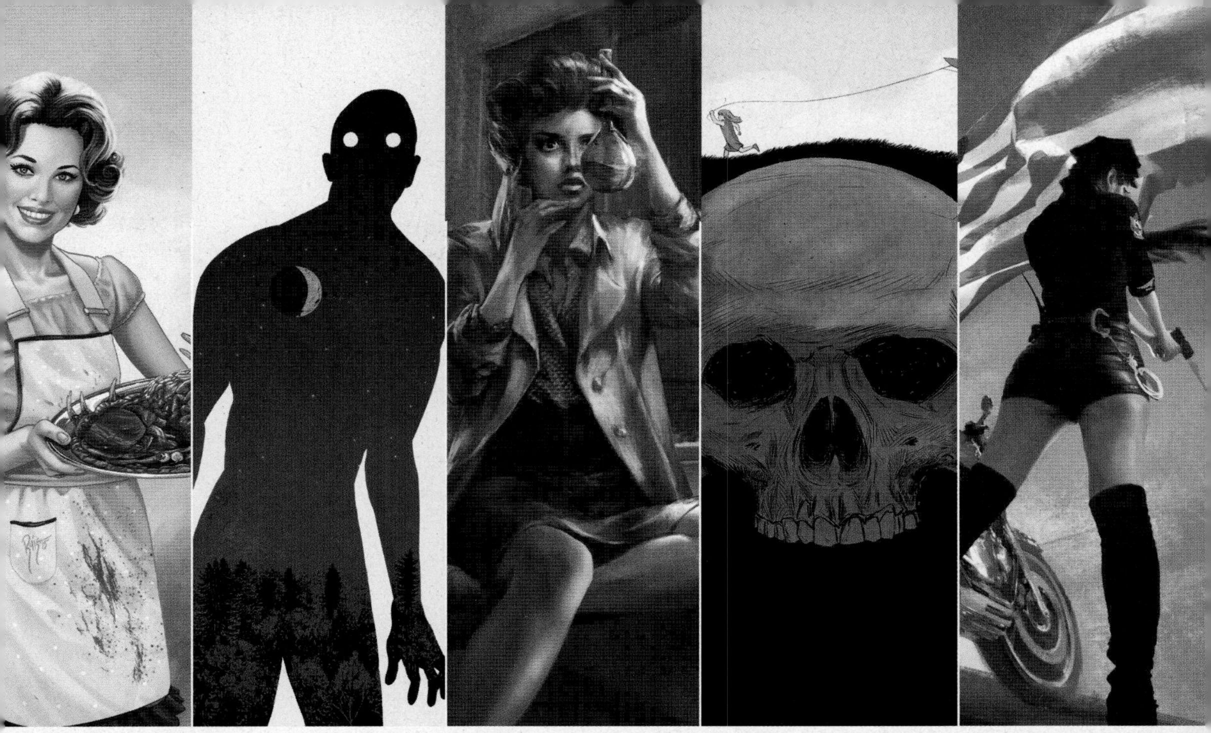

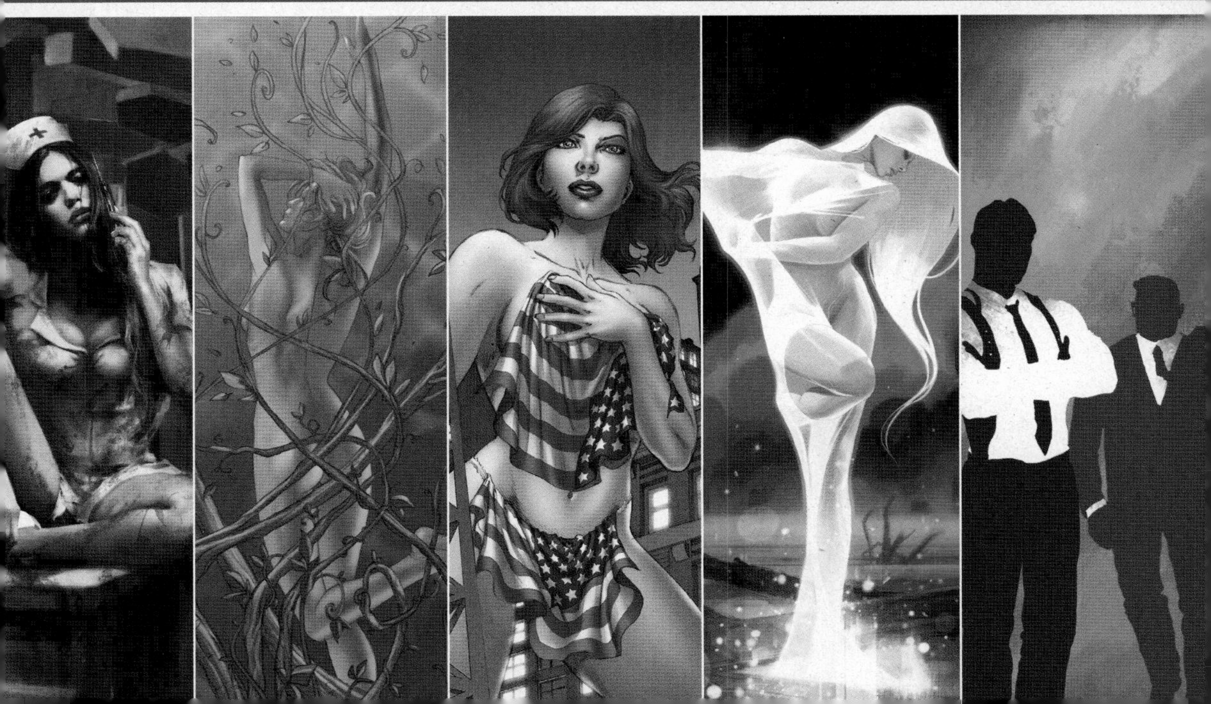

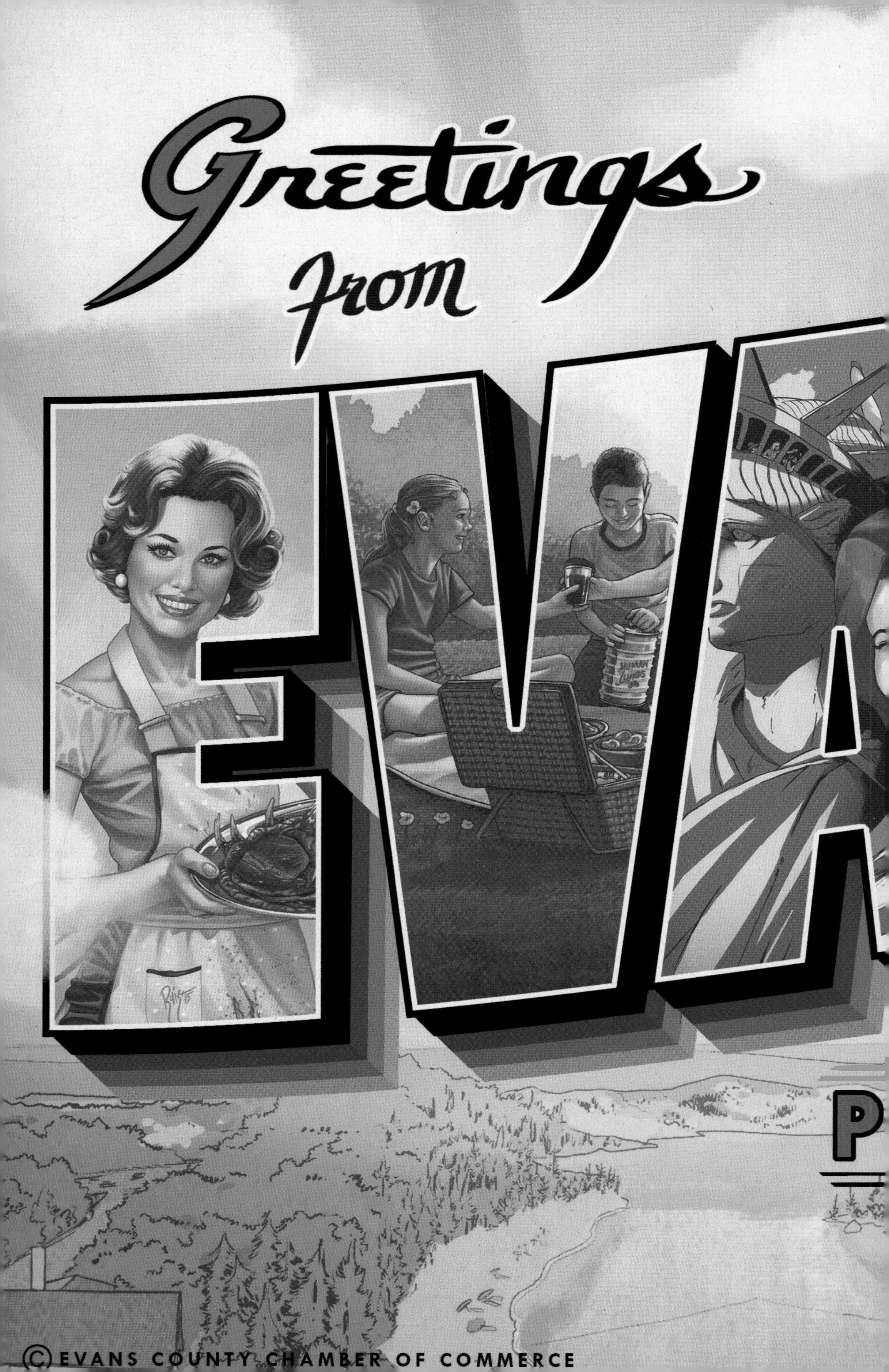
Greetings from
EVA
© EVANS COUNTY CHAMBER OF COMMERCE

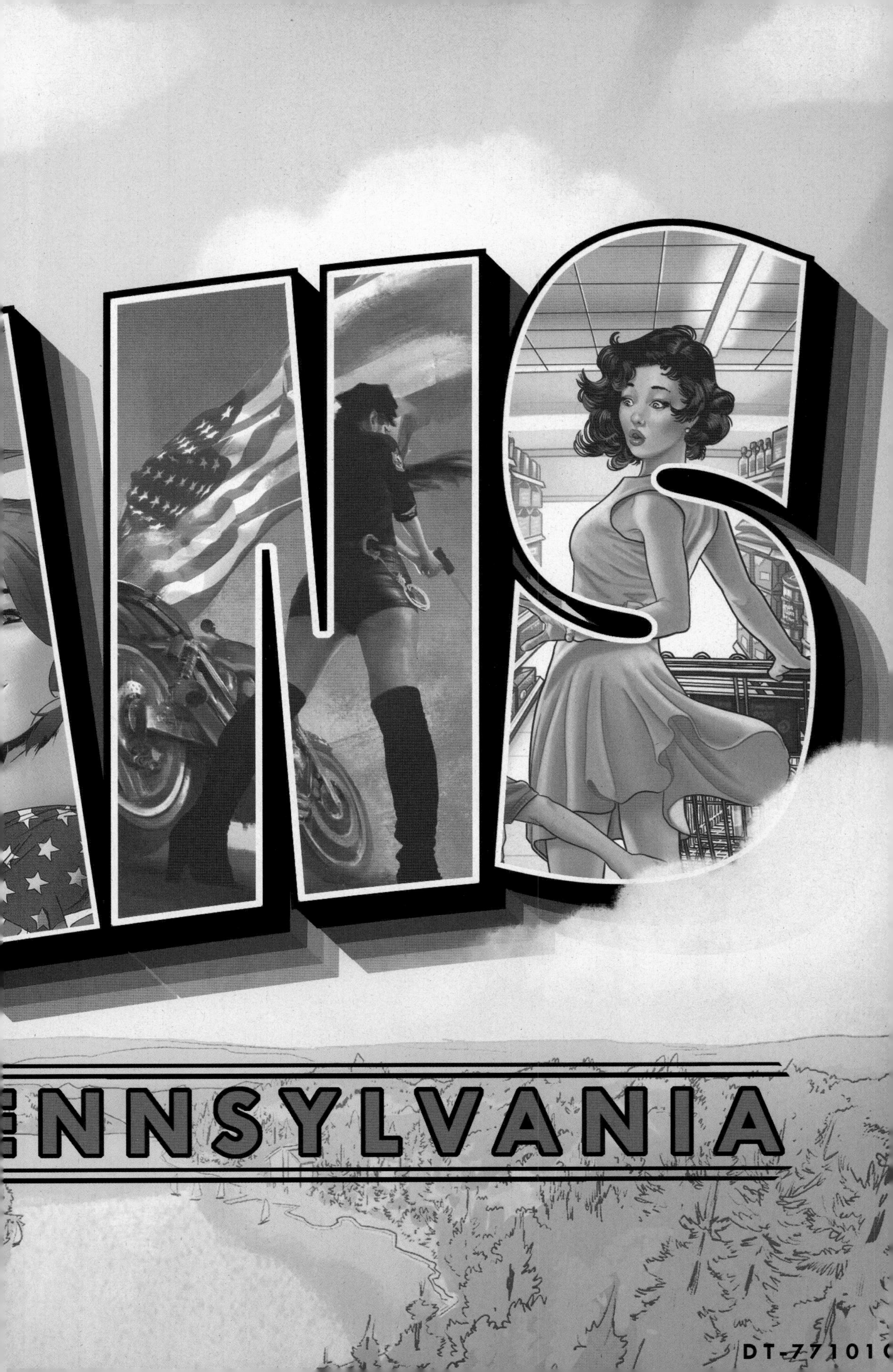
ENNSYLVANIA
DT-77101

They won't leave.

They'll leave alright.

You leave or I'll call the po …sh#t.

…This is Samantha Stanton, KBRF AM 530, with the latest news from the station that's first on your dial.

We have some description of the assassins.

Eyewitnesses say they are ordinary-looking people…

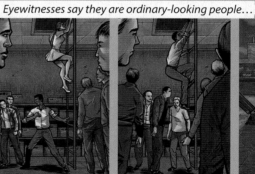

…who appear to be in a kind of trance.